D0277734

Mummy's Boy

LARRY LAMB

Mummy's Boy

CORONET

First published in Great Britain in 2011 by Coronet
An imprint of Hodder & Stoughton
An Hachette UK company

1

A CIP catalogue record for this title is available from the British Library

HB ISBN 978 1444 71527 9
TPB ISBN 978 1444 72024 2

Typeset in Plantin Light by Hewer Text UK Ltd, Edinburgh
Printed and bound by CPI Mackays, Chatham ME5 8TD

Hodder & Stoughton policy is to use papers that are natural, renewable
and recyclable products and made from wood grown in sustainable forests.
The logging and manufacturing processes are expected to conform
to the environmental regulations of the country of origin.

Hodder & Stoughton Ltd
338 Euston Road
London NW1 3BH

www.hodder.co.uk

To Jessie, my mum, who set the whole thing off and to Ron, my dad, who in writing this, I've finally come around to forgiving.

Acknowledgements

To Charlotte Haycock and Mark Booth at Coronet who gave me moral support I needed to actually write my story. Thank you to John Noel and Meryl Hoffman at John Noel Management for guiding me to Hodder and Coronet and taking care of me while I got on with it.

To my sister Penny for her patience in typing it all.

To Edward Duke who showed me a world I'd no idea of; to Lex Van Delden, my mentor and friend; to Steven Pimlott who finally truned me into an actor – three sadly missed men.

I owe a lot to Paul Bryers for his help and advice.

And to my glorious family who somehow or other put up with me and still manage to love me.

Contents

Finale

Act One

1

Beginnings

In the leafy London suburbs at 8 Greenwood Avenue, Brimsdown, out in far-flung Enfield, there's a party going on. But nothing like the party that Jessie White attended a few weeks before at Georgie Clark's council house. No, nothing like that party.

Whilst not in any way a sad place, number 8 is certainly not a particularly festive household. Other than early on, when they gave a birthday party or two for Jessie, their then newly adopted daughter, Fred and Nel White have never really done parties. They are two highly principled, forward-thinking, educated, working-class people. They just don't go in for that sort of thing.

But tonight is special and marks an important stage in their life as a proud 'modern' family. Jessie, the daughter they adopted when she was a toddler, has achieved maturity. This is her 21st birthday party.

And, in her own way, as a modern, well-brought-up young lady, Jessie has 'done her bit' cutting pit props for the mines as her contribution to the war effort. And so, to welcome her aboard the 'grown-up club', her mother, Nel, has organised a little celebration.

Jessie's headmistress from grammar school is there; her 'company commander' from the Timber Corps section of the Land Army and two senior members of the Enfield Highway Co-operative Society ('Ladies Section') have come along too, as well as Mr and Mrs Mitchell, the owners of the smallholding that still abuts Fred's allotment. It is quite a gathering.

The party is a big success. When they've all gone home, Jessie comes into the kitchen as Nel dries the last of the cups and saucers.

'Thanks for tonight, Mum.'

'Don't thank me, dear, thank your father.'

'I did, but Mum, it was you too, so thank you.'

'You looked lovely tonight, I was proud of you.'

'Mum, erm . . .' She just can't get it out. She tries again. 'Mum . . .'

Nel wipes down the draining board and turns. She smiles at her daughter, now a woman in her own right. 'Yes, Jessie?'

'Mum, I'm going to have a baby.'

Nel stands with the tea towel dangling, her eyes focused on Jessie's face like searchlights through the night.

'You are *what*?! Jessie Dorothy White!' Her face has completely blanched, her fine, dark features are drawn tight like bowstrings, taut and terrifying.

Jessie knows to watch it from that point on, but even so she isn't quick enough to completely avoid the wide-swinging smack that rings resoundingly through her head two seconds later.

'How dare you come home and tell me that?'

Bang! Again. Head ringing.

'Mum, I'm sorry, I'm so, so—'

'You're what? You're sorry? Sorry? What do you mean, sorry? You're sorry you are pregnant? You're sorry I'm angry? What are you sorry about? You stupid, selfish . . . How could you do this to me and your father – after all he's done for you? You thankless, ungrateful, dirty little thing.'

'Mum . . .' Jessie pleads.

'Just get away from me. I don't even want to be in the same

room as you. Just go away, just get up to your bedroom. Go, go, go. I have to think.'

★

A week later, Fred is eating the porridge that Nel has prepared. They are sharing the last drop of tea. It's about five o'clock in the morning.

'Six o'clock this evening they're going to be here,' she says to her husband.

'They?' He looks at her inquisitively.

'Him and his older brother.'

'And where is she?'

Nel doesn't answer.

'Nel, where is she?' Fred doesn't get noisy when he gets angry, he goes quiet. He says, so softly you can hardly hear him, 'Nel, where is she?'

Nel looks straight into his beautiful, deep, honest eyes. 'I don't know where she is, Fred. I've no idea. She went off this morning but I think she's gone to see Brodnick.'

'Poor bugger, I think he would have been just right for her,' Fred sighs.

★

That evening, Fred makes his home as ever on the trolley buses that run north out of London via Seven Sisters and Stamford Hill, all the way to Enfield Wash. He works for the bus company as an electrician; all the drivers and conductors that run out of the Chalk Farm garage know 'Whitey', and so he rides those buses as his own. He sits to the rear of the bus with the conductor. They laughed and joke a lot, but when the bus stops at The Angel in Edmonton, all the banter stops. Fred has spotted, amongst the crowd that comes aboard, two young men, both in demob suits: one tall and strapping – already prematurely balding; the other shorter, dapper, more Latin-looking.

He watches them go upstairs, where the big one lights a cigarette. And they sit very quietly, hardly exchanging a word.

Whitey spies on them via the conductor's mirror from downstairs. Just as he's predicted, they get off at his stop, Carterhatch Lane. He gets off after them and follows them, lagging behind, wondering which one of them it is.

They pause at the gate and he catches them up and walks through the gate into the garden. He pauses half way up the path. They look at each other as he turns.

'Ronald Lamb?' he enquires.

The taller one says, 'I'm William, this is Ronald.' He introduces his younger brother as though he is denouncing him and throwing him to the wolves.

Fred's memories of life on the rougher side of London are brought back to life by these two.

'I suppose you'd better come in.'

He leads them through the hall and seats them in the front room, which is dressed with all the best furniture, spick and span, not a single particle of dust, every surface polished and smelling of beeswax. The two of them sit uncomfortably as the big old clock on the mantelpiece ticks off the seconds.

'So you're . . . the father?' Nel is standing in the doorway, her eyes fixed on Ronald. Ronald starts to get up, as does William.

'Erm, look, Mrs White . . .' Ron smiles.

*

About an hour later, Fred closes the door behind the two brothers and walks back into the front room. Nel is at the net curtains watching the father of her grandchild-to-be disappearing down the street.

'Oh Fred. Who could ever have thought she'd end up like this?'

'Well, it's history repeating itself; her mother was in just the same boat.' Fred walks to the foot of the stairs and calls out, 'Jessie, come down here please.'

A door opens upstairs and a few seconds later Jessie walks into the room.

Fred looks at Jessie, his adored little angel. 'It's all sorted out,' he says. 'You're getting married on the fifteenth of next month. His brother William will be the best man and he and his wife . . . I can't remember her name . . . ?'

'Ruth,' snaps Nel.

'Yes, Bill and Ruth will stand as godparents to the child. Then the pair of you'll come and live here with us until you can sort somewhere out for yourselves. With things the way they are, Christ knows how long that will take.'

★

Liverpool Street Station the following morning is filled with the smell of coal smoke and oily steam. There are people all over, thousands of people scurrying everywhere. Amongst them, standing beneath the main clock, is a tall blond young man in the uniform of the Free Polish Army. He is obviously waiting for someone.

Nel and Jessie pick their way through the crowds. Jessie sees the man first from twenty or thirty yards away and stops.

'Go on, Jessie.' Nel shoves her forward, remaining where she stands herself. The man sees them through the crowds and smiles.

Jessie walks up to him, her eyes filling with tears. She hands him a brown manila envelope.

He takes it and says, 'What is this, Jessie?'

'It's your money, Brodnick,' she says. 'The money you've been sending for me to save. I'm not going to marry you, Brodnick. It wouldn't be right. I've got to go with him, he's the father.'

He stands holding the envelope. 'But Jessie, you don't have to. I've told you before, I will take you both. You and the child.'

She shakes her head and turns away and the tears start to pour down her cheeks. Heartbroken, she walks back through the crowds to Nel.

'Great start eh?!'

2

A Little Boy

My God, they were a complicated pair, my mum and dad: talk about a couple who should never have married. What a mistake, an absolute and utter mismatch. Jessie White caught Ron Lamb's eye in the closing moments of 1946. Two ordinary people, both of them average height: she with a warm and friendly face, brown hair and sparkly smile; he with darker hair, smoothed back with Brylcreem air-force-style.

They were both good dancers; he was always the joker and she was always ready for a laugh. 'If I said you had a lovely figure, would you hold it against me?' I'm sure he would have opened with something like that. And as they danced those final minutes of New Year's Eve away, something clicked between them. The spark was gone almost as quickly as it came, but it was already too late. After a hurried fumble in a shed on the edge of the local park in the first hours of 1947, nine months later this mismatched twenty-something couple were no longer carefree and single. Her father and my dad's brother had pretty much forced them to get married, as was the way back then. Neither of them were ready to settle down and start a family – and particularly not with one another. They hardly knew each other, but here they were, Mr and Mrs Lamb, and the only thing they had in common was me.

★

Ron missed my birth; he was still at work and my mum went through the struggle of labour without him. He peddled up to the hospital later on his old gas company bicycle. There I was, a brand new baby-boomer, all set to conquer the world, but hampered right from the start by those two poor souls who'd got themselves stuck in this situation.

For the first few years we lived with my mum's parents in Greenwood Avenue. It was a small red-brick semi. Cosy and immaculate, it had a perfectly kept garden at the front and a well-trimmed lawn and apple tree at the back. It certainly wasn't anything grand, but they worked hard and were proud of the home they'd created.

My granddad always referred to himself as the gaffer and I always called him Gabba. I remember him as he was, at about the same age as I am now. Medium height and balding, he always wore spectacles on his pointy nose and had a smiley, pleasant countenance. I always picture him with his sleeves rolled up, working on his allotment, which seemed to be where he spent all his spare time, growing his prize-winning vegetables: immense onions, leeks, parsnips and cabbages; glorious, long, even-looking runner beans and big fat hairy gooseberries – everything seemed to achieve incredible proportions. Every year he'd walk away from the horticultural society with medals, ribbons and rosettes. He used to drive a motorbike and I would sit on my nan's lap in the sidecar alongside him. He had survived four years in the trenches during the First World War and when he came home he got a job as an electrician at the General Bus Company, where he went on to work for forty-nine years.

My nan, Nel, was a well-educated working-class girl from Dorset, who came to London to go into service and later worked as a conductress on the buses. I have a photo of my Nan in a 1920s-style knitted swimming costume. She was rather a strict, austere, Victorian woman of average height and very strong political convictions. Gabba and Nan were both thirty-six years old when they adopted my mum, she was three years old, and they had finally accepted that they wouldn't be able to have children. They loved and cherished her as if she were their own daughter, so when my mum and dad needed help getting on their feet as a family, they naturally offered them a home to live in.

My dad's family, the Lambs, only lived a few miles away in Edmonton, but it was as if they inhabited a totally different world. They were a touch closer to London, in a darker, less salubrious, seedier area. Instead of the cosy and tidy lives Gabba and Nanny White lived, they had a large and lively family. There had been eight children, only six of whom survived. My dad was in the middle and he grew up at 192 Brettenham Road East, a tough area of terraced workmen's houses built near a big industrial estate along the River Lee in Edmonton. Down the road was the coal merchants, where there were stables for the horses that used to pull the local rag-and-bone men's cart and the shrimps and winkles cart on a Sunday afternoon. 'Shrimps and Whiiiiiiinkalls!', 'Old rags and bowwwwnns!' came the cries along the street; there was always some kind of shouting along there. It was a rough corner of suburban London; the street was full of families like the Tibbles, the Targets, the Slacks and old Mrs Wackett, the greengrocer whose cave-like shop on the corner always smelt of boiled beetroot and potatoes. She'd stand there in that same apron every day, swearing her head off. I recall she once asked my nan who the woman walking by with one of the local men was and, when she found out, her reply was hilarious. 'Gelfriend? That was 'is bleeding gelfriend? She looked like a fuckin' navvy wiv 'is bollocks chopped off!'

My granddad, Albert Lamb, was tiny – under five feet tall. I was bigger than him by the time I was eleven. He was a map printer by trade. As a lithographer, his was a reserved occupation and exempted him from military service. While men around him were going off to fight in the war, he kept working. Indeed he worked through World War I, the Depression of the thirties, World War II and right through until he finally retired at seventy. He made a good wage but he drank away much of what he earned. Granddad Lamb met his wife, Maud, my beloved Nanny Lamb, during World War I when she worked in a munitions factory.

Nanny Lamb was altogether bigger than my granddad – and she was really tough. She was a loving mother but she was never averse to giving her boys a clip round the ear and, as my Uncle Bill once said, 'If she landed you one, you knew it!'

*

My mum and dad did their best to make things work. Fourteen months after I was born, my brother Wesley came on to the scene. There were thousands of young couples thrown together by World War II, ill-matched and with nowhere to live but with family. That can put a strain on the strongest of relationships, to say nothing of one as tenuous and destined to fail as Ron and Jessie's. After four years of scrimping and saving, they managed to get enough for a deposit on a newly built house. They were free and all set to make a life together; surely if they had their own home, things would be better between them?

The place they bought was in Trinity Lane, Cheshunt, just north of London. In a rare romantic moment, they called the house 'Wedlands', a name that came from happy days my mum had spent with Nanny White's family in Dorset. Here we were, the four of us, a family. I think my mum and dad were caught up in a Hollywood-inspired make-believe world. They were of a generation that watched romantic wartime love films, and I think in some way they were following that unobtainable dream. She had been a Land Girl serving in the country and he was a Brylcreem boy. They were returning heroes after the war and this was what you did: you built a home, raised a family and lived happily ever after. But of course it wasn't like that. They weren't right for each other, they weren't right together. They argued and fought constantly.

Gradually the realities of married life, with two young boys, where neither party was happy, began to start forming cracks in their relationship, and neither of them was emotionally equipped to deal with the situation. They were kids, after all, both of them much younger than my son is now. With all that pressure to try and make it work, they were on a bobsleigh ride to hell. Night after night I'd wait for the rows to start, hoping that I would hear them before it got too stoked-up and I could grab the opportunity to run down the stairs and get between them, beg them to stop. Sometimes it worked but other times it didn't.

They're arguing down there, I thought to myself, *I can't believe it. They were friendly all day today but there they go again . . .*

I crept out of my bed and across the little landing so that I could hear more clearly what they were actually saying down in the kitchen, but they had closed the door. They must have been aware that I would be 'on alert' and they were keeping the volume down. But even though the words weren't all discernible, my trouble antenna told me that what was going on between them wasn't friendly. I could hear the odd word but it made no sense. Their rows rarely did. It always seemed to be about 'someone else', 'some other man' who likes my mum. That's all it ever seemed to be about, this 'other man' or all the men she looks at and likes more than him. And it always finished up the same way, with Mum crying and him shouting louder and louder. It was so frightening and now I could hear Mum saying she will leave him. I recently heard her say, 'I'll divorce you!' and when I asked John and Alan – the boys who live across the road who Wesley and me sometimes play with – what divorce means, they both said that 'it's where a mummy and daddy go and live in different houses', but when I asked them what happens to the children, they said they didn't know.

Suddenly the hallway door flew open and my mum came out and saw me crouching on the top stair.

'What are you doing there, Larry? I told you to go back to bed and go to sleep.'

'Why are you crying, Mum?'

The back door slammed and she looked through to where my dad must have gone out into the garden.

'Mummy and Daddy were talking and I got a bit upset. Now come on, you go on back to bed.'

'But why are you crying, Mum? What's wrong? Is Dad still angry?'

'Just a little bit,' she said as she wiped her eyes with her handkerchief.

'But why? I thought he was better? What's made him angry again? Why does he get so angry mum?'

'Questions, questions, you're always asking questions. Come on, silly, let's get you off to sleep.'

She led me up the stairs and walked me back to the bedroom. 'Why don't you sleep like your little brother? Look at him – Wesley's fast asleep like a good boy. Come on, you climb into bed and I'll give you a cuddle.'

'But I can't sleep when you and Dad are arguing,' I told her. 'It makes me frightened. Where is he?'

'Oh he's gone out into the garden.'

'But it's dark out there, what's he doing, he can't be doing the garden in the darkness, can he? Why doesn't he come in?'

'He'll be in soon. He won't be long.'

She cuddled me and swung her legs up on to my bed, curving her body around me. 'Mum, what does divorce mean?' I felt her draw a breath very quickly, then it went quiet for a long time. I heard the back door open and then close. I could feel her tension increase as she struggled with my question and as she heard my dad coming back in.

'JESSIE!' We both jumped at the sound of his loud whisper from the bottom of the stairs.

'I'll be down in a minute, Ronald, I'm just getting Larry off to sleep,' she called back, as softly as she could so as not to wake the deeply sleeping Wes. She wasn't answering me.

'What does it mean, Mum?' I was determined to have her explain this seemingly impossible state. How could John and Alan be right? I had to hear it from her.

'Tell me. Speak, Mum. I heard you say it again tonight!'

'Well,' she said, and I could feel her tensing up again, 'it means . . . it means . . . when two people who are married to each other live in different houses.'

'What? Like next door to each other?'

'No, not next door. Sometimes a long way away from each other.'

'But Mum, where do the children go if the mum and dad live in different houses? They can't live in two places, can they?'

'No, dear, they can't.'

'So where do they go then? And what happens to the house that they lived in before. Who lives there?'

'Well someone else comes and lives there, another family.'

'So does that mean that the mummy and daddy and the children that don't live in the house any more aren't a family any more?'

'Oh my little Larry,' she sighed, 'you do ask a lot of questions.'

I half turned my head to her and whispered, 'Are we going to stop being a family, Mum?'

I suppose I must have known already that it couldn't go on; for one thing I wouldn't have been able to put up with it continuing the way it was. They seemed to hate each other, but of course that was impossible: they were married, which meant they loved each other. That's what they said every time they made up after the latest row, that they loved each other. They rowed endlessly but they would always make up. When they kissed and cuddled again, that wonderful feeling of warmth would flood over me and through me and just for a while I would feel good. We were a normal family in those brief moments. But I'd begun to lose confidence in their shows of affection. It was all too hard, all too sad and all too frightening and, I think, more than anything for a child – forced to grow up very quickly by the disastrous antics of their parents – it was just too much to take on and, frankly, too embarrassing, even for a kid.

These two adults, the two most important people to me in the world, just so very obviously didn't like each other. Even a child could figure that one out. So who were they trying to fool with their shows of affection? Themselves? Ron and Jessie were misfits most of the time – it seemed they utterly detested each other. I still can't understand why they didn't just call it a day and break up. That now would seem the obvious thing to have done, but back then, in the final gasps of a Victorian world, I suppose they had to try and make a go of it.

If I started to consider how they might be better off apart, I would be forced to think again about what the children did when their mummy and daddy lived in different houses. That was just too difficult to comprehend.

I felt my mum shiver and then she hugged me even more tightly to her. 'Of course we won't stop being a family, son. Don't you worry, Mummy just said that to Daddy in a temper. Of course we're going to stay a family, don't you worry.' I'm sure now she was trying to convince herself as much as me.

'You promise, Mum? You promise you didn't mean it? Promise – cross your heart and hope to die?'

She kissed me on the back of the neck. 'Cross my heart and hope to die. Now come on, you've got school in the morning. Give mummy a kiss and you go off to sleep.'

She gave me a last hug and kissed me on the forehead before she walked to the door. She started to close it behind her.

'No, leave it open, Mum, so I can see the landing light.'

We both knew what I meant and she gave me a knowing smile. I heard her steps go down the stairs and the door to the kitchen click shut, and I strained my ears to hear any tell-tale sounds but it had all gone quiet.

I thought about going back to my stair-top listening post, but I was just too tired. That was it: another day – much like every day with its turmoil and tears – gone.

When I opened my eyes the next day those same thoughts were swirling around in my head. *What does happen to the little children?* I suppose it must have ended peacefully last night or I'm sure I would have woken up. Wesley is still fast asleep, untroubled by it all. I wonder if he does just sleep through or whether he just ignores it? Or perhaps he is just too sensitive to be able to believe that it's going on?

I crept down to the kitchen, the bare boards of the staircase cool under my feet. One of the steps was starting to have the beginnings of a creak; Dad said we wouldn't notice that once the stair carpet went down, but I didn't want to wake anyone so I gave it a miss and almost tripped. It was ten past, according to the kitchen clock: perfect timing. I filled the kettle to the bottom of the spout, and lit the gas with the pistol on the wire of Mum's pride and joy – and the source of many delights – her New World cooker. I put out two cups and saucers and got the milk and sugar from the larder. This had been my job for about a year now. I was always keen to be doing something to help, so when I'd turned five and started school, Mum and Dad – I think mainly Dad – had decided that I was old enough to make the morning tea. Having been meticulously

instructed on the way to scald the teapot and exactly how
much tea to put in, how long to leave it brewing, how to stir it,
how much milk to use and exactly the right amount of sugar
to put in each cup, I'd finally been let loose on what would
become the routine of a lifetime.

They were still asleep when I walked through their bedroom
door, but Dad's eyes flicked open the second I put his tea
down next to him.

'Hello son, what time is it?'

'About half past six I think, Dad. Morning Mum.'

'Morning son. Ooh tea, lovely, what a good boy you are.'

'Is it all right, Dad?'

'Perfect, couldn't do better myself,' he said as he turned his
back on Mum.

I could sense that things hadn't been totally resolved and
that perhaps it might be best to leave them alone.

'I'm going to get Wes and go to the brook,' I told them.
'Wes! Wes! Let's go fishing, come on.' I ran into our room,
shaking him as I pulled off my pyjamas and pulled on my
shorts. 'Come on, it's sunny! Where are the nets?'

And that was how we lived, two little boys only fourteen
months apart; we were close enough to be friends who did
everything together. We lived in a brand-new house on a
little street on the edge of pastureland where big-horned beef
cattle grazed and we had our very own brook that ran along
the front of our house – it even had a little bridge to cross
it – and in the brook there were sticklebacks and redthroats,
water beetles and all sorts of creatures to catch and keep in
bottles, tins and jars. It should have been an idyllic existence,
if only those two indoors could learn to love each other! Then
it would all be perfect.

They could be such fun. Sometimes we laughed and
laughed – all of us – we laughed until we cried. Wes and I
would wait for Dad on the little bridge and when we saw him

walking down Trinity Lane we would run to meet him and he would pick us both up in his big strong arms and carry us on to the house. Our dad, then the best dad in the world and our mum, the best mum in the world. Mum was a brilliant cook: the cakes, the sponges, the pies – she made us some lovely things; we were so lucky. On the occasional happy days everything seemed blissful.

'Come on boys, it's time for school. Larry, Wesley, come and get your shoes on.'

School was fun. We lived almost opposite and Mrs Robertson the head teacher was a real mother hen; all the children in her care were coddled and cared for in those daunting early years at school. Trinity Lane School was housed in an old building at the back of the church and that was where I began to enjoy being 'a clever boy'. Mum had had me reading a year or so already and so I had a head start over most of the other children. I enjoyed those days at school, but when the bell rang I was keen to get home.

I walked back into the house alone. Wes had gone straight down to the brook to see the fish we'd caught before school. As I opened the front door I caught the heavenly smell of cakes cooking. My mum called out from the kitchen, 'Is that you boys?'

'It's just me, Mum. Wesley's down at the brook,' I replied.

'Well go and tell him to change his clothes. I don't want him all covered in mud.'

I ran back down to find Wes. 'Mum says you've got to come in and change, come on!'

'Oh all right, I'm coming.'

I ran back up the path and into that kitchen full of wonderful cake smell. 'Can I clean the bowl, Mum?' Even as I said it I had the big brown mixing bowl in my arms and was already licking the remains of the cake mix from the spoon as though it were a big lolly.

'Save some for Wesley though, don't be greedy!' she said, laughing at me.

I heard Wesley giggling and there he was with Dad in the doorway. My mum looked at him and smiled. 'You're early, I haven't even started the tea. What's that under your arm?'

'I'm going to make some brawn so I got this from the butcher's.'

As he said it, my dad unwrapped the grubby white paper and plonked half a pig's head down on to the kitchen table. It was rather weird but Wes and I were both fascinated. But Mum turned her back and walked out of the kitchen. 'Ughh, that's disgusting,' she said turning her head.

Dad looked at us and winked. He carefully slid open the table drawer and, taking the carving knife, he dug out the one blue, staring eye and, having severed the various connecting nerves and blood vessels, he held the thing to his forehead and followed my mum out into the hallway like a cyclops.

'Jessie! Look at this, come on, look.' My mum turned to look at what he was talking about and screamed. She took off for the living room and then through the French windows and into the garden. Wes and I were highly amused but Mum was obviously terrified. She wouldn't let Dad near her; he chased her all around the garden. By now my mum was really shrieking in fear. She ran back into the house and locked the door.

And so it went on, the ups and downs; amongst the tears there were moments of hilarity, but the one constant was the fighting. Hardly a day passed, it seemed, without them being at some stage or other in some sort of row.

I remember a holiday in a holiday camp, Warner's at Dovercourt in Essex. It was bad enough to be at home with them when they were at each other's throats, but it was even worse in a tiny chalet with 'Hi-Di-Hi' coming down the loud-speakers. The journey by bus and train to the camp was like tiptoeing through a minefield, fearful that at any minute Dad would start off. When we got there it might have been a dank, evaporation-soaked hut but it was a holiday. We'd go to the funfair and to the boating lake and we'd have walks around the dockyard in Harwich. But the holiday couldn't last forever and they just couldn't seem to become the happy man and wife that they strived to be, like the glamorous stars of their favourite Hollywood movies.

This was all supposed to be a good time for the whole family.

That word again, the 'f' word.

3

Fish-shop Boy

I was seven and I already had my first proper job – apart from making the tea for my mum and dad, but that didn't count.

'More chips, Larry.' My dad would stick his head around the doorway from out the front behind the fryers.

'Coming up, Dad,' I'd call back.

'We only fry with peanut oil. None of your beef dripping at R.D. Lamb's Wet, Dried and Fried Fish Shop.' That was the name on the side of our crisp white Kraft paper carrier bags.

How on earth we ever finished up in that situation – owning a fish and chip shop – I have no idea. In the way that a lot of young couples do when the relationship isn't working, my parents decided that a change of life and home might just get them back on track. And all of a sudden we were on our way to a new home in a new town and a completely new life.

The shop was in Burgoyne Hatch, a tiny five or six unit mini-mall built to service local requirements. Our new home was in one of the recently constructed neighbourhoods out in the Essex farmland where Harlow was being developed. The New Towns were being built by the government in an initiative to provide public housing to take the pressure off the capital, which was still recovering from World War II. Thousands of new homes were being built on land just outside the green belt around London. Harlow was laid out neighbourhood by neighbourhood, each given names like Ladyshot, Felmongers, Harefield and Churchfields. They were often quite a distance from any shops so, as the development of those estates progressed, small parades of mostly family-run businesses were built, to provide local shopping for the rapidly expanding population.

Neither of my parents had had any experience of running a business of any kind, let alone a chippy. But they had somehow or other managed to get premises and we lived next door. What on earth ever possessed my dad to take that jump, I do not know.

We had no car and he couldn't drive anyway, so he'd be up at 3 a.m. to get a taxi to the old Billingsgate Market twice a week to stock up on fish. The shop was fitted out with counters and a great big stainless-steel frying range. I can still summon up that smell of cold cooking oil and fish. No matter how much my parents kept the shop clean, the smell still lingered on. It would get into your hair, your skin, your clothes; it permeated everything.

I very quickly learned how to use the potato peeler and chip the peeled potatoes, I even learned how to fillet plaice and cut the other fish into portions – nothing like starting young. And my dad paid me a farthing per tub of potatoes peeled – that meant in a couple of hours of peeling I could earn about sixpence, which would buy me a Mars Bar back then.

'You be careful with that knife, boy – it's as sharp as a razor.' Dad was definitely one for letting you learn the hard way. 'And don't drop it or you'll blunt the b— thing and you'll never fillet plaice with it blunt.'

Funnily enough, it never occurred to me that he could stand at the bottom of the stairs – I'd seen him do it many times – yelling up at my mum, calling her the most disgusting things, words that I should never have been exposed to: the 'f' word and the 'c' word both featured strongly, along with other endearing terms like 'slut' and 'trollop'. Yet he would stop dead on 'b—' when he was talking to me or to Wesley. It was as though a beast were unleashed in him when he got into a tantrum with my mum. And boy could he throw them.

'You fucking slut!' he bellowed. This time he was standing at the top of the stairs. To make it all slightly surreal and even more terrifying, he was absolutely stark naked. My dad had long ago learned how to make those scenes – because that is what they were, scenes or stunts – as terrifying as possible for us. I suppose it must have been cleansing for him; it was a way of releasing all the anger inside as he stood there at the stop of the stairs like some primeval beast screaming his head off. 'You fucking slut. I WILL KILL YOU!'

The decibel level was unreal; he projected his voice with such control and volume.

I have no idea what was going on – he's dead now so I suppose I never will – but I remember being totally transfixed with fear. The image is branded on my brain.

The climax of the scene saw him reach down, crouching as he gripped the edges of the brand-new and newly laid stair-runner. He stood up slowly, gradually straightening his legs, and using every joule of energy in his being, he curled his arms and yanked that runner from the floor.

Flip, crack, ping, clatter, clatter, clatter.

All the fixings, rods, brass brackets and tacks pinged, flipping, slipping, sliding and bouncing down into the hallway.

All the while he was roaring blood-curdling obscenities at my mother. I can see and hear him to this day.

'Nice one, Dad.' That's what I should have been able to say as a son, but I'm sure there was nothing else to do but find shelter with Mum. But he dominated us all. My mum and I would be cowering in fear of what would come next. He never went so far as to hit any of us, but there was always that threat of abuse or violence, a suggestion that there was more to come. He'd been quite a drinker at one time but he'd stopped it totally by this point. He was stone-cold sober, which

I suppose makes it even more terrifying; it was very sinister now I come to think of it. The violence that he used in the way he shouted at us and in the stunts that he pulled kept us living in fear. Just like his father before him, this crazy little man would seemingly do anything for attention. He wasn't afraid to make a scene, to throw and smash things and scream and shout. He would flip out over the tiniest things; he would just fly off the handle for no reason. All of a sudden the atmosphere would change.

My dad had had a rough time as a kid: according to him my drunken granddad picked on him no end; he bullied and tormented him. My granddad went so far as to beat my father. He'd slept three to a bed with his brothers and he told me of one night being pulled from the bed whilst asleep, his father really hitting him hard. At the age of eighteen Ron finally sought escape by joining the air force. According to him, he didn't have a good war. Years later, in a rare moment of intimacy, Ron revealed that he'd been terrified of going out on operations after the sights he'd seen and the things he'd had to do. He'd flown on bombers and he'd seen a lot of friends chopped to pieces by machine-gun fire. He used to have to lift them out of the planes and he couldn't face having to scrape up the remains of his mates any more.

Each time he went up in a plane his life expectancy got shorter, and with each flight the chances of him not returning increased. It had a terrible effect on him, and he finished his duty guarding prisoners of war rather than taking to the skies again. He was traumatised and there was no support to deal with his feelings after the war. In fact, one day an NCO came to wake people from their bunks and grabbed him from his bed. Of course, buried deep inside him was the memory of his father doing the same to him and instinctively, fearing another beating like the one his father had dished out, he'd hit the NCO. He almost got thrown out of the air force for that. So,

without any support, years later, everything that he'd interal-
ised would come erupting to the surface without warning and,
in the way that his father had been towards him when he was a
boy, my dad would turn into a wild animal at the drop of a hat.
I remember his brother Bill saying to me, 'He's potty, your old
man-bom-boms.'

The 'stair-runner scene' had sort of put the kibosh on life
in Trinity Lane. So now it was a new school, new home, new
life. In a new shop.

Harlow seemed to be mud, mud and nothing but mud.
That's what it was like living in a town being developed on
ancient Essex countryside. For a seven-year-old boy, this new
life seemed like an adventure, and for my dad it was the first
time he had worked for himself. 'I'm my own boss,' he would
proudly say. It was a big change and seemed like such a step
up the social ladder, as we were born into the working masses
and grew up where putting in long hours for local companies
was a way of life. But it didn't make any difference where we
were, my mum and dad didn't stop fighting. It wasn't really
fighting; it was her getting picked on by him. He wasn't satisfied with her, it's now patently obvious: he wanted someone to
blame for being trapped.

So they fought for two more years.

My dad was always accusing my mum of cheating on him,
though of course she never was. He was a jealous and posses-
sive man. It was a frightening form of possession, his jealousy was totally unfounded, but in his mind he wanted to
control her and was fearful that he couldn't. Evidently granddad Lamb had been the same with Nanny Lamb, some deep
dark vein of jealousy passed on from father to son. It was
completely groundless.

I think the saddest moment for me – and perhaps the
moment my father really took his rages a step too far –
happened when I was out one afternoon. I was always fearful

of what would happen when I wasn't there. Scary as it was to live under that roof and watch it all, I was even more frightened when it came to spending time away from them. I was a member of a church-based youth group called the Junior Covenanters. I'd only really joined because if you went to ten consecutive meetings you got a shiny badge. I did, and soon after I also got to go to their annual jamboree in London without my parents. I'd never done anything as exciting as that! We met up with other groups from all over the country and sang jolly songs and ate sandwiches and played games. I had a brilliant day, and when the coach dropped us off again I ran back from the community centre full of stories from my trip. But when I opened the front door I could tell something was wrong. I knew I shouldn't have gone and left them. It was quiet, too quiet.

As I closed the door behind me I listened intently. I could hear my mum crying very softly. I walked in to the tiny front room to where a set of glass double doors opened into the little dining room. My mum was standing there, the sorriest sight I have ever seen. In a fit of rage my dad had emptied the teapot on to her head and there she stood with a very neat cone of steaming tea leaves piled on top of her hair. As she wept, her tears mixed with the brown stream of tea running down her face, her nose and chin and on to her dress. My father lurked somewhere like a caged beast. I could sense him somewhere upstairs, his silence simply terrifying. He started to stomp around, wanting attention.

As he stomped around upstairs, I looked at my mum.

'It's alright, Mum, come on, let me wipe your face,' I said.

'I didn't mean to leave the tea standing so long, I was only gone a minute.' My mum sobbed.

That was all it would take for him to fly off the handle: a cup of tea not quite to his liking.

I didn't know what to do. I think a part of me wanted to run and hit him, for all the good it would do from a small boy, but I just stood there and held her. How had my parents come to this?

★

I look back now at that time when I was eight or nine and my parents' violent and turbulent marriage was on its final legs and I'm not sure how I coped. On the outside I think they seemed like a normal couple and other people didn't have a clue what went on in our house. If they were rowing and someone turned up unexpectedly they would switch to being a happy couple but I knew what was going on and that was so difficult to deal with, that pretense. Why couldn't they keep that act up for *us*? The reality was that the rowing had become more and more frightening.

Throughout that time, though, Gabba would come and visit regularly. He must have got a sense of what my dad was like from the time we'd all lived with him and Nan. Gabba now had a car, so he would help out, and he would always arrive with gifts: usually things he had made for Wes and me. He was a very skilled amateur carpenter and could more or less turn his hand to anything. He made us a soapbox cart, the likes of which no one else had. It was solid with matching pram wheels and it even had a brake and a ledge on the back for one of us to stand on. He was the one to get me my first bike too. It was second-hand but he completely refurbished it and gave it a new coat of paint. I was so proud.

Next door to the fish shop was an open piece of ground that used to be our playground. It was where we made a bonfire on Guy Fawkes Night and we would keep the embers going, making new fires for days. We'd burn things on the fire, melt things, we'd cook things on it and use it to harden arrow tips. Dad taught us how to make really powerful bows and we'd fire our arrows up into the sky, watching as they disappeared.

But that land was the site for a new neighbourhood pub. I didn't know it then, but from the day they began digging the foundations with picks and shovels, the clock was really ticking for us as a family. The blokes on the site started to hear the ructions and the rowing – they couldn't avoid it – and so Ron's bad temper actually led to his being set free.

'She was a little smasher, your mum, always was, my Jessie.' Gordon 'Lofty' Bartrip, one of the labourers on the site, came into our lives. Well over six foot tall, he was the strapping son of a head gardener who worked on one of the big posh estates around Loughton, Essex.

Gordon had taken a shine to Jessie. She had offered him a cup of tea one day and of course as a working-class boy he'd been properly trained on how to accept that courtesy. They'd hit it off. And more than fifty years later they're still together. Still making each other cups of tea.

Of course it didn't go down well with my dad. Even before Mum and Gordon got together, my dad had his suspicions, and that was all it took. When my mum fell pregnant with my sister Penny, my dad was evidently suspicious of whether the baby was his – though of course it was. One afternoon when I came back from school I was worried when Ron wasn't in the backyard of the shop: he should have been there preparing fish for the evening's trade.

'Wes, where's Dad?' I asked my brother.

'He's gone after some bloke and he's taken the big fish knife with him, rolled up in newspaper.'

This was typical of Wesley; he was unperturbed and would just wait and see what happened. I, on the other hand, went flying out of the shop.

'Which way did he go?' I shouted back.

'Down the lane I think,' he said, though I wasn't waiting around for any more directions from Wes.

My heart was pounding and I could feel the adrenaline

rushing as I ran along the tarmac as though my life depended on it. A minute or so later I saw him ahead of me, shuffling along in his old mackintosh and wellingtons.

'Dad! Where are you going?' I shouted.

He turned and said something that I didn't quite hear. I ran up beside him. He was spitting with rage. I pointed at the bundled-up knife he had gripped against his chest under the raincoat.

'What's that?'

'A knife,' he spat back.

'What for?' I pleaded.

'I'm going to kill that fucking bloke, that's what for.'

'What bloke, Dad?'

'The one who's chasing around after your slut of a mother. I'm going to chop his fucking head off.'

'Dad, you can't, you'll go to prison if you kill someone.'

But by now Ron was striding away from me and there was nothing to do but grab the tails of his coat.

'Dad, Dad, come back! You can't do this, Dad!' By now I was screaming at him.

He tried to pull his coat from my hands but I just hung on, refusing to let go. I think he actually needed someone to stop him because he suddenly turned and looked at me.

'Dad, come back to the shop,' I pleaded. 'If you go to prison, what will happen to us?'

'You'll probably be better off without me anyway,' he said.

But he must have realised that this was all a bit too much, that this had gone beyond a tantrum and that the consequences could be very grave. And so, almost as quickly as it had started, the situation calmed down and I, my dad and the great big fish knife all headed back to the shop. I think at this point he was actually going mad; some time afterwards he realised he needed help and he took himself off for electric shock therapy.

My sister, Penny, arrived on the scene, and to see her as a baby there was no doubt that my dad was her father. I think things calmed for a little while, but the writing was already on the wall. While Penny was just a baby, my father ran away with her one day. He just disappeared – there was no note or word to say where they were: they'd just gone. My mum was beside herself but there was just no sign of them. Some time later, the phone rang and it was my dad calling from a phone box. He was in the middle of Piccadilly Circus in his fish apron and wellington boots, with Penny in his arms. Gabba drove into London to get them and calmed everything down, but I think this must have been one of my father's final stunts before the whole thing just blew apart.

Eventually my job at the fish shop disappeared. But gradually, certainly not overnight. Dad started staying at Nanny Lamb's back in Edmonton and the shop just stopped being opened. I got sent out from school one day to get my teacher a fish-and-chip lunch. When I got there I found the shop empty. I walked back to her and gave her the 2/6d. 'Sorry miss, the shop was shut . . . I think they . . .'

I'm sure when it first happened, I instinctively made an excuse, but gradually – after the same thing occurred again a few times – I didn't bother. I'd tell the teacher up front that they might not be open and avoid the embarrassment.

I remember when we first moved there, my dad told me, 'Yes son, we'll have a whole chain of shops: R.D. Lamb & Sons. You wait.'

But it just slowly turned into a sort of mausoleum. I remember scrunching up my eyes, and shading them from the glare with my hand as I desperately sought some sign of Mum through the front window. But she was never there any more. The shop was locked and silent, still.

I really don't know where she was. We were obviously being

fed, I remember that much, but Mum just didn't seem to be around. She was preparing for her escape. And not just hers – we were a family of five by then with little Penny.

School was hard for me; with my world falling apart at home, I found it so difficult to make friends. There was no one I could confide in. Teachers would never get involved back then, and if anything they would mock me for coming in with uncombed hair and for being untidily dressed. But then my appearance for school was the last thing on anyone's mind, with all the tension in the house.

I began visiting Nanny Lamb's in Edmonton every Saturday, and I would stay for the weekend. Wesley stayed at home with Mum and Penny, so I got to go on my own to see my dad, who was always a bit calmer away from Harlow, and spend time with my nan and granddad. I used to have a lovely time there.

As we went through the summer of 1957, just as I was approaching my tenth birthday, it all finally fell apart. The war was over, of course, there was that to it – I didn't have to live around that any more. But now they weren't going to be together, it had finally happened just as I'd reluctantly accepted it would. The divorce thing was out in the open. Mum moved out, taking Penny with her, I can't remember there even being a goodbye. I didn't know where they had gone; for years afterwards I didn't know where my mum lived. Wes and I were going to live at Nanny Lamb's with Dad, so there were good things coming out of it, our life at home would be more settled. But somehow or other I had to deal with this totally impossible truth. I wasn't going to be living with my mum any more.

How was I going to face up to that?

I have absolutely no idea how I dealt with it. But knowing what an emotional volcano I am even now, I must have cried two oceans. And to think that somehow or other I've managed to forget how bad I felt as I mourned my loss, that it's all scarred over, is a miracle. The strange thing is that Wesley has the same missing link in his memory of it all.

How does a child cope with a loss like that?

4

Life at 192

I have to say I think I was resentful about this step backwards, this apparent demotion. When it had been a case of visiting Nan at 192 Brettenham Road East, it was all rather fun, something of a sideshow or a trip back in time but of course I'd never really lived in the place before. It was always somewhere we visited, the family home of my father. He was full of stories about the place; it was where he'd spent his childhood and where he'd left to join the air force. To me it was a complete contrast to everything that I'd been used to in terms of a place to live.

My life up until the break-up and the move to Nanny Lamb's had been pretty much a suburban affair. Enfield, where I'd first been lodged, and then Harlow New Town were a far cry from the grimy corner of Edmonton I now found myself in. Low brick walls and privet hedges fronted the small terraced houses; we'd call them workers' cottages now. There was just a tiny space, in no way a garden, in front of the bay-windowed 'parlour', or the front room as it was coming to be called. It was always the 'parlour' to Nan and Granddad, even though for a long time before Wes, Dad and I had sought refuge there, Nan had made it her bedroom.

The house was tiny. I'm sure now it would feel like living in a matchbox. The front door opened into a tiny passage that led directly to the staircase. Off to the left was the door to the parlour and then just next to the stairs another door led into the room we called the kitchen. It housed the table and four or five chairs and in one corner was a two-seat settee. The fireplace had a big old mirror over the mantelpiece and, in the other corner, beneath a big sash window that looked out into the backyard, was a matching armchair. Taking pride of place in that corner was the telly.

There was a cupboard under the staircase where the coal was kept. I can still remember Mr Lawrence the coalman, blackened with coal dust, hauling in those big hundredweight sacks on his back. With great bangings and rumblings they were tipped into the bunker. 'There you go, Mrs Lamb, that should see you through for a few days,' he'd say over the sound of the dogs barking and growling and having to be restrained from attacking this big noisy creature. I can still smell the unmistakable scent of the moist, hand-cut coal, which drifted through the whole house.

The kitchen was where we lived: it was the heart of the house. All meals were taken at that table and everything was done on it. The dogs both lived under it: Mick, a poor, much-loved, tired old Labrador mix, and Nipper, a hugely overfed spaniel with a back so wide and matted he felt like a smelly old rug. Beneath that table was their den.

One step down from the kitchen was the scullery, which was what we would now call the kitchen. There was a big old china sink in the far corner with a cold tap and, by the side, an 'Ascot' gas water-heater, a draining board, a gas cooker, a little refrigerator and a small 'meat safe' with fine wire mesh over the door to keep food fly-free. That was it. The door from the scullery led out on to a small side yard and that ran out into a garden, but that was just a repository for anything on its way out of the house on the way to the dustman. It wasn't very tidy, it was primarily a space to hang washing, I suppose, and of course to accommodate the 'Chamber of Horrors', the 'Khazi' or the 'Throne Room'. A toilet inside was one thing

I did miss from my 'modern' suburban lifestyle; the alfresco variety just brought it all home that in a sense we had been downgraded. Creeping out there in the middle of the night in the rain for a pee? No thanks. But we were stuck with it. No conveniences.

Baths were considered a bit of a luxury. I think the family had long dispensed with the zinc model in front of the fire because a few pennies (and a fifteen minute walk to the Town hall) got you a big, freshly laundered towel and a bar of soap and a huge tub full of water so hot it would melt you. Once a week was enough. Wash-downs in front of the sink were the order of the day, and when Wes and I realised that the money intended for the 'slipper-baths', as they were called, got you a session in the second-class swimming pool next door (the division of facilities into first- and second-class still existed in the 1950s), there was no contest. We smuggled out our trunks and a towel and came back just as clean.

Moving to Nanny Lamb's was a huge jump backwards. It wasn't as if we'd led a privileged existence, although having been shopkeepers I guess it was a step down, and our new, lower class felt a bit of a burden. More than anything, though, it was the way this new environment just seemed so old-fashioned; this new life with no Mum to cushion the blow was just not good enough. Nan was great, but she wasn't our mum.

Did I start off crying every day? I do know my darling nan used to cuddle me to her bosom when I was missing my mum. It didn't happen every night, but it certainly happened more than once. The sense of peace that her embraces induced, just as I was drifting off, cuddled and beloved: it's so vivid.

At the time, though, particularly when I was a teenager, I made up bald-faced lies to the kids at school if they ever asked where Mum was. 'She's in the clothing business and she works all over the country, she doesn't come home much.' That was the sort of thing I told people on the odd occasion

– just when needed – when talking 'mums'. Sometimes I think I even tricked myself into thinking it was the truth. How I must have missed that motherly presence in my life.

Where did my mum live throughout that whole time? We didn't know. She was *persona non grata* – we were absolutely forbidden to talk about her. We were still little boys and we were hardly happy about this half of our world being blotted out of our lives, but when I talk to my brother now about that time, we both realise that we can't remember much of what we were feeling; thankfully all these years later much of it has scarred over.

Each week we met Mum at the bus stop on Angel Road, just around the corner from Nan's. We knew only roughly when she would arrive and we would wait for the 191, 102, the 144 and the 84 buses. Sometimes we'd stand there for hours if she'd been delayed, but in the end she would arrive with Penny. I seem to remember Woolworths was a favourite place for us to go or we would walk round and round Pymmes Park.

Now all those visits, all those Saturdays seeking something to do, they've all blended and become a single memory. I really can't differentiate between them. It was all just waiting at the bus stop and wandering around the park.

Just around the corner, back at Nan's, we had to make a new life, a life away from Mum and Penny. There was no point wishing for something else – that wasn't going to happen. Life was now at 192.

5

Life with the Lambs

There were bonuses to the new life without Mum, and having Uncle Terry at home full time was a big one. Terry was my dad's youngest brother and he was always fun to be around. Living with Nanny Lamb meant we saw a lot more of the family. We were now, after all, resident in the family seat of 192, and all the boys would drop in to see Maud – although never my granddad 'Gurgling Bert', it seemed. I, seeking out male role models to replace the damaged one I instinctively knew my dad had become, would relish these visits.

My uncles were all characters. Great Uncle Wally, my granddad Albert's brother, would visit on most Sunday mornings. He collected the paper money from his customers every week and by the time he'd come in for a cup of tea at the end of his round, the leather pouch he wore over his shoulder like a satchel would be swollen with coins. In the end, I'd get to do that round myself, and it made me feel so important, aged twelve or so, to be carrying all that money.

His real name was Walter and he was a veteran of World War I. He'd been a crewman – a machine gunner, in fact – in the 'Little Willies', the first ever tanks, and had come home unscathed.

He lived well off the newsagency business that he'd taken over from his father H.T. Lamb; now into his sixties, he enjoyed days at the races and living the life of a 'gentleman of the turf'. His world was far from anything that I could relate to, but it evoked a certain mystery and sophistication that certainly wasn't too much a part of my life.

His namesake and nephew, Wally, my dad's eldest brother, despite having been crippled in childhood by polio, was a completely self-educated, self-made businessman. He'd been tormented by other children as a boy and had channelled his phenomenal physical strength – which was doubtless inherited from Nan – into his one good arm. His punch was lethal and, by the time he was a young man, all taunts had long since faded into silence.

He made bows and arrows and catapults and hour after hour would aim at targets that he would set up at the end of that disastrous old backyard. In years gone by he would apply the same dedication to practising his boxing skills by filling a canvas kitbag with sand and hanging it up out there in the yard. His good arm and deadly fist became toughened and toned through years of slamming it into that unforgiving punchbag. By the time I got to know him, he had a successful TV sales and repair business in Hayes, Middlesex, and had become a highly regarded fly-fisherman. Every Saturday afternoon of the season he would leave the shop and drive the hundred or so miles down to Somerset where he would fish for every possible second, his 'deadeye dick' aim dropping the fly right on target time after time. We got the salmon and trout to prove it.

Uncle Alec was the gentle soul of the Lamb brothers, the one destined – it turned out – to outlive them all. He was a real family man. He'd married his beautiful Irish wife, my darling Auntie Martha, during the war, and they and their children, my cousins Johnny, Patricia and Eddy, were the family I longed to be a part of. Uncle Alec had been in the air force and was always a source of fun. He was never without a joke and he was always doing something for somebody. He's an old man now, and his doting family still wait on him the way he always looked after everyone else.

Auntie Pauline, my dad's sister, was a gentle, loving soul, Nanny Lamb's only close female companion in that male-dominated household.

Uncle Bill was my godfather. He was the one I was always most like. There seems to be one tall Lamb in each generation. Bill was the one in his and I in mine. Everyone else was of average height. He'd suffered the same quips as a boy as I did: 'Must have been a big milkman that year!' But, unlike me, Billy was a fighter – a boxer in the Royal Navy. He'd been a divisional heavyweight champion and if crossed was known to hit people hard enough to lift them right off their feet.

He'd been torpedoed and was listed as Missing In Action on three occasions, but every time he had made it back to 192 for the thirty days' survivors' leave to which that entitled him. He'd swagger down Brettenham Road East, every inch the victorious matelot. He'd pull the string through the door that opened the latch and yell down the passage, 'Oyy! THE NAVY'S HERE!'

Bill was my hero. His wife, Auntie Ruth, and their daughter Carol lived just around the corner from Nanny Lamb, so I saw more of them than any of the others. Carol was a sort of big sister to me and, once I got into my teens – my very awkward teens – she would give me records and teach me how to dance. She even let me – as a gawky, spotty-faced sixteen-year-old – dance with her and her mates at 'The Royal', north London's number one dance spot. She must have had a heart of gold even to be seen with me, let alone to dance with me!

Living with Nanny Lamb, there would always be someone dropping by. It was a busy house, which I guess made a big change from the haunting silence of our old family home. The week days were about work for the three men and school for Wes and me but the weekends meant a leisurely timetable that revolved around that little kitchen. As we listened to

Uncle Sandy on the radio playing children's favourites like 'The Laughing Policemen' or 'Mud, Mud, Glorious Mud', nan made the ritual steak and kidney pie, the fixture for a Saturday lunch. I helped her cut up the meat and make the pastry for the crust. Everything had to be just so and it was a real taste delight. The afternoon would end with tea which meant perhaps big fat sausages and mash and all this served up as we listened to the results of the football and the men filled out their pools coupons. Saturday evening ended quite late with *The Perry Como Show* and *Bilko* on the telly. Sunday meant *Two-Way Family Favourites* while the lunch was roasting and filling the whole house with its glorious smells. *Round the Horne*, *The Navy Lark* and then an old black and white film would follow. We'd have high tea with shrimps and winkles and then finally, to round it all off, *Sunday Night at the London Paladium*. Sheer, organised, regular bliss!.

We all knew that we wouldn't be at Nanny Lamb's forever and that one day we'd get our own place. I'd learned how to do everything about the house at Nan's; she really prepared me for the inevitable moment when we'd go away. Washing, ironing, cleaning shoes. Wes and I washed and dried every dish.

I remember her teaching me to make a stew: a sort of a mince and tatties, London-style. I never learned how to make bread pudding, Nan's *piece de résistance*, though, that was left to my nan, and over the first few months, when we did eventually move out, once a fortnight I would go and visit her and carry one away with me. But they never made it all the way back home!

Dad had got a job – with a house included – back in Harlow. There was a perfectly good grammar school there but I couldn't face another change and all that that involved. So I inadvertently made life easier regarding Mum by deciding to commute to school from Harlow on the train. The long journey meant that as soon as the bell rang at the end of the day, I would head off for my train, so any small friendships that I'd managed to form were left there at the school gate. There weren't as many opportunities for people to ask questions about my family life or my mum. Now my life was completely split: there was home, 88 Radburn Close – 'Two Fat Ladies' as bingo callers would say – and there was school.

I was already starting to fall 'off message' as far as study was concerned. The homework thing came as a big shock to me and I just couldn't deal with it. Coming home after school was all about getting the tea ready for when Dad came in from work. As long as that was under control and the table was all set on time, then any spare moments were surely for mucking about, weren't they?

And to make it worse, I'd found myself a job!

History repeated itself when a mate of Dad's mentioned that the boy who worked at the shop where his wife worked was leaving and had to be replaced – they needed a fish-shop boy.

6

Mother's Love

Wes, Ron and I were living on our own now, experiencing the bachelor life, but I had some fond memories of my time living with Nanny Lamb and the rest of the family.

'I'm gonna sit right down and write myself a letter and make believe it came from you,' Terry sang. Terry was always singing. As a boy born just before the start of World War II, he'd spent his youth and early adulthood absorbing American music. He would tell us that 'this is the sort of music you'll still be singing when you're sixty, not that fucking rock-and-roll nonsense.'

I'd bought my first ever record, 'To Know Him Is to Love Him' by the Teddy Bears, but as Terry had the gramophone, I could only ever play it when he was out. He was so dismissive of everything that wasn't to his taste. 'I'll be glad when his balls drop!' was his response to a heartfelt aria sung by some soprano that happened to be on the radio once when he walked into the room.

But he was right: his music – Ella Fitzgerald, Fats Waller, Billy Eckstine, Dinah Shaw – eventually distilled into my music. And the songs by those stars that he sang along with are the songs I still sing now in my sixties.

As he sang, Terry was shaving in front of the kitchen mirror. The kitchen at 192 was where we did everything. We really lived in it. As Terry turned from the table where he'd rinsed the soap from his razor, he stepped over something before continuing his shave. Dad, Nan, Wes and I stood watching him. We'd just come back from the Isle of Wight. My dad bent down to see what it was Terry was stepping over. 'How long has he been there? He went missing at Waterloo Station.'

'He was there when I came in about half an hour ago.'

'He' was Granddad Albert – Gurgling Bert, as he'd been dubbed by his sons, since he was now such an old sot he could hardly be understood – and there he was, laid out prone on the floor between the kitchen table and the fireplace.

'Is he all right?' My dad was now next to the old boy, checking him for signs of life.

'I've no idea,' laughed Terry. 'Might be in luck, he could be brown-bread!'

But he wasn't, he was just in a drunken stupor, which was pretty much par for the course.

We'd had a great holiday on the Isle of Wight, a huge treat courtesy of Nan and grandad; we'd stayed in a hotel and gone swimming every day. We'd sipped tea and munched cakes on the beach and ate out in restaurants. It was a happy time. But when we'd got to Waterloo on our way home we realised we'd lost my granddad. We'd looked around for a while and then, assuming he'd made his own way back already, we set off on our on buses and Tubes with our suitcases. It was when we finally got back to the house after our endless journey that we found him lying there, on the floor, amidst Terry's shaving ritual, clearly having stopped for a pint or two on his way.

There was a real upside to Albert's beer consumption: the deposits on the empty bottles traditionally went to Wes and me. Back in the pre-disposable container days, beer for home consumption was sold at off-licences, and my granddad was fortunate that there was one at both ends of the street. He was always too pickled to be bothered to take the bottles back, so we'd gather them up and return them at 3d per bottle. But it wasn't just Albert's empties that we cashed in. On a walk along the track behind the industrial estate, we stumbled across dozens of empty pale-ale bottles lying in the grass and nettles that grew by the side. We discovered the source of this potential gold mine: there was a beer-bottling plant on the estate and, as the lorries returned with the crates of empties, bottles would bounce out whenever the truck hit one of the many potholes on the track. It was too good to be true. We returned the next afternoon with plenty of shopping bags and an old push chair and cashed in more than two pound's worth of bottles that evening. It was like we'd won the lottery. And we harvested along that lane every two or three weeks.

My uncle Terry was the star turn at 192, but top of the bill, the grand empress, the real superstar was Nan – 'Maud', as all her boys called her. She was one of nine children raised in the East End. She had mothered six kids herself and, despite being led a merry dance by a dipsomaniac husband through-out their married life, she now absolutely ruled the roost.

She was funny and cheeky and bubbling over with love. She snuggled me and Wes under her wing and took over where Mum had left off.

'Don't waste all that, keep that peel thin, you'll finish up with no potato at all!' I spent a lot of time by her side at the kitchen table learning the basics.

'You can take that right back, it's not fresh . . .' she ordered the despondent butcher's boy who'd made the Saturday morning delivery of the week's meat. The boy watched Nan inspect every ounce of it laid out on the table.

'And change those kidneys, I want more suet around them!' And he knew he'd better be back with it put right.

Her rise to pole position in the household hadn't been easy. Albert, whilst always earning good money as a map printer, had 'pissed his wages up the wall' as Terry put it. In fact in the mid-1930s he'd drawn the winning ticket on the Irish Sweepstakes and won well over £600. It was an amount that in those days was enough to buy a house and completely change the status of the Lambs. But instead, as my dad told me, 'He bought all us boys a jumper, Maud and Auntie Pauline got a new dress each, he bought a three-piece suite and a piano for the parlour, and the rest went to Whitbread's.'

His drunken rampages were all a part of the family saga. It's hard to imagine it now: this tiny man was just five feet tall. He would sit at the table, in the place he always sat, with his bottle of beer and his glass as he slowly drank himself to death.

'How did you cope with him, Nan? When did he stop all his craziness?' It seemed the obvious question to ask her now she so clearly reigned supreme.

'I'd come back to the house later than usual one evening,' she said. 'I knew he was home: the front door was on the latch and the lights were off, I realised. I had to go back outside under the street lamp to find a shilling in my purse for the meter. I walked through the pitch-black passageway and stepped down into the scullery from the kitchen and realised I was standing in water.'

'So what happened, Nan?' I was transfixed, a teenage boy on the edge of my seat.

'I put a shilling in the meter and saw immediately what had happened. He'd stuck the garden fork through the side of my copper in one of his rages and all the soapy water that the clothes were soaking in had poured out all over the floor. I opened the back door and started to scoop it out into the yard with the coal shovel and then I just stopped dead, put down the shovel, walked up the stairs and burst right through the front bedroom door where I knew he'd be sleeping.'

'Up he sprung like a jack-in-the-box and I just landed him a right-hander, a real dough boy, right on top of his nose. And you know what? He was never any trouble from that day on – should have done it years ago!'

And so life at the Lambs with the six of us living there

– Wes, Dad and me sharing a room – muddled along nicely. And most importantly, there were no wars going on. Terry and Albert didn't ever speak a word to one another, which was a bit weird and uncomfortable, but at least there weren't the outbursts like before with my mum and dad. I remember happy times at Nanny Lamb's house.

Terry would surreptitiously sprinkle salt and pepper into Albert's beer when he wasn't looking and we would all wait for him to turn back from the television and take a long swig. There was never even the remotest recognition. Wes and I would be in hysterics as Terry smiled and egged us on; Albert would just stare at us through those beer-mottled eyes: 'What are you little buggers laughing at?'

But overall, living at 192 meant being part of Nan's life. She nurtured and loved us. Firm always, but beneath the bluff, gruff front she could put up, you knew she was a font of love.

Perhaps, after all those years of living in the shadows of a fearsome, drunk little man, and now in control of her life, she could help put right some of the damage he'd caused. Wes and I, offspring of her offspring, had come back into her charge, and now she had the time and no distractions she could put a bit of mother's love back in our lives.

7

Albert Hunt

One job wasn't enough, of course. I spent Tuesday, Thursday and Friday nights in the fish-and-chip shop earning the grand sum of thirty shillings (the equivalent of £1.50 now) for a total of twelve hours' work. That was good money for a teenager back then but I wanted more.

The fish-shop job was great and over the two or three years I worked there I really learned the ropes. Some of it was still the same as back in Burgoyne Hatch but now, as a young adult, I was able to work out in the front of the shop behind the counter serving and even learning to fry the fish and chips. The only downside was that I was constantly aware of the smell the fish and fat left on the skin and hair, but I think riding my bike everywhere must have kept me aired out.

Another boy called Larry – not a common name back then – a friend of Wesley's, was giving up his Saturday job in Harlow town centre's market and the man who ran the stall was looking for a replacement. I went to see him.

Back then I hadn't realised how many men named Albert would feature in my life: both my granddads were Alberts (although my mum's adoptive father was Fred, her real dad was called Albert) and now I was standing in the market square of Harlow New Town talking to Albert Hunt, a truly larger-than-life character.

I suppose he must have been in his mid- to late thirties,

perhaps a little older even, and he ran the busiest, noisiest, most colourful stall on the market. In fact he ran several stalls – he'd managed to bag a whole corner section, and by linking several spaces together he had the equivalent of a fruit and vegetable market of his own.

He prided himself on the fact that he sold more produce than any of the other stallholders. But shifting the amounts that were unloaded from his lorries at six o'clock in the morning took a lot of hard work, whatever the weather, the show went on. Albert could and would work harder than anyone. He taught me how to display his wares, all beautifully colour-matched and 'pretty as paint'. He taught me how to dress the fruit using the individual tissue wrappers so that each apple, orange or pear sat in its own little coloured nest with wonderful handwritten price cards. The whole thing was put together like a real work of art putting out 'the flash' as he called it.

He was of gypsy extraction and he was proud of it. In truth his passion was horses and he sold the fruit and vegetables to fund his equine pursuits, but whatever he did he made sure he was the best.

He dressed immaculately, in the traditional style of a successful horse dealer. His brown leather boots were always polished to a brilliant sheen, his hand-cut trousers with a tiny turn-up were tailored exactly to his trim waist and thighs. He wore exquisite jackets and waistcoats, with shirts worn open at the neck and a brightly coloured handkerchief or 'shtook' knotted in front of his Adam's apple. The whole thing was topped off with a cheese-cutter cap or, more usually, a neat, thin-brimmed brown trilby. He was so dapper!

This is the man who asked me, 'Can you shout, son?'

'Can I shout?' I laughed. 'In my house that's the only way to get heard,' I replied.

As he smiled there was a glimpse of a gold tooth just to the side of his mouth. It glinted between strong white teeth set against a skin constantly tanned by his year-round outdoor life.

'Right, come on. Get to work on them bananas.'

He took off his jacket and hung it carefully on a hook in the cab of his lorry. He rolled up his sleeves and took a money-pouch apron and tied it around his waist.

'Just copy me,' he said. 'Come on gels! Good lot a bananas 'ere! Ripe bananas, that's the way to buy 'em, mum! Bake, boil or fry, make a puddin', make a pie. Come on gels, what a lovely LOTTTTT!'

And that's all I needed, that was my cue. He gave me the strength. If he could do it, so could I. Sure I was a bit self-conscious, but there was something bold and slightly outrageous about it, and in all honesty I guess it really was my first public performance! My first big break, put in front of an audience.

Week by week, the patter that had been passed down from generation to generation passed on to me. All that vocal tradition: the costermongers from the East End came out into the country to a market in a new town where a boy descended from former East Enders had picked up the patter that his grandparents and probably their grandparents would have heard. 'Nobby Brussels', 'Good ripe tomatoes!' 'Cox's, right out of the boxes!' Who knows how long those little sound-bites had been used to peddle produce.

Albert took me with him to the wholesalers' market at Stratford where he did his buying, and he taught me how to load a van or lorry so that nothing shifted and not one scrap of space went to waste. He even let me drive his lorries long before I had a proper licence. One of them was a big old flatbed five-tonner with a funny old gearshift that sat above the engine and right back in the cab, about as weirdly placed as it could have been. He showed me what to do and trusted me to drive it out of the car park and onto the market square. Thrilling!

I worked hard and was never late. We always sold more of what he had to sell than anyone. Sometimes he and I would get into a competition, both of us shouting and 'serving up'. With old-fashioned weights and scales and totting everything up in our heads: no tills or calculators, not even a pencil and paper; you kept your wits about you all day long.

The biggest treat of all was going with him on the non-market days to buy and sell horses. I watched him at Southall Market looking at a horse being run up and down by whoever was selling it, looking at every detail of the beast in question: mouth, teeth, eyes and hooves – no detail overlooked. When he'd given it the once-over he always used to say, 'Go on, run him up again. Go on son, git up!'

This was his world, whether at a rather smart country fair or at the weekly horse market, he was just as much at home as any of them. There was always a wad of notes in his back pocket with a fancily tooled money clip. He was unforgettable, and to see him on the end of a rein with a big rearing young shire horse, only half 'broken', was something to behold. He was absolutely fearless.

The women idolised him. They were forever coming by to say hello and 'taking a look inside his horse van', even on afternoons when it was empty apart from a bale or two of hay! Some of that showman, just a little of his style, must have rubbed off on me. He gave me a bit of a boost that helped me realise that what I knew as my world was perhaps not for me, and that there was a different world out there – and it was there to be grabbed.

Something of his spirit inhabited me, infected me; so, with the fondest of memories and the greatest of respect, I say, 'Wherever you are, Albert Hunt, good on yer, guvnah! I owe you one. It was thanks to you that I got my first break in show business.'

8

Tangled Teens

Our new home was in Radburn Close in Harlow New Town. We each had our own bedroom, which was such a relief after the three of us sharing for four years. We had a garden and a shed and there were woods just a few minutes away. We had some nice neighbours in our new street, next door but one. Tommy and Barbara Coates had moved from the tougher area of Bermondsey; a newly married young couple, they seemed to take pity on our situation and invited us in. Wesley and I would sit in their happy, warm kitchen, drinking tea and eating toast, and it was a world away from our sad menage two doors away. I craved the comfort of being around them because they loved one another, they were comfortable and happy together, they were everything I wished my parents had been.

My dad was working as a draughtsman for British Oxygen. Wesley was going to the local comprehensive. People used to think I was more intelligent than him and I teased him a bit but it was simply due to the fact that the eleven plus had been dropped and he'd never gotten the chance to take the exam.

My teens were a mess. My mum was gone and now I was fourteen and Nanny Lamb was out of the frame too. I really needed some sort of female in my life. To complicate matters, I myself was cast in the role of housekeeper, head cook and bottle-washer. I don't remember feeling resentful about having to do all the daily chores. I think I'd taken on board the fact that those things would have to be done, and that if Ron was out earning a salary, he would need support, but it didn't leave much time for anything else.

I'd not really done myself any favours by staying on at Edmonton County. The commute involved taking two buses to the train station, a half-hour train ride, a quarter-mile run and then another bus – and then the whole bloody thing in reverse at the end of the school day. In winter I never saw the house in daylight. As soon as I got home, I had to get Dad's tea ready. Wes and I would eat on the hoof, but the ritual of setting the old man a place at the table and making him a simple meal – anything other than fish was OK; he had a bad psychological hangover from our days in the shop – had to be observed. I became the woman of the house.

Ron was very bitter and he played the role of jilted husband to the hilt. Of course it was a huge handful trying to raise two teenage boys as a single parent, but it would have been so much more pleasant if he hadn't been constantly badmouthing Mum. A teenage boy who is struggling to cope without his mother shouldn't really be told by his father that she is little more than a common whore. It didn't do anyone any good, not even my father.

Little Penny was getting to come for weekend visits during this period, which meant that we were spared those hours spent wandering around trying to find something to do in the park on our weekly visit with Mum. Wes and I would meet Penny and Mum at the bus stop up on the main road and have a little time altogether while she waited for her bus back to wherever it was she came from – we still had no concept of where or how she lived – then back the three of us would troop to Radburn Close.

I really can't think of how we entertained a five- or six-year-old but I suppose a large part of the reason she was there was to see Ron. We went for walks to the nearby woods, and sometimes we went on trips to the swimming pool.

Those weekends weren't all about happy family time, though: we had rows too. Somehow or other, one weekend Mum had sneaked us off to see Granddad White, dear old Gabba. We barely got to see him and he'd left a real big hole in our lives. Penny let it slip. In all innocence she started to talk about it. Ron went into meltdown mode. 'You ungrateful, disloyal little bastards! How could you be in that man's presence?' he shouted and bellowed at us. He was so sanctimonious, he played the part of the poor deserted and put-upon ex-husband well. His attitude was all about wondering how that evil woman could have abandoned him, and he was very good at putting on a 'poor me' performance. Wes and I had to defend ourselves for going to see our beloved granddad. What a way to treat kids. It was bad enough that we were denied our mother's love, but then to deny us access to a grandparent too just felt so unfair.

Instinctively I must have known he was nuts. Try as we might, there was no defence: in his view we were guilty of this transgression and it was marked down on my dad's list.

9

Grammar-school Boy

It had all become so important. This 'passing the scholarship' thing, becoming a grammar-school boy. When the brown envelope finally did arrive, it was addressed to Ron so I had to wait for him to come home from work.

'Well, sorry to say, son ...' My dad slowly dragged his words out. My heart almost hit the back of my throat: had I not made it in? 'Only joking, you've got a place at Edmonton County!'

It had been my first choice, influenced by the fact that some of the other boys in my class had made it their first choice too. David Dow, Robert Birch, Tony English and I were all accepted along with three or four girls whose names have long since escaped me – at that stage I wasn't as interested in girls as I later became. My dad's view of women during that time we lived our bachelor existence was that they were prey. He was of the 'find 'em, feel 'em, fuck 'em and forget 'em' school of thought. I think he could still charm them, but ultimately women were sexual objects. Perhaps because of that I was sexually driven but it didn't really get me anywhere. There were no major physical encounters with the girls until I was almost eighteen.

Right from the first moment of walking through those gates at the boys' entrance – girls were strictly assigned to the other end of the school – I was very much a square peg in a round hole. I had been one of the brighter boys at junior school but grammar school was something I just wasn't prepared for. It was nose to the grindstone from day one.

There were the unofficial 'greeting ceremonies' to be suffered: caps were torn off by the newly promoted second-year boys and heads dunked into sinks and soaked in freezing water – but it was nothing too serious and probably something that did in fact bond us all together. But the homework, and all those rules and regulations; the prefects and head boys and girls and the teachers wearing long black flowing gowns: that all took a lot of getting used to. What had I let myself in for? It was all so formal, all so strict and all about one thing: getting your name up in glittery gold-leaf letters on the timber-panelled wall of fame in the school hall. The staff were uniformly dour and distant. Among them all there was only one bright face, Miss Burbidge, my biology teacher was warm-hearted and kind. To me she was to one to give off any sense of friendliness which is something I badly needed. She is a friend to this day

They made no bones about it: exhibition scholarships, state scholarships, this was what we were here for. O levels and A levels were just the ticket you had to earn. I was totally unprepared.

The lessons were hard enough, but no relief came when it got to 'games' at the end of the day. I was really overweight from about eleven onwards; my breasts were bigger than most of the ones the girls in my class were sporting – not that I ever got close to seeing them! I can see that Nanny Lamb was trying to make me happier by giving me plenty of sweets and treats – on top of all the glorious meals she cooked. I got picked on a bit as a fatty, although fortunately not too much as I was also fairly tall, so all but the biggest of bullies steered clear. There were always some who couldn't resist taunting me, though.

When it came to putting a little direction into the programme and starting to decide where my strengths might lie so that I could work towards the future, they made a big mistake and let me interfere.

'But I want to be a surgeon, sir, I want to save people's lives,' I told them, having watched too many episodes of *Emergency Ward 10*.

'Yes, Lamb, but that would mean you studying sciences – physics, chemistry and biology – and they are obviously not your strong subjects, whereas your history and geography marks are definitely more promising and your aptitude in French would certainly indicate you should take up German as a second foreign language.'

Maybe it was an early aptitude in the gift of the gab that led them to give in. For the next five years – I had to repeat the fifth form – I slogged away at physics and chemistry and to this day am still mystified by them. All I've done over the years is prove that my teachers were right in their instincts: I'm an absolute history nut and a geography freak and, after doing German at night school, I've also learned basic Spanish and Italian off my own bat. How much simpler would my life have been if I hadn't been so stubborn?

I suppose that by the time I left with a handful of O levels, my only real achievement was to have gone from a fat boy who was assigned as a marker during the annual torture of the 'cross country running' season, to one who ran for the school in the county championships. Finally, after getting 'half colours' for athletics, the one who always 'should do better' *did* do better!

10

Escape From College

I found the change from grammar school to what would today be known as sixth-form college pretty startling.

'Mr Lamb, what is the main difference between the British Constitution and the American Constitution?' a smiling lecturer asked me. My mind started racing. Does he even mean me when he says Mr Lamb? I looked around; all eyes in this classroom – the eyes of fifteen or so equally new students – were on me. He had to mean me then; I wasn't used to the formality. But now I had a big problem because I didn't really understand the question, primarily because – in a last-ditch effort to find something to study in the field of commerce and business at A level – I'd opted to study the British Constitution without even bothering to find out exactly what it was.

'I don't know,' I stumbled. 'I haven't done the British Constitution at O level, so I . . .' I let my words drift off, hoping his attention would be off me soon.

The smiling lecturer, Mr Lyons – or 'Dave', as he told us to call him – switched his attention to someone else. *I'm off the hook*, I thought. *At grammar school I would have been really humiliated for not being able to answer this.*

But that easiness and being treated as a young adult was more than I could deal with. It was like coming out of prison and getting to live in a holiday camp – even the 'guards' here were friendly. Needless to say, I took it all for granted, and half the time – because there was nobody dishing out punishments

– I didn't even bother to turn up to the lectures. It wasn't as though there were a lot of them, either. I'd been used to a full timetable of seven periods a day, five days a week, and now I had a total of about ten hours of actual classes to attend and nobody to keep me to it.

And there were girls to chat up at college, too: girls dressed in proper clothes, not encased in drab school uniforms and policed by imperious old spinsters. They all seemed so friendly and chatty and free – obviously we didn't know it at the time out there beyond the suburbs, but the sixties were happening, the times they were a-changing, and shaking off that uniform was just the start.

There were parties every weekend; there were dances that we organised ourselves, and there was sex. At last.

My seventeenth summer. I'd gone down to Devon with Wes. We travelled to Exmouth, which was eight hours on the coach from Victoria, but the long journey was worth the agony to be away on our own. We'd been going there for about three years running. There was a bed-and-breakfast place that we'd stayed at with Ron where the landlady really looked after us. She gave us big meals and we went on trips out on the fishing boats with her son David. But by now there was only one sort of fishing we were interested in, and there always seemed to be so many girls down there. We'd realised that on our one and only trip there with Ron and so had managed to get shot of him the very next year.

I was absolutely bound and determined to lose my virginity before turning eighteen. Wes had said goodbye to his a long time before, and I was fourteen months older than him. I'd finished with school and was about to start college; I would be eighteen in October and the clock was ticking.

St David's Hall in Exeter was where it happened. Wes got talking to a group of boys from Sutton in Surrey and we were really impressed because they had a car. At that time I was still busy failing my test. Between them and us, somehow or other we all started dancing with a fantastic-looking girl from the West Indies. She was just so lovely, she was such a great dancer, and after a while I realised she actually seemed to be interested in me! 'Do you want to come outside for a breath of fresh air?' seemed a reasonable question to ask, and I was certainly up for that, so off we went. We finished up round the back of the place just snogging like crazed people. We were both groping at each other; as there was nowhere to get ourselves comfortable, I took the plunge.

'Shall I go and get the keys to the car?'

She smiled. 'What for? We going for a ride?'

'Well,' I laughed, 'I haven't passed my test yet, but we could certainly have one of those.'

The car was a Zephyr Zodiac with a big bench seat at the back, and that's where I finally 'did it' – or I think I did. I'd been carrying a Durex with me for so long that the packet was almost worn through and after the initial fumbling to get each other undressed, I then got into a terrible muddle about getting it on. Of course, once that was achieved and the green light flashed, I was so over-excited. It was all over in a heart-beat and I wasn't really sure whether I was where I was meant to be or somewhere between her bum and that bench seat.

However, lady that she was, we met up the following day at a park near her home and there, in a little hidden corner, she took me where I wanted to go, and that time there was no mistaking.

11

Leaving Home

At my nan's house, my dad fell into line and his behaviour had seemed milder but when Wes and him and I had our own place, some of his old rages returned. My mum wasn't there to row with or torment, so my dad turned his attention to me. I didn't just take my mum's position when it came to the house-work, I became the doormat that my mum had been. I was his surrogate wife looking after the house and all the shouting he still longed to direct at her for leaving him was now launched at me. I was now the focus of his episodes, the victim of his torment. For some reason or other Ron felt it necessary to redecorate at least one room every year. It became a ritual that I dreaded to the point where even now the mention of wallpa-pering sends huge painful echoes reverberating through me. The problem was that he was hopeless at it and as sure as he would screw it up, I would try and be good-humoured about it and become, yet again, the whipping boy. It happened with-out fail. He would mismatch some ghastly pattern we'd chosen and somehow or other I would get the blame. I'd be yelled at and made to feel worthless but his clock was ticking.

I used to agonise over why I was the one who caught the brunt of my father's mood swings. Looking back now, though, I can see why. If it hadn't been for me coming along, my dad's life probably would have taken a different path. He wouldn't have ended up marrying my mother and having three chil-dren – one whom he barely saw and two he had to raise single-handedly. I'd always been a mummy's boy. I could be quite a cry-baby and always sought comfort in my mum's arms, and later my nan's. Despite everything he had done, I had always loved my father as a child. I still looked up to him in that way a boy does to his dad. But when my dad had lashed out at my mum, I guess my reaction was to go to her side. I looked like my mum too, so even when she had been gone for months and even years, I must have been a constant reminder to him, like looking into my mother's eyes.

Ron and I were locking horns with ever-increasing regularity. I would question him on things like why I had to work for my money and Wes got pocket money. He must have sensed that his dominant male act couldn't last for ever; there was only so long it could run and time was running out. I was growing taller, and in some ways I was getting more confident. I was seventeen going on eighteen and his threats were beginning to ring a bit hollow. I'd been hearing them for just a little too long; the time was coming when we'd have to sort things out once and for all.

Any seventeen- or eighteen-year-old boy is likely to lock horns with his father, even without the background that we had. I was in that strange area where a boy starts to become a man; like any male adolescent moving through this stage of development, I needed a bit of careful handling. Ron, unfortunately, was not the man to do that: he'd been brutalised himself by his own father and he appeared to have no inclination to avoid a repeat performance. He was always keen to recount tales of his paternal mishandlings, of how he'd been picked on and beaten by his dad, but he didn't seem to see – or perhaps care – that he was doing all the same things.

I was starting to question my dad more. For a long time I'd taken everything he said to be right, and I'd assumed that when we argued I was always wrong, but now I was starting to see him for the man he was. I was itching to break away from his control. All those part-time jobs I did were a means of gaining independence, and I guess I had an eye on getting away. We'd lived together so closely and for so long and I had put up with so much, I was reaching the end of my tether. Finally, after years of bubbling away under the surface, the big showdown happened between us.

It all came to a head over weeding the garden. The front garden had never really been touched since we'd moved in, and I recall we'd been warned by the local housing officials that we had to clear it up. Always the one to do the chores, there I was on my hands and knees in the garden. I started to weed between the rose bushes that had been stuck in that hard-baked Essex clay when the house had been built. I made it clear to my dad that I wasn't happy having to do it. He stood right behind me.

'Just get on with it. I'm sick and tired of you making excuses.'

'Why don't you do the fucking thing yourself?' I blurted out.

'Don't you talk to me like that, you ungrateful bastard,' he roared.

And with that, he turned and walked into the house, slamming the front door behind him. Determined to finally have it out with him, I was right on his heels. As the door in front of me hit the frame, there was a great smashing of glass as the entire panel shattered to pieces and scattered all across the front step. One chunk of glass dropped on to my foot, piercing my shoe and cutting between my toes. It wasn't that serious, but coming after years of terrifying words, taunts and threats, it was enough to make me realise that this couldn't go on. This was the moment we'd been building up to, the climax of all the tension and verbal abuse. I stepped through the gaping hole where the glass had been and confronted him.

'You see what you've done? You've cut my foot open!'

'It's your own fault! You should just do as you are told.'

'Oh yeah,' I challenged, 'and if I don't, what are you going to do about it?'

'You watch it, boy,' he said. 'You think you are big and grown up, but I can still handle you.'

And that was it, I looked him square in the eye and said, 'All right then, Ron, you just do that. You've been telling me for long enough about what you are going to do to me. Come on. Come on. Do it!'

By this time I was yelling at him. He stared at me with a shocked, affronted look and said, 'How dare you talk to your father like that?'

I couldn't believe what I was hearing. Surely he must be kidding after all the things he'd said to me before? But he was absolutely serious, playing the poor, offended, loving father card.

Well, that was it for me, I could never take him seriously from that moment on. After years of cowering in his presence, I had finally stood up to him and shown that he couldn't dominate me any longer.

Coincidence? Maybe. Good fortune out of bad? Perhaps. But things changed dramatically very soon afterwards. A year or so earlier, poor dear Uncle Terry had died. His doctors had predicted he would die young, back when he was a little boy. They'd tried to control the scoliosis he suffered from with the prosthetic 'suit of armour' he'd refused to wear. His curving spine had finally done its worst and blown one of the valves in his heart. I remember visiting him in the hospital as he wasted away to a rack of skin and bones – his insides crushed by the force of his own body. He died there in the North Middlesex Hospital where he had been born. Just thirty-two years old, Nanny Maud's baby boy looked like an inmate of Belsen.

I got a phone call from my uncle Bill, my godfather and

hero. He asked me if I would go and live with my nan back in Edmonton. He and Uncle Wally were prepared to pay all my living costs and travel expenses. They wanted Nan to have some company. Now granddad and Uncle Terry had both died, she was on her own. She needed a companion and a helping hand around the house. After all she had done for me as a child, looking after me and helping bring me up – those happy years we'd spent together when I was a little boy – now, as a young man, I could – in part at least – pay her back. And what a break! Just when I needed it. 'See ya later, Ron Lamb. I'm going back to someone who really loves me, not someone who hijacked my life.' If I could have put my feelings into words back then, I'm sure it would have sounded just like that.

The reverse commuting to college from my nan's was so different from my daily slog back and forth to school. Now, with just a few hours of lectures each week, it was a breeze. And I'd met a girl through friends who was doing the same commute – and did that ever put a bit of a sparkle into the journey? 'Heavy petting' was the order of the afternoon on that almost empty train from Harlow back to Edmonton, only pausing for breath when it made a stop. What fun we had!

It was around this time I'd finally confronted and endured another rite of passage: the driving test. Ron had never driven, so there was no car to learn in and that meant paying for driving lessons. For about six months or so, that's where all my money went. I was determined to get my licence as soon as possible, so that meant at least a couple of lessons each week. I seemed to be taking two steps forward and one step back, because the first half-hour of every session was spent re-learning what I'd always forgotten since the last lesson. It was so frustrating, made more so by my desperation to succeed. I needed the licence. It was all part of the plan. Escape. I needed to put as much distance between me and Ron Lamb as was humanly possible. But every time I got behind the wheel of that car, it was as though I'd never done it before. In the end Alan, my long-suffering Scouse driving instructor, figured the best thing to do would be have a crack at the driving test. Nothing to lose, he reckoned.

I failed miserably over about a dozen different points. It wasn't even a near miss. I wasn't happy, but it did serve to focus me, and after another ten or so lessons I tried a second time. This attempt proved I'd come along since my first test, but not nearly far enough. I was just too nervous, and that was obviously being picked up by the examiner.

To me it was clear I just needed practice. Most of the people I knew went out for drives with their mothers or fathers to get used to being behind the wheel, but for me that only happened when I paid for a lesson. There was only one thing to do in my eyes. It was risky, but this was a situation which had to be sorted out. It was a real Gordian knot and I was going to have to cut it, or face an endless and expensive future trying to unravel it. So I bought my first car. A 1938 Morris 8 Tourer. This lovingly restored little gem was mine for thirty-nine pounds, money which I'd managed to save in preparation for the great day when I'd pass my test, but as that still hadn't happened, and a fellow I knew from college called Dick Prime wanted to sell it, I decided it was time to do – as my nan would say – 'what the old maid did' and 'take a chance'.

I thought through the ramifications of falling foul of the law and decided to put on L plates and drive with no full licence, assuming that – in the event of being caught – it would be better to have committed just one offence rather than two. And my scheme paid off. I didn't get caught and I built my confidence up sufficiently to sail through the test on my third attempt. In fact, I was so confident that within a fortnight of passing the test I'd had my first accident.

Completely misjudging my braking distance, I'd rolled in front of an oncoming vehicle at a T-junction – fortunately no one was injured – and got my first endorsement before I'd even taken delivery of my licence. But all that negative stuff aside, I was finally mobile. Nobody or nothing could stop me now.

Once again, Uncle Bill came to my rescue and helped in my escape. He worked for J & J Maybanks, a waste-paper company that was part of the Reed Paper Group, which in turn was part of the Daily Mirror Group. He was very close to the chairman, Jimmy Maybanks. The company had been built up from very humble beginnings. They'd started out as little more than rag-and-bone men. But Jimmy Maybanks had turned it into a major player in the paper business, so that when it was eventually purchased by the Reed Group he had become a very wealthy man. And as an employee with a long and trusted record, Bill had been promoted to become the manager of Maybanks' contract with HM Government, one of the company's most lucrative operations.

Thousands of tons of paper are generated by the government every year, and this was particularly true back in those days when so much of what now lies in the private domain was then controlled by HM Stationery Office. And, in theory, sooner or later a great deal of that paper finished up in Maybanks' yards, sorted, graded and baled as the basic raw material for new paper. Bill's job was to oversee the day-to-day running of every aspect of that contract, and he asked me if I would like to go and work for him, with a view, if all went according to plan, to taking over from him when he eventually retired. It meant starting off as a lorry driver's mate at the bottom of the ladder but that suited me fine; that's how Bill started. So why not? Bill made BIG money, he drove a BIG car and he lived in a BIG house. This was an offer I couldn't refuse. A job with amazing prospects, working for my beloved

godfather, and I wouldn't have to face the inevitable humiliation of sitting my A levels. I jumped at it without a moment's
hesitation. I was on my way.

Not only had Bill given me a job, but he'd also given me a
way out.

—— 12 ——
No More Nepotism

'You've been nicking sets of encyclopedias, haven't you?'

That was when I knew I was in trouble. That question was the one that I really didn't want to be asked and I certainly didn't want to answer.

'Tell me the truth, Larry, you've been nicking encyclopedias and selling them on, haven't you?' This spelled the end of my career in the waste-paper industry. I was standing in Uncle Bill's office, being eyeballed by one of his cronies, a detective from the flying squad who was one of his after-hours drinking mates. I'd met him before and chatted with him when I was simply Bill's nephew, but now he was an enemy and I had my back literally up against the wall.

He was scary, this little guy, and he knew it. 'Tell me about it, Larry, there's absolutely no point trying to deny it!' Now he was right in my face, under my nostrils, and the smell of lunchtime Scotch was still strong on his breath.

And there and then I understood why I would never fill Bill's shoes. I might be able to craftily drive out of the yard with two spotless sets of *Encyclopedia Britannica* – fresh from the printers, still packed in their original cartons, designated to be shredded along with the government waste – but when it came to facing down a tough guy like this I just didn't have the bottle. That was the difference between me and my hero: Bill would have fronted it out and told him he was dreaming, that he was barking up the wrong tree, but never would he have come clean.

'Yes, I did. I'm so stupid.' There seemed to be no use in trying to make excuses.

He turned and walked away with a sort of sneer that conveyed nothing but complete disdain. His mate's golden boy nephew had been caught red-handed with his fingers in the till.

He opened the door and called out, 'Bill!'

I stood there in total shame. How could I have been so stupid? Those pristine volumes were being deliberately kept off the market, and there I was selling them to the bookshops on Charing Cross Road. Bill walked in and exchanged glances with me. The detective walked out. 'See you later, Johnnie,' Bill called after him.

He stood and looked at me. He was impeccably dressed as always. He wore a smart blazer and tie and a football club pin in his lapel. He was every bit the self-made man. He shook his head slowly, in disbelief and sadness. Who knows what thoughts were running through that fighter's brain of his? But he was now sure that his godson, 'this chip off the old block', was not going to cut the mustard, was not going to take over from him. I was definitely no Bill Lamb. Not only was I stealing from the firm, but I was also doing so ineptly, and then admitting to it without even an attempt to bluff.

'You're a fucking idiot, aren't you, boy? A fucking idiot! You had a job for life here. You could have had it all. Why? Why did you do it? Aren't I paying you enough?'

I couldn't answer him I was so choked up with shame and remorse. I wanted to crawl away and die.

'Come on boy, you gotta go. Come with me!'

And with that we walked out of his office through the yard and out on to Norman Road. I felt such a fool. How could I have been so stupid, so ungrateful? Bill, my uncle, my hero, had rescued me from that world where I needed qualifications. He'd given me a chance in which those A levels that I never would have passed could be forgotten about. He'd made it all so easy for me to become a trainee manager – nepotism in its purest form. The boss's nephew had been taken on to take his place, and what had I done but disgrace myself? Now here I was walking round to Maybanks' main office on Deptford High Road. I was on my way out. What an absolute fool.

We walked through the main gates, past Jimmy Maybanks' Rolls-Royce parked in its special place outside his office. All hopes of me ever having one of those were now racing away from me like water down a drainpipe. *You stupid, stupid, ungrateful fool*, I cursed to myself.

I couldn't believe I'd done it, but I think if I am honest what I was really sick about was not that I'd done it but that I'd been caught.

The walk through the office, past all the jolly ladies who did the typing, the billing and the wages, was just too embarrassing. They all obviously realised something was wrong because they put their heads down and tried to ignore what they were seeing. We stopped in front of the chief wages clerk's desk.

'Make up his money, Mary, up to lunchtime today.'

I stood there, unable to raise my head. This was the ultimate in shame because all those people knew how proud Bill was of me. I was the son he'd never had, and here he was kicking me out, paying me off. He'd brought me in and now he was getting rid of me and everyone had to see it. I was his responsibility and I'd gone wrong.

I took the brown envelope and followed him back through that hall of shame down the stairs and out on to the street. There was nothing to say; there was no point in shaking hands. We walked back round to the yard and I got into my car and drove away. I drove away from an assured and comfortable future where all I had to do was work hard and everything would be right. I'd screwed it all up for a couple of hundred pounds.

It was so strange to be driving back along my normally traffic-filled route to Edmonton in the middle of the day. I couldn't bring myself to tell my nan. Shamed. When I walked away from that office, I walked out of Bill's life for years.

13

On the Way Out

Early in 1968, I'd met a young woman at a christening. My dad was the godfather to a colleague's child and she was the godmother. I can't for the life of me imagine why I'd gone along, Ron and I must have been under a temporary truce, but I certainly remember that one look at Anita and I was in love. At first she'd kept me at bay, but I was pretty persistent and in the end she'd agreed to go out with me. It was never going to be simple, though – she clearly had a boyfriend and, apart from anything, I was too young for her. I hadn't yet turned twenty-one and she was already twenty-five. However, both those details served to make her seem more of a prize to me: an older woman – what a coup – and she would have to give someone up for me. Double hit.

By the time Bill sacked me from my job at the paper company, Anita and I were seeing each other on a regular basis and we were, as they used to say, 'intimate'. But that wasn't enough for me. I wanted to own her, to possess her; I wanted her to be mine. Sure, she'd dropped the boyfriend, but he worked away for months at a time and the possibility that he might reappear on the scene was too much of a threat for me. I'm sure I realised at this point that I needed to focus on getting some sort of a career together.

I'd got a new job to bring some money in, but filling documents in for an import/export agency that sent millions of tampons on their way to Italy wasn't doing it for me. I had to

steer my career path back on course. The sense of worthless-
ness, of being completely rudderless, was too much for me.
I had to have a proper job, something that would lead somewhere. Maybanks had been laden with potential because they
operated in other countries, so I'd spent three months on an
intensive German course to improve my chances of getting to
work overseas. It wasn't just my instinctive wanderlust, I really
wanted to get away from this country and all that it meant to
me. But now I had to get a job, and quickly. However, with
just five measly O levels, the pickings in the 'Situations Vacant'
columns were pretty slim.

I was still living at Nanny Lamb's in Edmonton and
commuting up to Knightsbridge every day to work at the
shipping agency. I was depressed and so down on myself for
having squandered such a golden opportunity with my uncle
Bill. I was becoming convinced that I was destined to a life of
nine to five in a dreary office, having blown the job that held
so much promise.

And then I saw it, the little ad that – although I didn't know
it at the time – was about to change my life. It was in the
Thursday edition of the *Daily Telegraph*. An international sales
organisation was looking for 'Independent young people able
to travel: to work in Germany'. The most important part of all
was that there was no mention of qualifications.

I ran to the nearest phone box.

'Yes?' they answered.

'Yes, good afternoon. I'm phoning about your advertise-
ment in today's *Telegraph*.'

'Yes?'

I took a deep breath. 'Well, I'm interested in working in
sales and I can speak German.'

'Well, it's not necessary to speak German.'

I interrupted. 'Oh, I'm sorry, I thought the ad specified that
the job was in Germany.'

'It did.' I realised I shouldn't have interrupted, I could sense a slight tone of annoyance. 'The job would be in Germany but very definitely concerned with English-speaking people: American servicemen and their dependants stationed there.'

That's what it is about this voice, I thought. *It's got a real American twang to it but it's not American.* It was obviously male but difficult to pin down.

'Would it be possible to have an interview?' I tendered, hoping against hope that I wasn't too late or that my pushiness hadn't put him off.

'Yes, can you come tomorrow morning?'

I scrabbled around for a pen and wrote down the details. What a relief, I was in with a chance.

I stood outside the Park Lane Hotel at just before nine the next morning. I'd never set foot in anything like this place before. Apart from dragging bags of waste paper out of an office block nearby, and trying to be groovy in a Soho club for the odd night, I'd never had anything to do with this part of London. Despite the fact that it had seen better days and was badly in need of major refurbishment, I was really impressed. The top-hatted doorman nodded my way and I was relieved that I obviously satisfied the dress code. I was togged out as business-like as I could possibly be in my twenty-one-guinea, made-to-measure Montague Burton suit. I went straight up to the reception desk and spoke to a pretty young girl.

'You need to speak to the concierge, sir,' she said.

'Erm?' I looked around me vaguely. There wasn't much call for a concierge in Edmonton, so I wasn't sure what she was talking about.

She pointed to the smaller desk at the other side of the lobby and smiled at me in a way that told me just what a provincial I was. 'Over there, sir.'

I walked a seemingly endless stretch of carpeted corridor.

It was rather threadbare and a jaded shade of red, but for me it was reeking of promise and success and the great big world that I wanted to discover.

The room the concierge had directed me to was at the very end of the corridor. I wasn't quite sure what to do. There was no bell or knocker, so I tapped as hard as I thought proper and heard that voice, the one I'd spoken to on the phone yesterday. 'Yes, wait a minute, would you? I'll be right there!'

The door swung open and there before me was a truly unforgettable sight.

'Hi. You are?'

'Larry Lamb, I phoned you yesterday.'

'Hello, Larry. Come in and take a seat. I'm Hillier Kanerick, call me Hilly.'

This guy really had to be seen to be believed. He was average height and about forty years old. He had a mop of jet-black hair and a pair of horn-rimmed glasses with lenses that looked an inch thick. He wore a suit in a check so loud it was startling, like something a clown would wear. With his accent that somehow blended North American, South African and southern Scottish, he was spellbinding.

'Larry, let me put you in the picture. I'm the sales manager for the European division of Encyclopedia Americana based in Wiesbaden, West Germany. I'm here in London to recruit salesmen.'

A door to an adjoining room opened and in stepped a very expensively dressed man, who put out his hand straight away.

'Mr Lamb, I'm Bill Dunn, Divisional Manager. What experience do you have in sales?' He had a very smooth, well-tanned complexion and a very Italianate look to him. His eyes seemed to gaze right through me. There was no point trying any flimflam with him: I was on the spot.

'Well, only in shops, ever since I was a little boy. My dad

was a shopkeeper and I sell fruit and vegetables on a market stall on Saturdays, but that's about the extent of it. I'm good at it, though. My boss pays me more than anyone else.'

He and Hilly exchanged a smile. I was over my first hurdle.

14

On the Road

I had absolutely no connection with Germany other than a basic knowledge of the language. And now I was on my way to live there, indefinitely as far as I was concerned. I'd said goodbye to Nan – she was the only person I felt really connected to – and, with absolutely no sense of regret, I boarded that flight for Frankfurt.

I had a rough idea of the geography, I knew the names of the major cities, but most importantly I knew how to communicate. Those lessons at the German Cultural Institute were about to pay off. Not of course in the way they were meant to, my career in the waste-paper industry now ironically 'in shreds', but I could be independent in my new environment and that was something I instinctively knew I had to be. I could speak the lingo, which meant I was in control!

I was supposed to provide my own transport but I felt rather uncertain about my old grey and cream Wolseley 15/50 being up to the job, so I gave it to Wesley who promptly wrecked it. The flight to Frankfurt was on a British European Airways Trident, then the most up-to-date jet in their fleet – I felt as if I'd finally made it now I was travelling in style. I was revelling in the whole joyous experience of leaving my old world behind. This was momentous for me, so I didn't want to waste the experience by driving. I wanted to be up there in the sky, looking down as I left it all behind. What bliss, what joy. See you later, I'm out of here.

I'd taken a bit of a liberty by booking my flight. I wasn't alto-gether sure that the company would cover the airfare. They had said that they kept a few old cars at the office which could be loaned, and I reasoned that the plane ticket was about the same price as the car ferry, so I figured it was worth the risk. Flying on a jet to a foreign country where I was going to work and where I wouldn't have to have anything to do with my former life – it had to be the only way to go.

It was a Sunday afternoon in early September when I boarded the bus at Frankfurt Airport. It was warm but there was just a light sprinkling of cooling rain. The bus took me to the centre of Wiesbaden – the beautiful old spa town where the sales team for *Encyclopedia Americana* had their offices – and dropped me off just a little way from the guest house where I'd been instructed to stay. It was really an old-fashioned workers' hostel. It had tiny rooms, with nothing in them but a bed, a chair and a small wardrobe. Lavatories and showers were out in the corridors but there were plenty of them. The floors and stairways were as simple and unpretentious as smooth cement could be, and the lights had a dim orange glow to them, giving the whole place a strange, subterranean feel, even though we were three storeys up. I checked in and threw my bag down in the room allotted to me by the rather severe lady on the desk. When she demanded my passport with her curt '*Ausweis bitte,*' it had a rather officious ring to it. As soon as I'd put my bag down I headed off into the now darkening streets. I was abroad. I was free!

My new residence was on a street just behind Wilhelmstrasse, the main commercial street of Wiesbaden, and as I nosed my way around in the half-light, I had this slightly creepy feeling; not so long ago these rather quiet, damp back streets would have echoed to the sound of jack-boots. Perhaps it was a little dramatic, but to a boy born in the shadows of World War II, it wasn't too far-fetched. That aside, this was exactly where I wanted to be. I wanted to be somewhere alien, somewhere totally disconnected with where I'd come from, somewhere where I was in charge, with nobody to answer to but myself.

I felt sure that all the new colleagues I would be joining on the following morning would be out playing in the numerous bars that lined Wilhelmstrasse, but for some reason I was more drawn to my own company on that first night. It was as if I needed to experience being on my own. I think perhaps sharing the thrill of this new world with company would have diluted it for me in some way. I wandered around, half thinking that I might bump into someone I recognised from the Park Lane Hotel, but I was intent on just breathing in my new environment. Everything was different: every single detail. Even the drains in the streets had a strange, unfamiliar, soapy, sewery smell to them. The cars, the items of clothing in the brightly lit, luxurious shops that this place was famous for – I feasted on it all. Alone and happy, tired and confident, I went back to my new bed.

Suddenly, so soon after I had arrived, it was Monday morning. The sombre streets of last night were now hooting and banging and clashing, at seven a.m., Wiesbaden was alive and kicking after all. I stood under a boiling hot shower, shaved, and made it into the office just before eight.

'Hi Larry. Welcome. Get yourself a coffee and come meet everyone!' Hilly greeted me – still in his nightmare plaid.

'I'll be right there, Hilly,' I called. 'Just give me a minute.'

Everybody was already in. I walked into a meeting room and there were about twenty salesmen sitting around the place, chatting in groups. I remembered some of the faces and nodded across the room to Dave; I'd ridden home on the Tube with him after our interviews.

'Morning everyone, this is Larry Lamb, who is joining us today to start training. Welcome, Larry!'

And that was it, a couple of guys smiled my way but there was no mistaking that this gathering was about sales and not about welcoming me. The general function of the meeting was to assign territories for the coming week. Up on a board in front of us was a list of towns: Frankfurt, Mannheim, Darmstadt, Aschaffenburg. Gradually Hilly worked his way down the list, writing a name alongside each one.

'Larry, you'll be going to Stuttgart with Speedy. Speedy Sims is our most experienced salesman and he will be training you for your first two weeks. Dave Miller will be with you too this week; he's been working with Speedy for the past week already. Speedy has sold everything from pick-up trucks to whorehouse drapes and if anybody can turn you into a salesman he'll do it.'

Speedy Sims was a super salesman, a real old carpetbagger from Arizona. He was about forty-five or so but looked nearer seventy. He had that dried-apricot appearance that lighter-skinned people get when they live in a desert environment. He had dull blond hair, he was about average height and he had a bit of a beer belly. He smoked about three packs of cigarettes a day, every one of them flicked elaborately from the soft pack he always carried in his shirt breast pocket and lit with great ceremony with his thousand-dollar bull-horn-encrusted solid silver Zippo lighter.

Speedy was going to be my trainer, my guide to the fascinating world of sales, and to this new world in Germany too. We would be setting up stands in American army bases and selling to the soldiers. When we arrived we showed our letters of identification to the sentry at the main gates of the base and in we drove. We'd entered a mini-America: everything other than the old German barracks was American-style and everything was in English. We drove past the medical centre and the bowling alley towards the post exchange – or PX, as it was known. Here outposts of US commerce were licensed to operate on military property.

Speedy showed me how to set up the display of encyclopedias on the little folding table and how the other accompanying books were arranged for maximum effect. He showed me the entry forms for a free drawing – the American term for a raffle – and then he got to work.

An unsuspecting soldier had stopped to look at our display. Speedy called over to him, 'Sergeant, how are you? Would you be interested in entering a free drawing to win a set of *Encyclopedia Americana*?'

We were at the entrance to a snack bar; we were two civilians in a totally military world. 'What are you guys peddlin'?' he called over to us, and then, realising the possible jeopardy of getting into conversation, 'Encyclopedias? Man, I don't need no books. I'm on my way back to 'Nam.'

Speedy edged towards him, 'Well, Sergeant – ' he got himself into a position where he could read the man's name on his breast pocket '– McCabe, why don't you just fill out a drawing card and maybe you'll get lucky and win a set for your family.'

That was it, that was all Speedy needed: the net was cast and he could sense that this was a potential sale. 'I see you're from Wichita? I had a cousin lived there for a while.' The man had just filled in the section of the card with his address in the US and Speedy was zoning in, trying to 'qualify' the man, as the sales jargon instructed us. He needed to know whether he was regular army – 'RA' – or 'conscripted US'. This could all be gleaned from the details he entered on the card and would indicate the length of service to which he was committed, which was important for the payment part of the contract.

'I see you're RA. Will this be your first tour in Vietnam?'

'No sir, my third!' the sergeant answered, and Speedy nodded in admiration. He picked the 'Luckies' out of his pocket and offered the man a smoke. Both men instinctively reached for their Zippos; it was as if they were drawing their weapons. They both smiled and each lit his own. Having just drawn in a lungful, Speedy curled his tar-stained index finger round his cigarette and said, 'Buy ya a cup of coffee?' The sergeant nodded.

He should have said no, but he was on his way to do just that anyway. He got his cup of coffee, but forty-five minutes later he also walked out of the snack bar with a folded-up contract in his pocket and $25 less in his wallet. He'd been caught.

Speedy lit another Lucky Strike with the butt end of the one he'd just smoked and led me back out to the stand. 'So what do you think, Larry? Think you can do that?'

I was stunned. Speechless. I'd witnessed the impossible. I knew there was no way on earth I'd ever do that.

We were staying in a little hotel right in the middle of Stuttgart. The neighbourhood was inhabited by what seemed like hundreds of Turkish immigrant 'guest workers' or '*Gastarbeiters*'. The rooms in the hotel were cheap and clean and they served good hearty meals: a lot of pasta and meat in the local Schwäbisch style – and wonderful local beer too. Dave was working in Stuttgart as well, so we were all in the same hotel. For me this first night out on the road was rather significant. I was twenty-one years old at last. There was no party, no family, no cards or gifts to mark the occasion. It was just me and two new workmates a long way from home. I thought about the big twenty-first birthday bashes I'd been to, but in actual fact it really suited me. I was where I wanted to be, free of all ties, and making my own way in my own world on my own terms. So if that meant turning twenty-one in the Star Hotel on the seedy side of Stuttgart, why not enjoy it? So we toasted my maturity and moved swiftly on.

Speedy turned in early and left Dave and me to our beers. 'I'll see you guys down here for breakfast, say nine?'

'OK Speedy,' we chorused. 'You're the boss.'

I looked at Dave. 'You should have seen him sell this set of books this morning,' I told him. 'He was just incredible. The bloke just came in for a cup of coffee and mentioned to Speedy that he has two young brothers back at home and neither of them are doing too well at school. Speedy hooked on to him like a limpet: "Well, don't you think it would be a wonderful gift to those boys to help them with their education? This could be something that could help change their lives?" He just wouldn't let him go. He talked him round in circles and got him. It was amazing.'

Dave nodded and told me how Speedy had been just the same with him the week before. 'He makes it look so easy and I can tell you it's not. I've been out all day today and couldn't get anyone even remotely interested. No wonder they call him Speedy: he's got them signed up before they know what's hit them!'

We headed up the creaky old stairs and saw that Speedy's door was slightly open. Dave stuck his head into the room then turned back to me, trying to stifle a laugh. 'Look at this,' he whispered. I leaned in and there was Speedy, fast asleep, just snoring gently in his T-shirt and shorts, with a burning cigarette still gripped between his fingers. He must have lit the thing, taken a puff and then fallen asleep. It had burned right down to the filter tip and there it stood, a tiny twisted totem of ash, smoke still wreathing upwards.

We lifted the burning butt and he never moved. 'Good night, Speedy, sleep tight.' We were laughing as we turned his light off and closed the door. Dave grinned. 'Not so Speedy now, is he?'

15

A Close Call

Dave and I were working together again, breaking the rules. Already beginning to realise that I was no born salesman, and having spent days and nights alone on the road, I'd persuaded Dave to team up with me and we were back in the big American Shopping Centre in Patch Barracks, Stuttgart.

'Can I buy you guys a cup of coffee?' a man asked us. We both recognised him as the beautifully dressed, ultra-cool manager of the car sales team that operated in the shopping centre. 'I'm Frank Bufour, I work with the Chrysler Corporation. I'd like to talk to you.'

Dave and I looked at each other and smiled as we both shook our heads and asked ourselves the same question: 'I wonder what this is all about?'

'How would you like to go to Vietnam to sell cars?'

I don't think either of us could quite believe it. I asked him if he was kidding and he responded, 'No, no, not at all. We have sales teams throughout Vietnam and we're currently recruiting new men.'

'But there's a war on, isn't there?' said Dave, trying desperately not to sound like an idiot.

'Yes, there certainly is. But that just means there are a lot of guys out there earning hazardous-duty pay with nowhere to spend it.'

I was just incredulous: 'So you sell cars in a war zone?'

'Yes, sir. We have our main sales office in Saigon and we send salesmen out all over the country. We have several sales personnel who clear two thousand dollars per month.'

That was enough to convince me – $2,000 was a fortune. It was ten times what we could make selling encyclopedias.

'Where do we sign?' asked Dave. We were hooked.

'Hold your horses, buddy,' he laughed. 'You'll both need to get accreditation and ID cards, but as long as you're both fit and you don't have a criminal record, we should be able to get you out there by January.'

Of course it wasn't as simple as that. There were a lot of forms to fill out and we each had to provide twenty-four passport photos and go through a medical. After that we just had to wait and resist the temptation to tell any of the other salesmen that we'd been poached. For now we were still encyclopedia salesmen as far as everyone else was concerned. But I have to admit as I waited for a departure date, I wondered whether it was wise.

*

Dave and I were driving in convoy to our next destination. I pulled up behind him as he stood staring under the bonnet of his ancient loaner car. His car had suddenly died on him. We were almost there and eager to make a start, so I suggested that I try pushing his car forward using mine. Both of our cars were so past it that it was certainly not going to harm the bodywork. I got behind him and nudged him along the edge of the autobahn off on to the slip road and, as luck would have it, I hardly had to do any more as the road ran downhill all the way into yet another sleepy backwater of occupied Germany. We'd arrived in Brückenau, the closest place we could find to our destination for the week, the NATO exercise area of Wildflecken, just across the Iron Curtain dividing West Germany from East.

Mummy's boy.

Jessie, the lumberjill, cutting pit-props for the coal mines during World War II.

A proud young mum with Wesley and me.

A girl with a long way to go.

My junior school days.

Me in my early teens with my brother, Wes and my sister, Penny.

Desert rat.

On the Essex coast with my
mum in the late eighties.

Cuxhafen, north Germany,
in my salesman days

Posing in the
eighties.

Kate O'Mara keeping me at bay, *Triangle*, 1980.

Dragged up in *Fox* with Bernard Hill and Peter Vaughan.

Linda, me and our beautiful baby boy.

Barnes – as fit as I ever got, getting ready for *Christopher Columbus*, 1983.

Linda and George, my anchors.

Going loco down in Acapulco in 1988 with Phil Collins as we filmed *Buster*.

Buster and the boys. From left to right: Ralph Brown, Phil Collins, me and Michael Attwell.

We dumped Dave's car on the local mechanic and drove in my car up into the hills towards the NATO base, up and up until we were completely lost in a maze of dirt roads that went through the dense woodland. It was misty, and everything at this level had a fine dusting of snow. The track we were on suddenly followed a sharp slope downwards and, with hardly any tread on my old car tyres, we slithered on down the hill and ran right into a convoy of tanks: M60s, all moving along in line with their monstrous engines roaring and the ground shaking beneath them.

We skidded along the track, trying to get past, much to the amusement of the soldiers riding on top of the tanks. We were shouting at them, trying to get directions, and finally we managed to come up alongside a young officer in a Jeep.

'Excuse me, Lieutenant,' I yelled. 'We're from Encyclopedia Americana. Could you tell us where the PX is?'

He looked at his fellow soldiers and shook his head in disbelief. He shouted back to me: 'You need to stay on this dirt road for another two k and then when you get to a fork in the road you go to your right for about another kilometre. But you guys have picked the wrong time, the whole battalion is out in the field.'

We drove on and finally approached a guard post of some kind. It was only then that we realised that neither of us had our letters to get us through. We couldn't give up now; Dave found an old beer mat in his pocket which he held up as we pulled alongside this sad little shack. The guard himself was too busy grooving to his music – he hardly looked up and we rolled on to the PX. It had been a long and eventful journey but we were here now. As I began to think about setting up our stall, Dave headed to the Gents. He came straight back out. 'There's no doors to the toilets,' he said, stunned. 'They've all been taken off. Will you keep a watch out while I go in? I can't wait any longer.'

We set ourselves up in the lobby and two sergeants eventually wandered in and looked at us in total amazement. 'What are you guys doing here? This is a live fire zone, you could get yourselves killed!'

'Well,' I said, 'there didn't seem to be any security, so we just drove straight here.' I took my opportunity and went in for the sell. 'Would you like to enter a free drawing for a set of encyclopedias?'

We finished up buying them coffees, but there was no way either of them were customers. Dave had to know the answer to one specific question before we let the pair go on their way. 'Tell me, why are there no doors on the latrines? We've been on a lot of bases but we've never seen that before.'

'Well buddy, these front-line soldiers are pretty wild. We call 'em grunts, ground-pounders. They're just getting ready to fly to Vietnam and with all the drugs and the booze that get consumed on the base, there've been too many muggings and killings in the latrines. So it made sense to remove the doors.'

That put paid to our sales outing to Wildflecken. We didn't fancy our chances of sticking around, so we finished our coffees and loaded up the display. It was time to hit the road. I didn't intend trying to stop a bunch of drug-crazed GIs from going into the toilets if I had to stand on watch for Dave again.

Back in Brückenau, the mechanic trying to fix Dave's car had pointed out a little hotel just along from the garage, and by about eight o'clock we were tucking into schnitzels and chips and having a great time chatting up a teacher we'd been seated next to. Her name was Irmgard. She spoke wonderful English and was obviously really taken with Dave.

'Irmgard, is there anywhere around here where we could perhaps meet some other people, perhaps somewhere we could dance?' I asked her.

'Yes,' she nodded. 'I'll take you up to Bad Brückenau. There's a hotel there and they have dancing.'

Considering just how far we were from civilisation, the place was quite lively. There were already about thirty or so people there, mostly our age, and there was a little dance floor and a jukebox. I was surprised to find that the selection of records sounded quite good. Dave seemed oblivious as he focused all his attentions on Irmgard, so I wandered across to see if there were any of my favourites. As I stood there running through the titles, I realised there was a tall, really good-looking blonde girl standing right next to me. 'Play that one,' she ordered me. 'A-Twelve. Go on, push the button.'

I looked at her and smiled, toying with her. 'No, you push it.' After she had, I said, 'Go on, pick another one. But you'll have to dance with me.' This was getting interesting and I was half joking, but she smiled and nodded, 'With pleasure.'

We found a space on the dance floor, right alongside the now very hot-and-heavy Dave/Irmgard situation. Dave took his attention off Irmgard for just a second to praise me on the choice of records. He ran his eyes over my partner and we both realised who'd come up trumps on that particular night out.

My new friend interrupted, 'It was I that chooses the records . . .'

I asked my dance partner her name. 'It's Irmgard,' she replied. *Bizarre coincidence,* I thought. *I've never even heard the name before and now I've met two Irmgards in one day.*

She told me that the hotel belonged to her parents.

'Really?' I said. 'It's a lovely place.'

'Thank you,' she smiled. 'Why don't you and your friend come and stay here? We have very nice rooms.'

Dave took off the following evening. The mechanic had managed to find a spare part for a reasonable price and, although his Irmgard was very keen, Dave wasn't so taken. One night of romance had been enough.

'So what are you going to do?' he laughed. 'Spend a day or two with your new love?'

'Well, she's going to give me a room and dinner for the same price as this place, so why not? There are a couple of bases I can drive to from here . . .'

He knew as well as I did that there was nothing really doing in the area – we'd just spent a second fruitless day in another empty lobby – but I was hooked. I just wanted to spend the rest of my life with this girl.

'Bye lover boy. See you back in Wiesbaden,' he shouted, and with that he roared off out of town.

The room Irmgard gave me must have been the best in the house. It was up in the roof and it had a beautiful big bed with white linen – cool and crisp. She served me a fabulous dinner and, just as I was about to drop off – wondering if anything was going to come of all this – she slipped into the room, locking the door behind her. She slid out of her work clothes, pulled back the duvet and – try though I did to force her off, honestly – she took advantage of me. I was in love, big time, with a beautiful blonde Fräulein!

16

Coming Home for Christmas

I was back in England for Christmas and I didn't know why. I wanted to see Nan – at that stage I had nothing to do with either of my parents – and tell her about my exploits, but I was so besotted with Irmgard I desperately wanted to be back with her.

And then the phone rang and it was Anita. She wanted to talk. I'm not sure that I did, but we met anyway and seeing each other must have reignited something for us. Our 'intimate state' surged on back, but then almost as quickly the heat went out of it, and I was on my way back to Bad Brückenau.

When I arrived back in Germany, everything had changed back at the hotel. I was treated like a leper. I checked in and half an hour later I checked out again. I felt so sick, the way Irmgard behaved; it was as though nothing had ever happened between us. I'd brought my little portable record player with me – it had been a gift from Uncle Bill, back when I was his golden boy – and now as I threw it in the back of the car, all thoughts of romantic evenings with my girl listening to my records were gone. Everything was a mess; a total, sad, pathetic disaster.

I called my friend Don, a former US soldier who had settled in Germany and now worked for La Salle Extension University selling correspondence courses to the GIs. A while ago he'd made me a job offer and he'd also been kind enough to make it known that if I ever needed somewhere to stay his door was open. 'Don, I hate to do this to you, but you remember you said you could let me stay at your place for a few days? Well, I'm in a bit of a jam. I thought I would be staying with my girlfriend but she's got family problems and it's not convenient.' I don't know if I was lying to him or to myself too. 'Is there any chance you could put me up?'

'So what happened about the job with Chrysler? Did you chicken out?'

'No, although I don't think I would have made it past Saigon because the regulations all changed and only the citizens of countries involved in the conflict can get accreditation. So my buddy and I got dumped. Chrysler were good about it, they offered us both jobs here in Germany, but your offer sounded much better and – besides – I don't know anything about cars.'

'OK, Larry. You have our address, come on over.'

Don was a wonderful man, a great big football-playing, all-American boy who'd been fortunate enough to know that if you signed up for four years in the army instead of being conscripted for two years you were about 90 per cent sure to miss out on Vietnam. Don had been posted to Germany, where he fell in love with and married Heidi. By the time I came into their lives, Don had finished his service and was now the Frankfurt area manager for La Salle Extension University. 'Larry,' he told me, 'it's like shooting ducks in a barrel, and if the guy has been on active duty for two years, Uncle Sam will pay for the whole thing through the GI Bill!'

It had sounded too good to be true. I had to get away from the encyclopedias; I'd long since worked out that I just could not sell them. So when Don had made his offer contingent on the Vietnam job I'd sort of loosely agreed to start in the New Year, but we'd left it up to me to call him.

And so I began my next career. At this point I was absolutely penniless. Don loaned me his old VW Beetle and a hundred dollars to get me started. I was living in the cheapest room I could find anywhere in Frankfurt, and altogether I was in a pretty despondent state. It is hard to recognise now what it was that made me stay there. Perhaps it was the possibility that I could be successful selling correspondence courses and could earn some decent money. There were certainly people doing very well in other parts of Germany. But I think probably it was just the sense of adventure that I was still clinging on to. Complete and utter freedom.

I was working with another Englishman called Hal Green who had been living in Germany for about ten years. He spoke the language well and, as a thirty-four-year-old man-about-town, he was someone I really looked up to. Considering how I'd been foisted on him and that he now had to share the Frankfurt territory with me, he was extremely kind and did everything he could to help me. He also did his best to rub off some of my pretty rough edges. We had to eat in restaurants at least once a day and, although they were not in any way fancy, he taught me that there was a certain code of behaviour to be observed – greeting people, acknowledging the other diners when you came in, not yawning and stretching after a meal (I was *that* rough), how to order, what to order, the beginnings of an understanding of wines, and on and on.

Things were beginning to start moving. I made a couple of sales and then one afternoon I got a phone call at the guest house. It was Anita. She was pregnant. That passionate reunion over Christmas – twenty-one years after a passionate union in Edmonton had brought me into the world – was about to change my life. How ironic. The bottom just dropped right out of my world and panic set in.

I was absolutely floored. We argued back and forth: she wanted to keep the baby but I was all for an abortion. There was no way we could sort it out over the phone.

'Look, Anita, I'm completely broke, I can only just afford to keep going here. I have to buy petrol and a few groceries for myself, and if I don't work, nothing comes in. I certainly can't afford to get back there, why can't you come here?'

It seemed the obvious conclusion and so over she came. We spent the best part of a week with both of us equally determined to have our way, but finally as we waited for her train to leave the Frankfurt station – she in the corridor of the carriage and me out on the platform talking through a little sliding window – I weakened. 'OK, I'll come back and we'll get married.' And as I said it the train pulled away and I stood there having got it wrong yet again. Of all the things in the world I didn't want, I certainly didn't want to be married, but it seemed the right thing to do. Hal and Don – both older guys with much more experience of life – had both counselled me and told me that I didn't have to get married, that if she wanted to have the baby that was her decision and, while I would have to be responsible financially, it didn't have to come to marriage.

'I do.' I said it there in the Wood Green register office in front of witnesses, knowing that there was no way I could see it through. Anita was a wonderful woman and I still found her really beautiful, but I was just not ready to be married. I'd gone and done it, though, and instantly – just as those wiser guys had said – I regretted it. I knew this marriage was doomed. I could deal with the responsibility of a baby, but marriage . . . ? No way.

Back in Frankfurt, I suddenly got lucky in the selling department and made enough money to furnish a basement apartment out in a little country town, far enough from Frankfurt to be affordable and yet still within reasonable driving distance. But Anita had to spend her days in this lost corner of a country she had no interest in, and in the end, with me constantly out trying to sell, she flew home to London. But then, a week or so later, she came back.

It appeared that in the eyes of the law she had deserted me, and if she wanted to get a divorce that wouldn't be good enough. I had to tell her I wanted her to leave and that would be seen as the relationship having broken down. And so back she went.

I was in a really terrible state – I felt so responsible – and yet now she wasn't with me I felt so relieved too. Over and over I asked myself why I'd gone through with the whole charade instead of listening to the advice my friends had given me. I was married now and, whatever might happen, within a few months I would be a father. I threw myself into work, knowing that if I could make a success of this, it would at least boost my morale. Following up a sales lead, Hal and I took a drive out to Wiesbaden and found ourselves in the lobby of the Amelia Earhart Hotel. It was the accommodation for all the senior American military personnel – mostly doctors, nurses and officers – who were part of the massive US Air Force presence in the town, which at the time was the headquarters of the US Air Force in Europe.

There was a notice on a board that caught our eye. 'Castle Party! on the River Rhine. Bring a jug of booze and a sleeping bag.' That was enough for us; we invited ourselves along the following Saturday night. There were hundreds of people there. It was a really fantastic party but it was as though Hal and I were from another planet. Everybody else seemed to know each other but nobody knew us – and more significantly they knew they didn't know us.

I finished up on the top of a tower watching the sun come up over the Rhine Valley. I'd been dancing with this woman called Margaret and had enticed her up to the tower with a view to trying for the mile-high club, but she was involved in a long-term relationship and laughed off my advances. But after a couple of hours just taking in the beauty of that vista and chatting away like old friends, she said to me: 'You know something, Larry, you should be an actor.'

17

Showbiz

Margaret's suggestion about being an actor proved to be a turning point for me. She took me to see the theatre on the air base where she worked. It was operated by 'Special Services', the American equivalent of the Navy, Army and Air Force Institutes, or NAAFI, and had a full-time director of entertainment who had been brought over from an American university to produce plays. It was incredible.

'So Margaret, are there theatres like this on all the bases in Germany?'

'Well not all of them, obviously,' she said, 'but certainly in all the major headquarters where there are large concentrations of military and civilians serving, yes. Don't forget there are a lot of people in service who have broken off their education for a few years and many of them are interested in theatre. The pay-off for the military is that the plays they put on provide entertainment in English and an off-duty activity for a lot of people.'

I'd probably only seen three plays in my life at that point, but I had loved every moment of them. Like anyone entranced by the power the theatre wields, I'm sure I must have at least thought about acting at some point before, but it had ended there because life was about earning a living, getting a career and being a success. The thought of acting for fun, as a hobby, had never even crossed my mind. And right there in Germany was a golden opportunity to give it a go.

As chance would have it, I got transferred up to Bremerhaven in the far north of Germany about a month after finding all this out, and the first thing I did when I got to my new territory was go and introduce myself to the local director, Jim Robertson, himself a recent arrival too. He welcomed me with open arms; he was badly in need of some extra help backstage, which wasn't quite what I was expecting, but it was a foot in the door and my first job in show business! Putting the arm of a record player down on a cue and then, on another cue, lifting it back up again, that was my job. The play was *Mary, Mary* and I was a triumph.

After that, things started to move fast. The local star actor, a teacher at the Base High School, was really indignant that the new upstart director had found an 'unknown' to play Sir Thomas More in his upcoming production of *A Man for All Seasons*. This unknown was a naval warrant officer who had done a bit of acting at university but nothing since. He bore an extraordinary resemblance to Paul Scofield, who'd become an international star in the role both on stage and, fortunately for me, on screen – I'd seen the film. Disgruntled not to get the lead, the local star didn't think the offer of the part of Henry VIII was good enough for him. He didn't play supporting roles.

The director called me into his office, put the script in my hand and told me to read the part of Henry VIII with him reading Sir Thomas. Robert Shaw's portrayal of the king in the film was still fresh in my mind, so I just played him playing Henry and that was it. Jim offered me the part. My first role. Broadway here I come.

But of course I was meant to be in Bremerhaven to sell correspondence courses. I still had to earn a living and it was commission only, so unless I made some sales I wouldn't be there long enough to be in a play. I was in a real jam when a chance meeting with a young army lieutenant, Craig Parker a brainy boy from a steel town in Pennsylvania, turned into an offer of somewhere to stay.

When I'd first met Craig, I'd tried to engage him in conversation to edge him towards enrolling in a correspondence course. It was a joke really, me an educational disaster with five O levels to my name, and him with a masters degree in Business from the University of Pennsylvania's Wharton School. Talk about the blind trying to lead the sighted.

'Larry, let me be straight with you,' he laughed. 'I've had the best education that America offers and that money can buy. Let's you and me just be buddies!'

Now he said: 'Look, Larry, I have a two-room apartment here on the base. You can bed down there, there's plenty of room.' Craig was a real lifesaver. I certainly had enough money to buy the odd case of beer and to chip in for the groceries, but it was the rent that was going to be tough. I found myself being looked after by a generous stranger.

Rehearsals for the play started to dominate the agenda. I was determined to do this well. My personal life was a shambles, my professional life even worse. There had to be something that I could be good at. I learned those lines until I could literally say them backwards.

Lieutenant Ray Vrazell – like Craig – was a university graduate whiling away his military service trying to keep out of Vietnam. Ray was already an accomplished actor who had been performing since he was a boy. He was playing the duke of Norfolk and was my first actor friend. He was so good. I could say the lines convincingly enough, but it was the sense of feeling at ease on stage that only comes with experience that I needed to attain. I watched Ray move around so comfortably, and it certainly helped, but I couldn't learn it and it wouldn't rub off on me. I had such a long way to go.

And so inevitably the moment of reckoning finally came. We opened in front of an audience. Our new star was stunning in the role of Sir Thomas and, with Ray as the duke, I was working with really first-rate people on this, my debut. In the play the king only has one big scene with Sir Thomas but, as the director drummed into me week after week, 'the whole play turns on that scene. The audience have to feel the power of that man, they have to believe him, Larry.'

I was so nervous when I stepped out on stage all beautifully costumed and bejewelled. I knew I looked every inch a young king. But the nerves! I was so scared my knees were knocking like a pair of castanets, but somehow or other I kept it under control. I didn't let my fear take me over; even when I turned to walk up a few steps and caught the arm of a chair, my huge voluminous sleeve carrying it with me, I didn't let it faze me. I shook it free and ad-libbed, shouting, 'Goddamn it!' It seemed to me at the time the sort of thing a king would have said; the audience laughed and I ploughed on. I'd found something I could do, something that was mine and that – unlike school, unlike encyclopedias and correspondence courses – was within my power. I could do this acting thing.

But with the same inevitability that the show goes on, the show had to end. And so did my career in correspondence courses. It was hopeless. I phoned Don back in Frankfurt and told him I had to go. He wished me well and we both knew it had to be.

'So, what will you do, Larry?' he asked in his big-hearted way. 'Go back to England?'

I laughed. 'No Don, I'm not giving up that easily. Dave Miller, the guy I was supposed to be going to Vietnam with, he's got me a job selling cars near Nuremberg. I'm going down there in the morning.'

The old Beetle that I'd finally managed to reimburse Don for was my only asset. I sold it to Craig, which gave me enough for the train fare south and a few days' keep. Other than that, I didn't really have anything more to my name than I'd started with, but I now had this new part of me, this new interest, and somehow or other it gave me a sense of purpose. I wasn't the complete failure I'd begun to believe I was. I said goodbye to Ray and Craig, two friends I would have for life, two people who'd watched me become a different person on that stage – and started the next chapter.

But of course despite my joy in what I'd discovered, I was completely broke and on my way to another commission-only job. Worse still, I was the father of a child by now: somehow or other, probably via my father, I'd heard that my daughter had been born on 29 September. A child I'd never seen and possibly never would see. But I was free, and in the moments when I wasn't torturing myself over the mistakes in my life, that spurred me on. I was making a life, reinventing myself. I had to go on and deal with the downsides, I had to survive and prosper and maybe I would be good at selling cars after all. Next stop Nuremberg!

I was now working for Ford selling American cars to American soldiers, but in reality I was working for Niedermayer & Reich, the main German Ford dealer in the Nuremberg area. They had the franchise to work bases in and around the city. I got a car to drive: a very basic Ford Taunus with three gears and no frills, not even a radio. I was allocated a sales territory, given a stack of brochures and off I went. Or that was what was supposed to happen.

I didn't really have anywhere to stay. I was bunking in with Dave initially, but he needed to find somewhere cheaper so we decided to see what was available out in the surrounding countryside. Der Grüner Baum (The Green Tree) was a combination of pub, restaurant, butcher's and farm right in the middle of Puschendorf, a village within an easy driving distance of Dave's office and the area I was working. It was a family-run business. Three generations lived and worked there and they had a big room with two beds that, with break-fast included, was cheaper for two of us on a weekly basis than Dave was paying by himself in town.

Puschendorf was really a collection of farmhouses all clus-tered together and surrounded by fields and forests. Our new home was in the middle of it. The old granddad who ran the place was himself a farmer; he and his son-in-law looked after their land, raised pigs – which were then killed and butchered in the backyard – and sold the meat in the butcher's shop on the premises. The grandmother and her daughter looked after the children and ran the hotel side of the business, and cooked wonderful food for their family and guests.

The shop and hotel were absolutely spotless, but the whole village smelt just slightly of pig and horse, hay and straw. There was no end to the scents that wafted around the little lanes that wound their way between the houses of this tiny farming community.

'Larry, look at this!' Dave called down the stairs as I was making the final arrangements for the terms of our tenancy – my German was now getting quite good.

'Hang on, I'll be right up,' I called back. I walked into our room and there was Dave resplendent in the top half of a Nazi uniform, goose-stepping across the floor towards me with his right hand held high in a mock Nazi salute.

'*Heil* Hitler.'

'Where did you get that?' I pulled the door shut behind me.

He walked over to the old wardrobe in the corner, still in step. 'In there, *mein Herr*! Must have been the old man's. Just think, we're staying with an old stormtrooper!'

The pair of us became a bit of a novelty over the next couple of months. We always returned to our rooms long after every-one else had gone off to bed and we were generally woken up by the squeal of pigs either being fed or murdered in the yard below. We would go down to the dining room for our rolls and coffee to be laughed at and joked about by the farm labourers who'd been out in the fields since before dawn and who were by this time of day sitting behind big mugs of beer eating their chunks of bread and sausage as they tucked in to their '*zweite Frühstück*', or second breakfast.

I was driving backwards and forwards across country every day, desperately trying to prove to my employers and myself that I could sell cars – but it just wasn't working. I felt completely lost with all the technical jargon that car enthusiasts love to engage in and quickly realised that this would be another dead loss. But I had to give it a month or so; Dave had gone out on a limb to get me in. So I had to try. But the truth was I couldn't sell them, not even to people who actually wanted to buy there and then. It was a disaster.

A big old soldier wandered into the little shack I worked from in front of the base at Bamberg one day and said, 'Who's the guy selling Fords?'

'That's me, Sergeant-Major,' I piped up. One thing I had learned was how to read the military insignia on their uniforms. 'What can I do for you?'

'I wanna buy a Mustang for my wife. I'm taking early retirement and we want it waiting when we get back to the States.'

It should have been the easiest thing in the world, but when he realised that I didn't actually understand about the different engines there were to choose from, or the 'brake horsepower' and the 'torque' and all that other mystical mechanical mumbo-jumbo, he just wandered away, his interest had disappeared. He left me standing there speechless.

But one Saturday afternoon I found I wasn't lost for words. As Dave and I stood chatting in his sales booth, a nurse opened the door and stuck her head into the room. She looked so exquisite in her immaculate uniform with her little cap and white shoes. We both adored her immediately.

'Excuse me, could either of you split a twenty for me? I need some change.'

There was no point me even looking, I knew exactly how much – or rather how little – was in my wallet, but Dave managed to help her out.

'Are you an army nurse?' I asked.

'No,' she smiled, 'I'm a civilian. There are quite a few of us working at the base hospital.'

And we were off, just like that. Dave and I were entranced. She was so funny and friendly, such a character. We both started to chat her up and about an hour later she finally went off with her change. She'd invited us to a party that night and we were both in hot pursuit.

'She was amazing,' I said, 'Jacquie Parris.'

'And you know what nurses are like,' Dave laughed

'One of us is going to be all right tonight!'

And – much to my delight – it was me!

Within no time at all I was back in Bachelor Officers' Quarters again, this time sharing Jacquie's little flat on the base. Neat and tidy and decorated with her knick-knacks, pictures and travel souvenirs, once again I had a home and a loving female figure, one I'd longed for ever since my mother had left.

We discovered we shared a love for the theatre and, within the first two weeks of getting together, we'd both got parts in a musical, *Li'l Abner*, which was the next show at the base theatre. I was playing Abner and she was Mammy Yokum, his mother.

This was a really ambitious enterprise, but the show was a big favourite amongst the Americans. The satirical cartoon strip that it was based on had run for years and the musical was a real crowd-pleaser. It felt a little strange being an Englishman playing the part of this American icon, with an all-American cast and a very American audience, but the director and his wife, who were over there from Texas, both insisted that my country accent was impeccable. All those episodes of *The Beverly Hillbillies* I'd absorbed as a boy had now paid off.

Jacquie, apart from being far too young for the part, was certainly the genuine article as far as her background went. With her years away from home at university and then travelling and working abroad, she certainly had a 'citified' style of speech – but all the Appalachian country girl came back when she switched into being Mammy!

★

I'd finally had to admit to myself that I was never going to make it in sales. There was a construction site just down the road from Jacquie's place and they needed general labourers, so I wandered in there one afternoon. I chatted to the foreman for a little while and started the next morning.

They were building a colossal aqueduct to carry a major canal that was under construction across a main road. There were about 200 Yugoslavians (as they used to be called back then) all living in barrack huts on the site, which, with sleeping accommodation, mess hall, cookhouse and beer shed, was a little world of its own.

The site boss was a real jolly Bavarian with leather breeches and braces, feathered hat and all. Employing a young Brit amused him; he needed someone to keep the site tidy and he found it rather ironic that having helped knock the place down, one of us was helping to build it back up again. It held a double irony for me because I was mostly employed to stack the big timbers used for forming the concrete and I'd learned how to do that working with Tommy Coates back in Harlow. Tommy had learned that on the docks around Bermondsey, which had just been blitzed by the ones I was now working for. Round and round it goes.

At last I felt secure financially. I no longer dreamed about massive commission cheques; instead I got a wage packet with cash in it every Friday afternoon. It wasn't a huge amount, but it was enough to live on without me having to sponge off Jacquie. It was such a relief to have money in my pocket and not constantly have to borrow against the promise of a sale.

Dave meanwhile was doing well with Chrysler, and was becoming a very popular addition to the social scene at the American golf course. His low handicap and his high alcohol consumption – together with his innate ability to get on with everyone – had turned him into quite a celebrity in the club.

However, things had got a bit heavy between him and the daughter of a very senior officer and out of the blue I got a message to phone him.

'Larry, look, I've got to go back to London for a few days. I 'erm . . . it's a bit difficult. That girl I was with at the weekend, you remember?'

'Yeah, the pretty blonde, wasn't it?'

'Yes. Well she's up the duff!'

'Oh well done,' I said sarcastically. 'So what are you going to do?'

This all sounded so familiar. 'She wants to get an abortion,' he said. 'A mate of mine has arranged it all. We've got to be there for next Wednesday but obviously she can't just take off on her own, or with me for that matter, she's only nineteen. What I was going to say was: do you think you and Jacquie could come along? That way it would be kosher, I think. The four of us taking a little trip to London.'

'All right, I'll ask her.' I told Dave I'd get three or four days off.

How strange it seemed, driving back to London to sort out the same problem I'd been confronted with myself before. But this time it was much more straightforward; both parties knew it had been a mistake and that was that.

I made contact with my dad. There was no real reason to

when we were staying at a hotel close to the clinic in North London, but he asked me to come over to Harlow and see him the next day. We went out to Dave's family and I borrowed the car and drove over to see Ron. When I arrived, who should be there but Anita and my now seven-month-old daughter.

I sat for an hour with this little piece of me in my arms. My guilt, my sadness, my fears all turned over and over as I stared transfixed by this beautiful child. Whoever I was back then, I was so far from the person I am now, the person that I've become. I knew that this tiny being was there because her mum wanted her there; I'd made my decision and I'd walked away. I was on my own journey and there was no changing my mind. I've never set eyes on my daughter since that day. But I've never forgotten that hour I spent with her.

★

Back in Nuremberg, *Li'l Abner* was a huge success. The audience loved it. Jacquie had played Mammy in a neck brace, which was a bit of a novelty. We'd both been injured in a minor car crash when a young soldier – who was driving us to a 'hayride' and picnic that I'd organised with the local farmers – lost control of his car and rolled us into a ditch. Jacquie didn't let it stop her and the show went on.

Everything now was so cosy. The show was over and new productions were being discussed. I was earning good, steady money and Jacquie and I were having a wonderful time together. But then it all went wrong in another incident . . .

'Were you driving the car on that day, Mr Lamb?'

'I'm not sure. I had loaned the car to two Australians I'd met in Frankfurt.'

'What were their names, Mr Lamb?'

I lied without a second's hesitation, 'Robert Barclay and Philip Jones.'

The police inspector wrote the names on the form in front of him.

'So what happens now, Inspector?' I asked.

'Well, Mr Lamb. I will send this information to Munich and they will decide how to proceed.' I shook his hand and left. Dave was waiting for me outside the police station.

'What happened?' my friend asked me.

'It was what I thought it would be, that afternoon on the way back here. I knew it.'

'So what did you say?'

'I made up a story. I said that two Aussies had been borrowing the car. I can't even remember what I called them.'

'And what did they say?'

'Well, the bloke dealt with it as though it were just a formality. He didn't say what had happened, he just said that there had been a complaint involving a car which belonged to Niedermayer and Reich and that according to their records the vehicle was assigned to me.'

'So what are you going to do?' Dave asked.

'Nothing really. I'll just have to wait and see,' I shrugged.

Dave switched on the engine. 'So tell me again what happened?' He checked his mirror and pulled out into the afternoon traffic. 'It was on that dead straight stretch, wasn't it?'

'Yes, the stretch with double yellow lines for miles. I was behind this guy in a big BMW who wouldn't let me pass – typical German – and the road was deserted except for us. I dropped that old Taunus down into first gear and managed to get past him, but in doing so I stupidly edged him off on to the hard shoulder. What an idiot!'

About three weeks later the phone rang in Jacquie's living room. It was Dave. 'There's a registered letter for you at the post office. You have to sign for it yourself, the postman wouldn't let me.'

It was just before six o'clock on a rainy Friday evening. I walked up to one of the post office counters and showed my passport and asked for a recorded delivery item. I tore open the envelope as I walked back into the street. It was a summons for me to appear as a witness in the case against two persons. The two persons whose names I'd given who were accused of dangerous driving. And of course I realised that the police were calling my bluff, as obviously these invented people couldn't present themselves to the court, so as a witness I'd have been there on my own, easily identifiable as the culprit.

That was it. I rushed back to Jacquie's, packed my bags, and I was on the train for London within an hour. I wasn't going to risk that appearance. I kissed Jacquie goodbye and she promised to come to London as soon as she could.

And that was the end of that part of the adventure. Auf Wiedersehen, Deutschland.

—— 18 ——

After Germany

It seemed easy enough to say goodbye and run but, although I hadn't struck it rich in the sales profession, life back there in Nuremberg had been settled and comfortable. I had no real responsibilities and it was all so safe. A soul-searching over-night journey lay ahead of me. The train was jammed with Turkish workers sleeping everywhere: on luggage racks and in corridors. I finally managed to find a place to sit, next to the guard's wagon at the back of the train. It was draughty and noisy, but I was on my own and that was what I wanted.

I knew I was on my way back again to England, but to where exactly? To Harlow? I really didn't know where to go once I'd arrived and I hadn't been in touch with Wesley for months. He'd initially followed me out to Germany, but I'd been travel-ling about a bit with work and then someone told me that he'd gone home. There really wasn't anywhere else. Nan was in an old people's home and suffering with dementia and I had absolutely no desire to dump myself on Ron who was, by this time, settled down with Janet, his new wife, and her daughter Kay. I needed somewhere to live, though.

As usual I was completely broke, so earning a living would be my first priority. I sat in my little corner of that noisy old train, running through the list of woes, all the things that I felt were wrong with my life, all the things that hadn't worked out. In the end it was all a lot of self-pity: what did I have to complain about? OK, so I'd screwed up and once again

I'd burnt my bridges, but I was young, fit and healthy, I had a great girlfriend and I'd discovered that I actually did have some talent for acting. My co-travellers – most of whom had already spent three days and nights on this train – were going back to hard, relentless, mind-numbing jobs in an alien environment and they would have killed for my life. I shoved my bag into the corner as a pillow. *Stop moaning!* I told myself. As I shut my eyes to try and get some sleep I turned my mind to Jacquie, my girlfriend, the one who loved me and cared for me.

★

I headed back to Harlow and moved in with Wes. He was renting an old caravan parked at the bottom of someone's big, overgrown garden. It was cold and damp but at least it was affordable. He'd also got me some work with Michael, an old artist friend of his, who lived out in the country. He was trying to rebuild his house, which had been badly damaged by fire. He'd built the place himself as a young man but now was too frail to repeat the process and needed someone to fetch and carry and do all the things he'd done himself back in the 1930s.

He was a delightful gent. He'd been a close associate and colleague of Henry Moore, but they'd fallen out. He made a living teaching young artists at the college in Harlow. The house had burnt almost to the ground in some parts, but he was a dogged old fighter – determined to return it to its original form. It had to be his home again.

It was a good arrangement. He paid me a reasonable hourly rate and I did exactly what he wanted done. I was his strong pair of hands. But more importantly he was a wise man who'd really had a life. He was on his own but living the way he wanted, and day by day he made me understand that that was what one needed to do, not let someone else live it for you. That old house of his – a thing that he'd created himself – was slowly coming back together and the old man that he'd become was just as determined to see it reconstructed as he had been as a young man to build it.

Wes and I had been invited to a fancy dress party and were struggling to decide what to wear. In the end it had to be cheap and cheerful, something that we could throw together ourselves. We used some curtains which were a bit old and tatty, but pinned together in the right way – with a few strands of ivy pulled from the neighbours' wall as laurel wreaths – and off we went as two dashing Romans.

Graham Poulten was at the party, beautifully rigged out in a convincing Roman's tunic and kilt; it completely upstaged my and Wes's ad-hoc arrangements. When the laughter died down over our similarly themed outfits, I asked him if he was still working abroad. I'd known Graham a little through Wes for years and heard that he was in the oil business.

'I'm working out in Libya,' he replied 'on cathodic protection, anti-corrosion work.'

'What, with anodes and cathodes you mean?' I ventured.

'Yes,' he said, 'do you know anything about all that then?'

'Well,' I took a deep breath here. 'I did actually study physics and chemistry for six years. I didn't pass the exams but I have an idea. Why? Any chance of a job, you think?'

He smiled. 'Well, the thing is, the gas industry here is in the middle of a large construction programme, building a high-pressure pipeline network to handle all the gas they've found in the North Sea. They have to hire a lot of technicians to install temporary systems all along the pipes. The company I work for are looking for people to train so you might be in with a chance. I'll ask my boss.'

He was true to his word and about three weeks later I reported to his company MAPLE for an interview. I'd done some reading up on the whole subject of corrosion and had a story ready about how I'd been working on similar stuff during my time on the site in Nuremberg, but the man was actually more interested in the selling experience I'd had and the fact that I'd been working overseas. The boss offered me a job as a trainee technician at a starting salary of £1,000 per annum, which at the time was very generous. I got a company vehicle too and expenses. I walked out of that office on cloud nine. I had been saved.

I was assigned a section of pipeline under construction near Stratford-upon-Avon. I had to oversee the careful laying into the soil of the pipe and then to install temporary anti-corrosion materials at each point where the pipe crossed a road, a river, a railway or any other major structure. I'd always had a fascination for big engineering projects and now there I was, actually working on one. Watching the huge lengths of pipe being meticulously welded together and then X-rayed and then ultrasonically checked and finally lifted into the air like great swaying lengths of spaghetti amazed me. It was of course extremely dangerous; although the pipes themselves were completely rigid, they became really flexible when welded together in a 400-yard-long section, so much so that a ripple that started at one end would reverberate along the whole length as it was lowered into the trench. One day when this happened a poor fellow was under the pipe: it drove his head right down into his body and he was killed outright.

My part of the job was quite straightforward: install the systems, watch the pipe being lowered into the trench and – most importantly – keep on good terms with the chief engineer. I was lucky on that score: John, the man in charge of my section, was a really affable Irishman and we got along famously. So much so that six weeks after starting I got a call to go back into head office for a meeting with the man who'd hired me.

'We've been hearing a lot of good things about you, Larry,' he said.

'Oh. That's nice to know. Who from?'

'The Gas Council. Well done. They're not easy as clients and somehow or other you seem to have really impressed them. How would you like to go out to Libya?'

'What? To work with Graham?'

'Well, he's running things out there at the moment and could do with someone to keep an eye on the project when he's on leave. What do you think?'

I couldn't believe my luck. I'd only been back in the country a few months and here I was getting the opportunity to escape again, only this time with a proper job and a proper salary.

'I'd love to,' I said. 'When?'

Things had improved in my overall mental state. Having a job with a regular income had enabled me to sort things out financially regarding my daughter. The court had assessed my financial situation and set a reasonable percentage of my weekly earnings to be sent towards her upkeep. That, at least, made me feel that I was facing up to some of my responsibilities. But being back in England whilst the world was out there beckoning for me to make something of myself just wasn't satisfying me, so an offer of a job abroad was exactly what I wanted.

There were two of the older engineers sitting in the outer office when I walked out. 'What are you looking so happy about?' one of them asked.

'I'm going to Libya!' I announced.

The two of them exchanged knowing glances. 'Have you ever heard of a bloke called Gaddafi?' said one of them.

'No, why?' I asked.

'He's just taken over Libya,' the other one laughed. 'Wait till you get out there, you'll soon hear about him then!' How right they were.

My new job meant I would alternate between Libya and various projects in the UK on a three-monthly basis. It also meant I would be able to save some money at last. Jacquie came over from Germany so that we could talk the situation through. This was obviously going to mean big changes for us both, especially financially. I would be earning five times my UK salary, tax-free and all expenses paid.

We decided that for the coming year or so she would work on a short-term basis for an agency in the US whilst I was in the desert, and then we'd come back to England to be together there. She loved being in Europe, particularly England, and was – like me – never completely happy in her home country. Both of us had troubled backgrounds and I think perhaps the travel served to deaden the pain. The time apart would be rough, but this was a chance for me to start building a career in a well-paid field – and we both knew I needed that.

My ticket to Libya was via Malta, so we flew there early for a romantic farewell holiday. We found a cheap hotel in Sliema and spent a glorious couple of days exploring that fantastic little island. Unbeknownst to me then, Malta would feature strongly in my life later on. The place seemed to be populated by old ladies in black dresses and monks and priests in brown habits – they were everywhere – and little bright-coloured buses that bounced along on those potholed roads. The standard of driving, we noticed, was terrible. There seemed to be no reason about which side anyone took and when I asked a bus driver why things were that way he said, 'Ah, in England if you want to drive, first you pass the driving test. In Malta if you want to drive, first thing you buy a car!'

All too quickly we were saying our farewells at the airport. Jacquie had to stay on the island until she could get a flight home via Rome, but I was on my way to a whole new way of life in a country supposedly in turmoil. Libyan-Arab Airways was an outcast airline operating from a country that had been ostracised by the whole world community and couldn't land in many places outside the Middle East. As the Maltese Government had remained an ally, a lot of their flights went via the tiny island republic. It's only a short hop from Malta to Tripoli, Libya's capital, and we landed right on time at about 8 o'clock on Sunday night.

It must have been a really hot day; as I walked down the steps to the runway, the smells of the place and the heat made a heady combination. There was smoke, donkey, straw and earth all mingling together in the still night air; there was hardly any movement at all. I knew this place was going to be nothing like anywhere I'd been before.

The international terminal was just a big old hangar with a series of police and customs checks to get through, all manned by very officious, not at all friendly, uniformed men. The place was teeming with armed soldiers.

There were about forty passengers on the flight, and by the time we'd all been processed three or four times it was pretty close to 10 o'clock. The airport bus took us over really rough roads into the capital and I finally made it to the Tripoli Palace Hotel just before eleven. I went in search of a nightcap but of course there was nothing to be had unless you wanted something strictly non-alcoholic. The first thing Colonel Gaddafi had done when he'd taken the country over was to implement strict Sharia law and ban all sales of alcohol.

I sat down next to a huge guy in a Stetson hat and full Western regalia, alligator-skin boots and belt, silver buckles and all. He looked at me over the top of his glass. 'Man,' he said, 'this is one sorry son-of-a-bitch of a country: no booze in the bars? That's about as much use as tits on a bull. It's a helluva shame, this place used to be jumpin' on a Sunday night. That old Gaddafi boy, he's killed this place dead.'

He was right: there seemed to be no life there at all. The lonely waiter served coffees, teas and soft drinks, and up on the walls behind the now-empty glass shelves of the bar, etched by sunlight and desert dust, were the silhouettes of the bottles that had stood there for years – signs of a bygone society all swept away.

'Have you been working here long?' I asked my fellow travellers.

''Bout five years now, but I don't think I'll be here another five.'

'Has it changed that much?'

'Too much. It was never the easiest place, but now these guys are taking control of everything and they just aren't ready to do it. They think that since the oil business has been nationalised they can run the whole thing themselves . . . most of them boys don't know their ass from a hole in the ground!'

We chatted on until about midnight but, as I was booked on the Esso plane at seven in the morning, that was late enough.

The early morning flight along the coast to Marsa El Brega was spectacular, the bright blue Mediterranean rolling up against a green coastal strip, with what seemed to be miles and miles of orange groves gradually petering out into scrub and then empty desert. There were very few signs of people and there was just one road that ran all the way along the coast, linking the country to Egypt in the east and to Tunisia in the west. There was very little in between. There was so much to take in, not only in terms of the place itself but also in learning about my new job too. Finally we landed at Brega, the capital of Esso's Libyan concession: thousands of square miles of desert sitting on top of billions of dollars' worth of oil and gas.

Graham was standing on the landing strip waiting for me, looking every bit the oil engineer in a neat khaki shirt and slacks. He was very tanned and fit. 'Welcome to Brega, Larry. Get your bags and I'll show you around.'

Then he added: 'I'm going to take you down to Zelten

where the project is first, and then we can drive back at the end of the day so you can have a look round up here in the big city!' The road was 120 miles of tarmac that ran dead straight over the desert; it made just two bends in its entire length.

'So you're on your way back to England, are you, Graham?' I had to shout to make myself heard over the engine noise.

'Just as quickly as I can get you settled in, yes!' he yelled.

MAPEL were installing an anti-corrosion system to protect the steel linings of oil and gas wells in the Zelten field that went anything from 5,000 to 10,000 feet underground. Down to levels where heat, moisture and chemical reactions gradually corroded the top-grade steel tubing.

'It's pretty straightforward at this stage,' Graham told me as we stood looking up at the rig we were using to install our equipment. 'You just have to keep an eye on things and make sure the crew are fastening the wires in line and marking them properly. This is an easy job for them, they're loving it!'

Zelten itself was basically a collection of Portakabins set in lines around an administration block and mess hall. But in reality it was the control centre of an oil and gas field pumping out millions of dollars' worth of fuel every hour. I was assigned a bedroom and we had a quick lunch in the mess hall before Graham introduced me to my immediate Esso boss, a lovely old electrical engineer from North Carolina. 'Pleased to meet you, Larry, make yourself right at home. I'm Dougal McCormick. Anything you need, you come and tell me and I'll do my very best to help y'out!' His accent felt so familiar from my days around all those soldiers and I felt at home right away.

Graham and I began the drive back to Brega. Just as the evening was beginning to draw in, I noticed there was something lighting up the sky above the horizon. 'That's the flare stacks,' Graham told me when I asked. 'They burn off gas that they can't use and at the moment they're negotiating a new price for the gas so they're burning it all.' As we drove over a ridge in the road, the flames came into view: they were lighting up everything for miles. 'Those stacks are 350 feet tall and the flames go up about another 100 feet and they've been burning day and night for months,' he said.

I got to know this road well. Graham managed to hold on to a room in Brega so there was always a bed up in the 'big city', and compared to Zelten it really was. Esso's facilities on the Mediterranean coast were really a self-contained American town built to accommodate the 3,000 or so staff and dependants. There was a school, a hospital, cinema, golf club, supermarket: everything, in fact, to make it a real home from home.

And unlike in Zelten, there was a very active social scene. When I was in the desert I worked, ate, wrote letters and slept, but up there in Brega there was a life! And whilst I was determined to stay on top of the job, the odd trip back to civilisation was very welcome.

The Esso staff had their own club, a bit like an old-fashioned country club, and invitations to functions didn't often filter down to lowly subcontractors like me. However, the lady who ran the whole thing happened to find out that I'd done some acting, and as she was also the chairperson of the drama club, I found myself welcomed into the inner sanctum. The complete ban on alcohol had cast a bit of a dark cloud over the party scene, but there were a lot of chemical engineers working in the oil and gas processing plants and, with a little ingenuity – and no small measure of courage since the punishment for even touching alcohol was instant deportation – a steady stream of 'White Lightning' helped to keep the social wheels rolling. Made from sugar instead of the usual grain, the local experts learned how to colour and flavour their hooch, and apart from the fact it left one with the most lethal hangover, it did the trick. Down in Zelten, bottles changed hands for fortunes, and in the market outside Brega, fifty-pound sacks of sugar sold like hot cakes.

As well as running the drama club, Noel Robertson was also the wife of the vice president in charge of Esso Libya. She and Harold, the boss, were Canadians, and had been in Brega for years. They were both in their mid-fifties and lived a very comfortable, sedate life. They hosted parties and receptions and altogether had a very busy social calendar. Harold had come to Libya straight after World War II. 'We landed on the beaches just near here,' he told me, 'and then with local labour hired in Tripoli we swept a path through the minefields that the Germans had laid all the way to Zelten. I've pretty much been here ever since.'

Noel was in a jam. 'Larry, I'm having a problem casting our next play. It's a lovely old English parlour drama called *Goodnight Mrs Puffin* and there's a part of an American. The man I've offered it to feels it's a bit too small a part for him . . . do you think you might be interested?'

The star system again, I thought to myself. 'Yes, of course, I'd love to, but rehearsals will be a bit difficult. I'm down in Zelten all week. The weekends would be all right though.'

'Oh, you leave that to me,' she said. 'I'll talk to Harold. I'm sure we can work things out.'

And so I was enrolled as a member of the Brega Players.

And for the next six weeks I commuted in and out of Zelten every day on the company plane, travelling 120 miles up in the evening with all the big shots and then back down in the morning for the day's work. What a life!

This high-flying commute did almost turn very ugly one morning, though, when we took off from Brega and the whole area around Zelten was covered in dense cloud. After three attempts at landing, even the hardened desert hands aboard were getting a bit nervous. The pilot took one more go at getting us down when there was a sudden break in the clouds and we all let out a huge yell, 'Power line!' It was right below us and the pilot pulled the plane up just in time. That line carried 37,000 volts down into the desert, so if the pilot hadn't pulled the plane up in time we would all have fried.

The play was a great success and put me well and truly in Noel's good books. So much so that she invited Jacquie to come out as her guest and fixed her up with a room in one of the secretary's houses. I had to keep my girlfriend's arrival hush-hush, as unmarried sexual relations were taboo and punishable by whipping and stoning, but it didn't stop us. We were at it everywhere. We came very close to being caught one night on the beach in the moonlight when the headlights of the police patrol criss-crossed the sand as we clung to each other giggling like school kids.

I'd been caught in a sandstorm a week or so before and it was a really frightening experience. I was out about three or four miles from Zelten with the plant clearly visible across the sand dunes. After a really hot afternoon, the wind started to come up, and gradually the plant at Zelten was blotted out. It was as if the whole desert was being lifted up and blasted in every direction. Thankfully, I knew what to do. I got into the cab of the Land Rover, closed the windows and covered my mouth and nose while I waited. Whatever happened, I knew to wait and stay right there. It was pretty terrifying, the sound it made, with the wind roaring and the sand battering the steel bodywork; despite all the windows being closed, by the time it blew out a couple of hours later my nose and throat were completely lined with a fine dust.

But of course it changed the whole area, and right on one of the bends in that dead straight road was a big sand drift. Early the next evening, two engineers from Zelten – one American and one British – came roaring towards that now half-covered bend in opposite directions. At the last moment they both swerved to miss the other, but they didn't manage to avoid a crash: they collided. They were lucky to be found by a Libyan driver who radioed the base and got them driven back to the medical room in Zelten. They were both in a really serious condition and the medic called through to Brega to get the plane dispatched. He was asked whether or not they were both Esso personnel: the plane could only be dispatched if they were. John Sigmund, the chief engineer, a long, lean, taciturn Texan, got on the phone. 'Now, you listen to me,' he drawled. 'Both these men work for me and, frankly, whether they are Esso or contractors, I don't care. You get that goddamn plane up in the air or I will close this plant down – and you know I mean it!'

They got the message, and half an hour later every vehicle that could be driven left the base for the airstrip. We lined them up all the way along both sides, their headlights illuminating the tarmac so that the pilot could land and take those men to the hospital in Tripoli.

It was definitely John Sigmund's high-handed action that saved them. They both made it to intensive care, but there was no way they would have survived had he not been prepared to go out on a limb like that. Working closely together in out-of-the-way places binds men together like brothers, and so perhaps what he did was what any of us would have done if we had his rank.

Most of the men who lived down in the desert flew in there to work and flew home on leave. That camp was their home from home. They worked on different schedules. Some did it to save money to buy a house or to enhance their family's lives quickly; others did it to be away. They were a really extraordinary mix of guys, always looking after each other. It was great to be a part of such a band.

Of course the isolation was the big problem. There was no communication with the outside world down there. We had letters, but that was it, and the Libyan postal service was laughable: it was nothing to get six or eight letters all backed up and to find yourself reading things completely out of sync.

And in the same way there was no telephone, there was no TV, no radio, no computers – nothing. Our only real entertainment was one film a week on a Wednesday night. The projectionist was Libyan and couldn't read English, so quite often a shout would go up in the darkened mess hall a few minutes into the second reel of a film. 'Ali! Have you got the reels muddled up?'

In a way it didn't really matter whether you saw the last reel before the middle one. We tended only to get the B movies, which I found to be mindless twaddle anyway. But when they were the only entertainment of the week, they soon became important and, as the camp gag went, 'Don't worry, next week we've got *The Guns of Navarone*.' Needless to say, we never did have.

Thanks to Jacquie's visit, the separation hadn't been too excruciating, but the work schedule in Libya got changed and I was spending more time there than in England. We seemed to be living most of our life via letters and though it was obvious that the situation had to change, there didn't really seem to be an alternative. Towards the end of 1971, Jacquie issued an ultimatum.

Off to America

So there I was on my way to America, on the next leg of the journey. In my heart of hearts, though, I knew that I'd got it wrong again. I absolutely adored Jacquie; she was everything that a man could want in a wife: funny, sexy, a great cook and, most importantly to me, she was a real mother, although at the time I didn't realise I was on a quest to replace the mum who'd had to leave me. I certainly wasn't ready to appreciate all these wifely qualities, but there I was facing another wedding that I instinctively knew was destined to fail. Jacquie was a few years older than me and, as she'd made perfectly clear, she wasn't prepared to wait around and leave it too long to have children; her body clock was ticking and she was ready to start nest building.

The plane had been delayed leaving London; about an hour into the flight, the captain made an announcement. 'Ladies and gentlemen. This is your captain speaking. On behalf of Pan-American Airways I would like to apologise for our late departure from London and to inform you that the bar will be open on a complimentary basis on the flight to Washington DC. Thank you. Enjoy your flight with Pan-Am.' A huge cheer went up right through the plane but my mind was in a real tangle. What was I going to do? I'd been there before, standing in front of witnesses and promising all those things that I knew I couldn't honour. How could I do it again?

Who was I kidding? Not myself, that was for sure. I knew what would happen in the end but, having met this amazing woman who wanted to be with me forever, how could I possibly risk it never happening again? I had to get married to her. If I didn't, I might regret it for the rest of my life. It was all arranged, the wedding would be held at the baptist church and the reception at the Daniel Boone Hotel. The dress had been made, the invitations sent out and my in-laws-to-be were all set for the big day on 18 December 1971. But there I was, 35,000 feet over the Atlantic, getting extremely cold feet. Beyond cold, they were close on Arctic.

I couldn't just arrive there and say I'd gone off the idea: that would be too cruel and Jacquie would be broken-hearted. I sat in my window seat staring out at those endless blue miles of ocean, turning the whole thing over and over, but really all I was doing was talking my way into it, not doing what I should have been doing and talking myself out of it. Just the short-term view of how Jacquie would feel was influencing my decision, and I was giving little thought to the way things would be when the inevitable occurred and the whole thing disintegrated. I was bursting with wild oats that I was absolutely determined to sow. But here I was running into a trap. I think I knew even then that it was a trap that, without doubt, I would escape.

It was an endless conundrum and I didn't break out of it until we were flying over Canada, but of course instead of deciding to make myself face the facts, be brave, tell the truth, I just got into a panic and resigned myself to going through with it. Just as I'd done before, I was going to take the easy route. How much better would it be to face the truth? Jacquie would understand that, love her though I did (in as much as somebody as screwed up as I was could ever love anybody), I just wasn't ready to settle down. It was only the fear of finishing up alone, of having found 'the one for me' and rejected her that led me to find myself in this situation. Of all the people in the world, I was about the worst possible choice she could have made, but I was too frightened to tell her. I couldn't deal with her sadness.

We flew over Quebec and New Brunswick, Maine, Vermont and New England, right over New York City and Philadelphia, then the captain told us we were beginning our descent to Dulles International Airport. And that sort of put the cap on it: I was about to land in America. I'd come too far. I just wasn't brave enough to tell her the truth.

I was twenty-four years old and so had qualified for a Pan-American young flyer's ticket for £40 for the round trip, London–Washington–London. My final destination involved an onward flight and that meant a transfer from Dulles International, way outside DC, on to National Airport, which is now Ronald Reagan Airport and close to the city. We were still over an hour late, so Pan-American met me as I came off the plane and escorted me through all the formalities. Before I knew it I was sitting in the back of a limousine being sped onwards to my connecting flight! And so the first American I ever had a conversation with on American soil was the limo driver. He was a thickset black guy who was a native of Washington but whose family on both sides had come up from the Deep South.

'Appalachian Airways? They's real hedge-hoppers, they just bounce their way over the mountains,' he told me. 'Where you flying to anyways?'

'West Virginia.'

'Oh you got a ways to go. You hold on to your hat, man. Weather like this, that thing gonna shake you up!'

I could have done without his comments, I was nervous enough as it was. He drove us brilliantly and just made it in time. Within ten minutes of saying goodbye to him I was walking out across the rainswept tarmac to board a plane not much bigger than the twenty-one-seater that flew me in and out of the desert in Libya. *Oh boy,* I thought. *I can do without small planes: give me a big old jumbo jet, a flying cathedral; this is all I need on a rainy, windy night – a flight over the mountains in a little plane!*

There wasn't even a cabin attendant on the flight. The second officer collected tickets and then checked that all ten or so of us were strapped in before he disappeared through the little door to the flight deck. And that was it. The pilot gunned the engines and that old familiar smell of aviation spirit wafted through the plane. We thundered over the runway and with a very definite lurch we were airborne.

My thoughts turned back to the torture of my situation, but very quickly they were interrupted by the second officer's voice. 'Ladies and gentlemen, we are likely to be experiencing a lot of turbulence on this flight, so please keep your seatbelts fastened securely and refrain from moving about the aircraft.'

Just as he finished his speech, the whole plane dropped as though it had fallen out of the sky. A man across the aisle from me shouted out in surprise as we felt ourselves dropping into the void. And so it went on, propellers roaring. As we dropped again, the sound would change. I found the whole thing terrifying. What on earth was I doing here? I could see the headlines flash before me: 'Young Englishman with bright future ahead of him, killed in a plane crash on the way to his wedding!' The wedding I didn't want to go through with. That was it; I would have to come clean. I would have to tell Jacquie that – despite the fact I really loved her – I just wasn't ready to settle down.

And then we plunged downwards again. I was desperately trying to stay calm but I suddenly felt sure that this was the end. I'd come all this way to crash in the mountains of Virginia. It was there that I made up my mind. If I made it through the night I was going to tell her the truth the moment I set eyes on her, no matter what.

With all of this going on and the fear spreading through the plane, I had completely forgotten that we were due to make a scheduled stop. With the engines roaring, we very quickly taxied to a halt at what looked to be little more than a hangar and a few sheds. The second officer came through to let off a couple of passengers and then called out, 'I'm going to the snack bar for a shake and fries. Can I take an order for anyone?!' I sat and laughed to myself: it summed up the contrast and everything I loved about it. Only in America . . . and here I was at last.

It wasn't long before we had to take off again and instantly the plane started to buck all over the place. *I should have got off back there.* I cursed myself for being so indecisive; surely that was my chance to escape the future that had been mapped out for me. *Why are you so flaky?* I asked myself yet again.

The second stage of the journey was even worse than the first, and by the time we banged down on to the ground for the final time, I was absolutely wrung out. I walked off the plane and into the tiny terminal building and there was Jacquie. All my resolve melted away and there I was hugging her, telling her how I'd missed her and carrying all that heartbreaking baggage with me, lie after lie after face-saving lie. Of all the people in the world to do it to. Jacquie was so kind and understanding that I'm sure if I had expressed what I was feeling she would have dealt with it. She would have been angry, of course she would, and she'd have been hurt too, but at least she would have been dealing with the truth. Who knows, that way I might even have kept her as a friend? But I was just totally spineless and went ahead with it.

Jacquie's father had died some years before, so her mother Louise, her old aunt Elsie and her brother Fred all made me very welcome in the family home in Clendenin, a small town twenty miles or so from the state capital of Charleston. They were straightforward, plain-speaking American people, a real united family who welcomed me with great warmth and incredible hospitality. 'D'jeet?' they kept asking me. 'Did you eat?' I remember gorging myself on red beans and onions with leather britches (a sort of preserved bean) on the side and platefuls of fresh-baked cornbread. Food, food, food: it was as though they'd found me starving in the street and were determined to build me up.

A bachelors' night out had been organised by some of the male relatives and they were taking me to Charleston with some of their friends. Most of the group were much older and a little more on the wild side. They were real country boys up for a night on the town. We drove to a bar in Charleston and proceeded to buy round after round of beers. We laughed and drank on into the night. At about one o'clock in the morning I was absolutely starving, and one of the boys suggested we drive to a burger joint a few blocks away. I got into a car with some of the other guys, I didn't really know who they were. We drove a bit further than I'd assumed we would, and arrived at an area of the city that had been completely demolished in preparation for some civic development project. All that remained was the street network; every building had been removed except one: a real tumbledown two-storey affair with a dim red light burning outside on the veranda.

'Is this the place?' I asked. 'What kind of food do they serve?' My new friends seemed to find this hilarious.

'No, Larry, this ain't the place for food,' the one who was driving laughed. 'This is the place where you get laid!'

That brought the house down, but I wasn't finding it as funny. I felt like some silly teenager. 'Come on fellas,' I pleaded. 'I'm getting married in the morning.'

'Don't you want a little poontang on your last night of free-dom?' the guy who was driving asked.

'No, no really. I don't think that would be a good idea at all, let's just go and get something to eat.'

'Well, Larry, if you don't mind waiting, us boys are gonna get us a piece of tail.'

'Hey lookee here! How you doing, honey?'

He pointed towards the now well-lit veranda and there, smiling a big toothy grin, was an extraordinary black woman with long wavy brown hair that had to be a wig. She was missing her two top middle teeth and as she spoke her tongue kept playing through the gap.

'Hi boys,' she called. 'Y'all looking to have some fun?'

Our driver took charge. 'Wait here, boys. I'm gonna get us a deal. I bet she does group rates!' So we sat and watched the negotiations play out in front of us. She went back inside, 'She's gotta ask her momma!' our man called back. When she reappeared, she beckoned him over, and after a minute or so she disappeared again. The driver returned. 'She'll take us all on for twenty-five bucks. Get your asses up here, boys! Larry, if you're coming you get to go first, I told her you's getting married in the morning. She said she'd never had an Englishman before.'

So there I was on the eve of my marriage, sitting alone, half drunk in a car, parked up outside a brothel. It was all a bit surreal. I waited for what seemed long enough for my comrades to return, but there was still no sign and in the end I started to get a bit worried and decided to go and make sure all was OK. I walked up the rickety old steps and across the veranda; the door was ajar already, so I pushed it open. There, in front of me, was a colossal black woman, obviously Momma, lying on a filthy old bed fanning herself with a newspaper. 'Is you with them boys in theya?' she asked.

'Yes I am.' I couldn't quite figure out how to address her. 'I'm the one who is getting married tomorrow, we're having a bachelor party.'

'N'you didn't want no pussy?'

'No, no offence, but it just doesn't seem appropriate.'

20

I Do

I do.

There I'd said it again, but I couldn't live up to it, and I knew it even then. After all my drawn-out resolution on those two plane journeys, I still couldn't accept the settled-down status.

We were due to drive up to Washington DC to stay at an address soon to become world-famous. A friend of Jacquie's had loaned us her apartment in the Watergate complex for a week as a wedding gift. Before we set off, however, we took a drive through some of the beautiful mountainous country-side around Charleston, West Virginia's capital, dropping in on friends and family who hadn't made it to the ceremony.

We drove up a long rocky valley, 'a holler', following a flowing brook, 'a crick' – hence the 'cricks and hollers' that the locals speak of when they refer to the backwoods areas. We finally arrived at our destination – a clearing overlooking the road and a big mobile home that appeared to be teeming with children. Our arrival drew all of their attention, and out from behind the screen that covered the main door to their house stepped a big burly man in his thirties, dressed in dungarees and a baseball cap. He ambled down to greet us, accompanied by a woman who seemed tiny alongside this colossus.

'Hi, m'names John, this here's ma wahf, her name's Julie. Y'all can call her Heifer!'

The look on Jacquie's face was priceless; it said everything. *You wanted to meet your new in-laws.* The little heifer just grinned.

One of her other cousins had a brother working in Philadelphia who evidently worked in the corrosion control business – an amazing coincidence, as I'd never met anyone who even knew what it was. 'Why don't you go visit with him on the way to DC?'

So when we got to Philadelphia, the first thing this new part of my ever-extending family did was ask me if I wanted a job.

'Well,' I said, 'I'm working between England and Libya at the moment and I don't really think it's going to work out long term, so I guess the answer is "Yes".'

He took the phone and called his old boss. 'Hey Regis, I've got an English guy here married to my cousin Jacquie – he's been installing cathodic protection systems out in Libya for Esso. Wanna talk to him? Says he might be interested in a job.'

I found myself sitting across the desk from Regis Kubitt, the charming, handsome forty-something boss of the Engineering Division of Henkels & McCoy, 'the largest privately owned utilities contractor in the US'. I was pretty impressed but wanted to keep things straight.

'I have to tell you, Mr Kubitt—' I started.

'Call me Regis, Larry.'

'Well, Regis, I know from experience that you would expect me to have a degree, but in fact I only have some very minor academic qualifications. I got lucky and started work in corrosion control just by chance.'

'Let me stop you right there, Larry. If I want a guy with a degree, I'll put an ad in the paper and I'll get a coupla hundred of them sitting out there, but none of them will know much about anything. Just tell me about what you've been doing – where was it?'

'Libya,' I said. 'In the Esso concession.'

We discussed the project – fascinating to him, as nothing like that had been attempted before – and after about half an hour he said: 'Right, when can you come and join Henkels?'

I was back in Libya about a fortnight after the meeting, the paperwork for my prospective emigrant status all in place, but there was one little fly in the ointment: my application had to be accompanied by a police clearance from any country where I'd lived for more than six months – and that meant Germany. I was really sweating over my non-appearance in court for that traffic violation – but in fact there lay my salvation: evidently the fact that I hadn't turned up in court for a traffic case didn't enter the realms of police affairs.

I arrived at JFK in April 1972, a new immigrant. They managed to issue my green card with a typing error for posterity, but other than that I was now a resident alien. I tucked my newly minted identity into my wallet and loaded my bags on to the Philadelphia-bound shuttle bus – they called it a limo but I'm certain it wasn't. But no matter, I was there. A new job, a new life in this new land that fate and chance had drawn me to. It all just felt so right.

21

A Pittsburgh Pirate

By the middle of 1973, I knew that all those months of living a lie couldn't go on. It was a lie that I'd pursued on that journey over to America to get married and that I continued to live every day as I went out on the road in America. It was too much deceit to bear. I knew how much Jacquie loved me, but it wasn't enough and I wasn't prepared to go on with it for a lifetime. I knew that in the end I would be tempted and it was only so long before that would defeat me. I'd given my life to someone else; it had to be mine again.

Within a couple of months of setting up home just outside Philadelphia, we were already trying out a trial separation. I'd answered an ad in the local paper and was sharing an apartment in a young professionals' condomininium. The social scene: the gym, the pool and the bar were just what I thought I wanted. But I soon ran back to mamma – in this case Jacquie – still wanting my freedom but also comforts of a wife and home. The only memorable moment of that whole episode came one Saturday afternoon as I sat in the main lounge, alone, when three big good-looking guys came in and were ordering drinks at the bar. I realised instantly that I recognised one of them and as bold as brass I walked up to them saying, 'You certainly gave Henry Cooper a run for his money!'

It was the man himself, Cassius Clay as we knew him then. He turned towards me, a big warm smile on his face, and took up a mock sparring stance, those big famous fists only half closed. 'Hey Englishman! What you doing here in Philly?'

It was my first brush with celebrity. I was so innocent, so impressionable, but he took it in his stride – a true gentleman with a big heart.

On a fateful Saturday morning in our little rented house in Grove City, Pennsylvania, the moment – that had always been inevitable from the minute I'd said 'I do' – finally came. I told Jacquie that I couldn't go on, that I couldn't stay married to her. I loved her deeply and I'm sure she knew that, but I just couldn't go on with it. I felt terrible for hurting her at the time, but when I look back I think I did the right thing. My feelings were perfectly natural, and all I was doing was releasing myself from a bond whose obligations I couldn't uphold. I simply wanted out. I wanted out before there were children involved and before other people's lives were affected. I felt sad for her pain, and boy did we both cry our eyes out as we packed all her things into her car, but it didn't go deeper than that. I'd freed myself and I could be me.

Jacquie was a blessed angel of a woman, and from what I gather from my relatives who are still a big part of Jacquie's life, she remains very much the same person that she was back then.

She was the first person to help me understand how to make sense of all the things that screwed me up. It was a really big step forward to admit that I had problems, and she helped me work out how it had all come to be. She took me under her wing and made me face the fact that a lot of the truly slanderous stories my father had woven into my psyche were just fabrications of his own damaged character.

I was constantly running my mother down, calling her all the names my father had called her. I'd grown so used to the side of the story that he used to tell, and one day Jacquie stopped me in my tracks. 'Larry! Look, it's just not right you saying what you say about your mother. You owe it to her and to yourself to go and tell her what your father has taught you and see what she has to say!'

I did just that. I sat down with my mum and talked to her about the way I'd been taught to believe things. My mum was calm. She said, 'Look, Larry, I don't think it's my place to say bad things about your father but if he's saying this about me then maybe you should go and speak to my friends, the women who were around us when we were still married. Ask them about what you've been told. I think perhaps you'll find it's about the pot calling the kettle black.'

I learnt a lot about my father from that conversation. Even though I'd been the subject of some of his turns and tantrums, I'd always believed him when he said my mum had been unfaithful or when he laid all the blame at her door for the breakdown of their marriage and our family. Talking to my mum, I realised that none of that was fair and I had been believing it all for too long. My dad had had quite an eye for other women when he was married to my mum; he would try it on with her friends whenever she wasn't around. My mum was gracious about it: rather than tell tales about him, she suggested I go and talk to some of the other people, outside of the marriage, instead. It changed my mind about my family, and in particular my mum.

That was the beginning of me growing up, and for that, to Jacquie, I am eternally grateful.

With her gone, the house was cold – it was sad and empty. I ran into one of the guys who worked for me at the service station and he called across from his car, 'Me and a couple of the guys are going downtown Pittsburgh tonight. You wanna come with us?'

I have to say it did cross my mind to say no – Jacquie hadn't been gone long and I couldn't stop thinking about how sad she must be – but what the hell, I was feeling lonely and I was free to reboot my life. 'OK, where you going?' I called back.

'Walt Harper's Attic. We'll see you there about ten o'clock.'

For some reason or other, they didn't make it, but it didn't matter to me, it was one of those nights that I'll never forget. Sure I felt bad about Jacquie, but where was the point in going through all of this and breaking up with her to be myself if I wasn't doing just that: being myself.

Walt Harper's Attic was a huge old industrial loft. It had a cavernous ceiling with big iron girders holding it up. It was a massive space and it was full of people out to have a good time.

'Would you like to dance?' There were those words again. I'd noticed the woman I was talking to from the other side of the dance floor: she had been laughing uproariously with the woman she was with. They were obviously having a great time sitting in one of the big comfortable sofas that were carefully placed around the main floor.

Her smile was wide and bright and open. The answer wasn't quite the one I was looking for, though. 'No, I don't want to dance right now, but why don't you come and join us?'

It was quite an ironic meeting really. I wasn't the only one who had found themselves in a situation that wasn't right: this woman in front of me had simply had to get out too. But whereas my situation was my marriage to Jacquie, she was an ex-nun – an abbess, in fact.

I knew none of that at the time, Therese only told me it all weeks later. There in Walt Harper's, we just sat laughing and enjoying the extraordinary ambience, the freedom and easiness of the place. She and her friend were teachers. They were both good-looking women and in the end we did dance. The music that the jazzy, bluesy, funky band, fronted by Walt himself, was playing was irresistible: you just had to get up and groove. As the evening rolled into the night and it was

obvious my friends weren't going to show, I gradually realised that Therese was in fact Walt's date. I'd latched on to the
boss's girlfriend. But these were real grown-ups, their relationship could accommodate the odd stranger, so I finished
up the night going out to eat with them and, as the dawn was
breaking, I drove back out of Pittsburgh with a new friend.

Her relationship with Walt was her business, but within a
week or so our new friendship started to heat up. It was then
that she started to tell me something more of her extraordinary Catholic story.

Therese had been one of twelve children born into a
deeply religious French Canadian family who'd emigrated to
Woonsocket, Rhode Island. As was the custom, two of the children were designated as gifts to the church. One of her brothers went into the priesthood and Therese who was already a
'very, very sexually aware teenager', was locked behind the
walls of a closed convent for eighteen years.

The sexual torment of a life of abstinence was unbearable.
In the end it was her family that got her out. When she was
well into her thirties, they coaxed her into proving to herself
that she could escape. She managed it once but she caved in
to her guilt and went back. But still she couldn't take it, and
finally she broke away.

Therese was the warmest, funniest person and there was so
much in her that reminded me of Jacquie. She knew what she
wanted and it was not being married to a wild young buck like
me. She was into loving but she wasn't falling in love.

It was madness, I was pretty rampant back then, but, as
she used to laugh, 'Larry, I've got eighteen years to catch
up, eighteen lost years.' We spent a lot of time together that
summer and I think I might have helped her with about nine
of them.

★

My life was moving on in more ways than one. My boss, Ken Beamer, had laid on a big fun junket for about fifty or so of his main clients from the Pennsylvania, Ohio and New York state regions that we were servicing. Together they represented millions of dollars' worth of work for the company, so the outing was a big thank you from Ken and the company.

My buddy Gene called me. 'Hey, Larry, that fuckin' Beamer's organised two busloads of clients to come see a Pirates' game Saturday week, and he wants you there!'

When the buses arrived and all those men came into the stadium to take their top-priced seats, the heavens opened up and Pittsburgh got hit by a monsoon. You couldn't even see across the ballpark, the rain was so heavy. There was nothing else for it. I'd been smart enough to draw a large wad of cash just in case I needed some, and so with Gene doing the intros I stood at the bar getting the drinks in. Over the course of that seemingly endless downpour, I got every one of those guys so hammered that by the time the game was finally called off, they'd had such a party they didn't really remember what they'd come for. It was after that night that I got promoted to go and handle a difficult situation in Nova Scotia, all on the strength of that afternoon at the Pirates' Stadium.

22

Big Apple

If you crack away the crust of New York City, just a lick below that surface, you'll discover a myriad of wires and pipes and passageways and tunnels. And cutting right through the city, running the whole length of Manhattan Island, is a major, high-pressure gas pipeline. A big one, a bloody big one! Back in the 1960s there was an explosion on a section of that line right there in the Big Apple. A lot of people got killed. In the end, they discovered the cause, and – in theory – it was something that could happen again.

I was working for Henkels & McCoy's, an engineering division based in Blue Bell, Pennsylvania, surveying the anti-corrosion system that was specifically designed to avoid a disaster like that ever recurring. And so I spent the roasting hot summer of 1972 on the streets of New York City.

At one point I stayed just outside of the city in Hoboken and went in through the tunnel. I worked with another guy as a team and we would start work at 5 a.m. By 1 p.m. we would be hanging like Zambezi hippos in the pool of the Holiday Inn, hair, eyes and nose out of the water. We would switch between the pool and the air-conditioned room.

We'd worked the whole way through from White Plains, Tuckahoe Road, Yonkers/Bronx, South Bronx and on to Manhattan via the George Washington Bridge right down through Harlem. Harlem was the place I'd always been warned about during years living and working with Americans. The place was electrifying and there were something like fifty or sixty murders in New York City that summer; it was on the car radio all the time. One day I was sitting running through a set of readings I'd taken that morning when something made me take my eyes off the page. A pistol was not three inches from my face, albeit on the other side of the window. On the end of the weapon was a short bearded man sporting a beige lightweight jacket. As I turned to my left to take him in, I realised that in his other hand was a plastic-covered identification card marked NYPD, but in a second he'd already moved on, skipping along the street, car by car.

Harlem was the place with the reputation, and I certainly felt on edge every minute I was there, but the South Bronx was the area that really felt threatening to me. One neighbourhood just seemed to be garages and scrap merchants with dirt roads running between them. It felt back then as rough and raw as it feels now in the markets of an African capital city. A wild place, where all commerce of any kind was done behind barricades, where life was front line. There were wild dogs and wild people as well, but they were all too involved in their own survival to pay attention to us and, apart from some of our test equipment disappearing, we followed that line for about five weeks, unharmed all the way until it dropped under the water on its route to Staten Island. And, at a certain point, somewhere around the middle of Manhattan, I actually connected all my meters and technical paraphernalia to that massive pipe right under the Great White Way. I was actually there. I laughed when the guy I was working with shouted, 'We made it, buddy. We're on Broadway.'

And four years later, I was.

23

Blue Bell to Broadway

I was now a divisional manager responsible for a multimillion-dollar power-line scheme in Nova Scotia. The bosses down in Blue Bell, Pennsylvania, had promoted me.

I'd read an article about that part of Canada's Maritime provinces in a weekend supplement earlier in the year. It was a promotional piece but it looked like it needed no selling. And when I got there I could see that it didn't. There's about 5,000 miles of shoreline to the place, yet it's only about 400 miles from end to end. The water is so cold for most of the year you can't even dip your toes in and there are endless pine trees and countless coves and peninsulas.

I almost didn't take the job on, though. When I'd heard about the offer, Ken Beamer, the 'king' of Henkels & McCoy, had said to me: 'Larry, the goddamn job is a poisoned chalice. I wouldn't touch it with a ten-foot pole.' I normally wouldn't have had dealings with him, but I'd been working indirectly for him for some months, on some projects the engineering division had bid on.

'Yes, but Ken, it's a big promotion that Mr Henkels is offering. How can I turn a divisional management position down?'

'You can turn it down, Larry. There'll always be something else.'

And Gene Tangier, my buddy, Ken's leading foreman, cut in too: 'Larry, what the fuck d'ya wanna go up there for? You'll be living off seal meat and raw fish.'

Beamer grinned and huffed; he stood up from behind his desk. When he stood up he was colossal. I'm big enough, but Beamer really was a bear, he was at least six foot eight. His huge hand clasped mine. 'You do what you think best, Larry, and I'll be right behind you.'

Nova Scotia took me in and adopted me, and in turn I fell completely for Nova Scotia, and those roots that I put down are still there. When I'd been in the province for three months I felt like I'd died and gone to heaven. The sixties had already happened in the rest of the world, but in Nova Scotia they were just swinging into effect by 1973 when I arrived. I was young, single and extremely well paid, a young buck on the loose, and there were plenty of women experimenting in a new world order. After months of ridiculous sexual freedom I met two girls, Kathy, who was Canadian, and Barbara, a Brit. They took me to a party and I got introduced into a gang of guys my own age who'd just graduated from university that year. They took me in and I became one of them.

We drank in the taverns and ate steak, fries and coleslaw, guzzling bottles of Keith's and Labatts Blue and pints and pints of 'draft'. What nights. What unforgettable fun I had with my buddies in Halifax: Joe Scott, John Swayne, Bill Kilfoyle and David Howlett.

Having lived on the road for years, travelling to Germany, Libya and now here to Nova Scotia, I decided it was time to buy a house. I found myself in a village called Enfield right near the airport. How strange to be standing there in a place that shared the name of somewhere in which I'd spent a large part of my early life. It was far removed from the Enfield of my childhood, but it brought back memories all the same.

I pulled on to the gravel in front of a real estate agent's office – really little more than a shack – and met this tall raw-boned guy who looked like a Highland gentleman, complete with tweed jacket and cavalry twill trousers. He stuck out his great big hand and introduced himself as Tom Parker. I explained that I'd seen a house for sale down the road.

'Yes,' he smiled, 'that's my son Robby's house – he just built it.'

Within half an hour, we'd done the tour and were standing back in the drive. I asked, 'How much is it?'

He turned to me. 'Twenty-four thousand dollars.'

'Put me a stove in and I'll take it,' I told him decisively, and so I'd bought into the tiny community of Enfield, Nova Scotia.

Across the road from me lived Loretta and Cliff Isenor and their boys Michael, Jimmy and Tommy, who had grown up with Robby and had helped build my house. I'd bought a piece of local history. None of us knew it at the time, but Robby had a big career in construction ahead of him and this would always be 'Robby Parker's first house'.

I used to drag a lot of young women back from Halifax in my great big flashy white Ford 500, and that certainly did cause a bit of a giggle in the village, but as far as I was concerned I was young and single and totally free to operate.

Loretta and Cliff were highly amused by my antics and they became new parents to me. I was still young and I'd missed out on the ordinary relationship with my parents. I fondly watched them with their boys and they welcomed me into the fold.

And so there I was, running this really important project for the Canadian Government. But ultimately I realised that what Ken had said was true. It was a poisoned chalice. As Beamer had put it: 'There's North American time, Larry, and there's Nova Scotian time! And the two don't mean the same thing.' So when the Canadians insisted on us using local labour instead of our own teams, I knew we had our work cut out for us.

The local guys didn't really want to work for Americans. A lot of the guys spent most of their working lives lobster fishing or seal skinning, and we just had no hope of getting the work done at the rate we were supposed to. I lost heart.

But I found a way back into amateur theatre.

'The Drama Society of St Francis Xavier University here in Antigonish is looking to find potential cast members from the local community. If you have any interest in joining the society, please call this number.'

I'd heard the advert on a local radio station; about a month later I was rehearsing the role of Richard the Lionheart in *The Lion in Winter*.

'You want me really to kiss him? Full on the lips?' I hadn't figured that into the picture. I'd taken the part without ever having read the script.

'Yes, Larry, I do. Full on his lips.' James Colbeck, the head of drama at the university, smiled. 'Go on, you can do it!'

I was acting again. I found myself racing all over the province with work, and now there was a 240-mile round trip every evening for rehearsals slapped on top. It didn't matter to me, I'd got the bug. First, I played Richard in *The Lion in Winter* and now I was Jason in *Medea*. I wanted to do this. I wanted to be free of all my mountainous responsibilities. I had to be brave and break free. Something had to give and this time it couldn't be the acting.

'Regis, Ken was right. The job is impossible. I'm going to take a bit of a time-out and go back to school. I'm sorry to have to let you down,' I told the man who had showed so much belief in me and offered me the job that had brought me to America.

'Larry, you go ahead and do whatever you want to do, you know your job will always be here.'

I couldn't ask for better than that. And that was it. I'd cut my ties with Henkels and it was time to move on. I'd phoned dear old Margaret Snodgrass in Arizona, the one who'd first told me I should be an actor – ever a friend – and told her I was making a break for freedom. 'Come down here to Phoenix, Larry!' she yelled. 'You could be a star!'

As I made my plans to leave, the company sent up a man to take over from me. After one week in Nova Scotia, he summed it up. 'Larry, I tell you, these people could fuck up a two-dollar funeral!'

Then, right out of the blue, a new possibility presented itself. Bill Kilfoyle, one of my mates in Halifax, told me he'd cut out an ad from the local paper. The Neptune, the local theatre, was holding open auditions. But I was heading south and I rather fancied being a rock-and-roller. I told this story to Phil Collins years later. 'Larry,' he said, 'you should've, you'd have loved it. You'd probably be dead, but you'd have loved it.' And so day by day I prepared to hand on the 'chalice'.

A week or so later, on a Friday afternoon, I was with our client's chief engineer whom I'd just entertained with a farewell lunch. He'd parked right outside the Neptune and, as I said goodbye to him, I knew it was fixed in my mind that those auditions were going on right at that moment.

Three minutes later I was in a telephone booth at the local shopping mall. 'Is there any possibility of getting an audition? I know it's late in the day . . .'

'How quickly can you get here, Mr . . . ?'

'Lamb, Larry Lamb. I could be there in two minutes.' It was all set up.

When I got there I was asked, 'So Larry, tell me, what exactly does an . . .' He paused and looked down at the application card I'd filled in. '. . . electrical power-line construction manager . . . do?'

He laughed and looked to his right at a guy who was sprawled the length of an ancient chaise longue, and then to his left to another thirty-five-or-so-year-old man, smiling over the length of a grand piano, and I thought to myself again:

Don't worry, if they are negative in any way you can just keep on with your plan to head south.

I started to tell him and we all talked for forty minutes. I thought we'd go on forever but finally he paused. 'So, Larry, what are you going to do for us?'

'Well, I just did a play called *Medea* – do you know it?' I was that gauche. The three exchanged nervous looks. 'I played Jason and I can do one of his speeches to show that I can speak proper English. And then I can do "Albert and the Lion" as a contemporary piece and then I could sing you one of the songs my nan taught me.'

They exchanged looks again but I was ready to start.

Alan Laing, the guy on the piano, who turned out to be one of the biggest musical directors in Canada, desperately tried to keep time with my heartfelt rendition of 'Cecilia' but, despite his talent, eventually just gave up and hummed and smiled along.

Robin Phillips, the guy in the middle, was the one in charge. He had a year to put together a company of actors for his first season as the new artistic director of the Shakespeare Festival in Stratford, Ontario. He was sitting in on all the auditions across Canada. He sat in one of those woven peacock chairs, so hip in the seventies, and never took his eyes off me.

John Wood – the one on the chaise longue – was the boss of the Neptune. He just smiled.

I had a bit of a falter in my Jason speech but 'Albert' went over a treat and the singing seemed to have done the trick. Without a word passing between them, Robin lit another cigarette, looked me dead in the eye and said, 'I think we think that you should be doing this.'

I walked out of that room an 'Actor'.

The reality of what it meant only struck me when I handed the keys of my company car over to my replacement. I was an actor now, on 120 dollars a week. I had no car, no expenses, and no frills! I used to spend more on drinks each week than I would now be earning. All that aside, I already knew I'd got things right this time. The people I was working with were so vibrant, so exciting and alive. They were actors from all over Canada, drawn east by the lure of John Wood's direction and Neil Munro's *Hamlet*.

The rehearsals had started and it was time for me to have my first crack at showing John Wood, the director, just what a phenomenal actor I was. I was waiting to make my first appearance as the Norwegian sea captain. I was ready to go with a fruity Mummerset/Westward Ho! accent, gripping my text like my life depended on it. I finally walked out on to the stage and I was immediately greeted from the depths of the auditorium by John's voice roaring through the gloom, 'Larry, cut the limp!'

I stopped dead in my tracks. How could he do this? I'd lived and died this character for weeks. You can't do this to me!

'OK, John!' I called meekly. 'Just thought I'd run it by you.'

Joining up with the Shakespeare Festival meant saying goodbye to Nova Scotia, but my roots there ran deep. As has so often happened in my life, I walked away and into another life. But, sad though I was to leave, I knew I'd be back.

Having left Nova Scotia, I arrived in Stratford and it was a blast. My two buddies from *Hamlet*, Paul Shaw and David Hemblen, during one of the seemingly endless after-show parties that invariably finished around a bottle of 'The Irish', had put me on the phone to someone who might be able to give me a place to stay. 'Mrs Shields' – whose real name was Clayton Shields – was a strapping, six-foot-tall fisherman from Prince Edward Island who, as he himself had put it, 'only gets on with straight men; every time I let a fairy have a room it all goes tits-up.' So I had digs.

And my next part was a great one: the English soldier in

Saint Joan. I finished up getting a Tyrone Guthrie Award too in my first year.

And then I fell in love. A beautiful shy, really quiet cutter in the wardrobe department called Sharon Purdy came into my life. And we moved in together at the end of the season.

Gordon 'Gordy' Pinsent is a Canadian star from Newfoundland another part of Maritime Canada. He came to Stratford, Ontario to take over from our leading man, Brian Bedford, when Brian's back proved troublesome. Gordy and I exchanged a lot of banter in the Newfie style that I'd picked up in Nova Scotia. Gordy's play *John and the Missus* was about to be previewed in Halifax, Nova Scotia, so Gordy asked me to be in it playing a Newfie! Sharon and I rented a little house and settled in and then somewhere about a week or two into the run of the play I got my first part in a TV show as a uniformed policeman. I helped to arrest Gordy in his role as the protagonist in *Horse Latitudes*. I was on the TV; I was starting to make it.

I continued in Stratford for a second season and now, after a bit of time working in the business, I was getting bigger roles and more responsibility.

On the first morning of this second season I found myself at the 'Big Top', the immense structure that housed the main stage and 2,700-seater auditorium. I was so overwhelmed. I was going to be acting with Maggie Smith, Hume Cronyn, Jessica Tandy, Jeremy Brett and Keith Baxter, and I was like some terrible star-struck kid.

'You know, Jessica,' I said as I sat next to her on the carpeted floor of the rehearsal room, 'when you were on stage, on Broadway, with Marlon Brando in *A Streetcar Named Desire*, I was being born.' What a brilliant way to start talking to a woman of a certain age. Boy, was I a cracker.

The only play in which I felt well within my comfort zone was *A Midsummer Night's Dream*, when I played Tom Snout the Tinker. It really was pleasing the crowds. It meant a lot to me to see people enjoying what I did, I was loving acting. After years of trying to make it in sales and become the big businessman, I'd found something that I could turn into a success and that was a joy to do.

The actor Jeremy Brett, who had befriended Sharon and me, introduced me to his agent Janet Roberts, who was up from New York. She'd been after Jeremy to audition for Mike Nichols' production of *Comedians*: 'As a Belfast docker, darling.' He'd roared with laughter. 'Me, a Belfast docker?! But I've told Janet all about you and she's going to see if she can get you an audition.'

After that, everything happened in a whirl. Hume Cronyn called me into his dressing room and said, 'Larry, what's this I hear about you auditioning for Alex Cohen? I'll phone him this evening, he's an old friend.' It was very kind of him and I was honoured. A few days later he called me in again. 'Did you hear from Alex Cohen's office, Larry?'

I certainly had heard from them. That Friday evening, I found myself in New York, back in the Big Apple, on the bare stage of the Music Box Theatre. The stage doorman led Mr Cohen and his team on to the stage with me. I was introduced, 'Mr Lamb, Alex Cohen.' Cohen was of average height but he sported a black fedora of enormous proportions and he wore a priceless black cashmere overcoat wrapped about his shoulders like a cloak. He looked – and indeed was – the archetypal Broadway producer.

'Would you let me see your green card?' he asked.

I pulled it from my wallet and watched him look it over in such detail, he did everything but bite it. 'Thank you, Mr Lamb. Mike Nichols and Trevor Griffiths will be here momentarily.'

I stood on that stage with a borrowed hairbrush in my hand as a mike and I did the stand-up comedy routine from the second act of the play. I was so nervous but out in that half-lit, echoing auditorium, I heard a laugh. And then another.

When I'd finished my audition I headed straight to my hotel. No sooner had I handed the porter his tip as he brought my case to the room but the phone rang. 'Mr Lamb, this is Alex Cohen. Subject to negotiation with your agent, I would like to offer you the role of George McBrain. Thank you very much, and I hope the Algonquin is comfortable. Goodnight.'

I phoned Janet Roberts. 'Janet, they've just offered me the part. Is this really Broadway?'

'Larry, Alex Cohen producing and Mike Nichols directing at the Music Box Theatre? It doesn't get more Broadway. Go down to the lobby, get in a cab and come down to the Village. I'd like to congratulate you.'

I returned to Stratford and when I crept back into the Festival Theatre for the Saturday matinee, the place went crazy. There were actors running around everywhere shouting, 'Larry's going to Broadway.' The word had leaked out.

Two weeks later I stood in my sitting room the tears rolling down my cheeks whilst Maggie Smith and Beverley Cross, her husband, together with the entire company sang, 'Give my regards to Broadway'. And I certainly did.

Act Two

24

Baptism of Fire

It all happened in such a blur. My move to Broadway was a huge moment for me and, with everything happening at such a pace, I needed a moment to take stock of how I had got here.

I'd been so fortunate to go from being a young man working in the oil business, indulging my theatre passion only in my spare time with amateur dramatic societies, to suddenly becoming an actor for real with the top company in Canada. Stratford Ontario was by far the best place to be employed as a journeyman actor – that was the title they gave me; I managed to skip the apprentice level. I'd done very well and I was so pleased when they hired me for a second season.

I think up until then it had all been a bit too easy. I'd obviously impressed everyone with my original audition but then I had to prove myself. Frankly I was just too bloody lazy and blasé about the whole thing.

In my second year I'd been given some good parts to play and as a measure of the confidence that the director, Robin Phillips, had in me, I'd been entrusted with some major roles to understudy. Unfortunately I just wasn't ready for such big opportunities. It was such a waste. Actors on the way up would kill for the opportunities I was given and I just took it all for granted. As an understudy, my contract required me to learn the role and be ready to go on by the time the play opened. However, three months into the season and I was still faffing around trying to learn the words. Nick Mancuso, the actor who was playing Bassanio in *The Merchant of Venice*, wanted out of his contract and he said to me, 'Are you ready to take over? Because I think I'm ready to quit!'

I freaked out. I didn't even know the words, let alone how he played the role; I just hadn't bothered to learn. I panicked and lost the chance of a lifetime. Careers have been founded on an understudy getting a lucky break like that and I squandered the opportunity I was given. What was I doing? How could I have been so stupid?

Maggie Smith was enjoying phenomenal success playing Cleopatra and people who knew her work were constantly saying how this was her at the top of her game. I used to stand backstage, watching her perform, trying to absorb some of her brilliance. All the canny young members of the cast – and a lot of the older ones too – had been wise enough to watch her rehearse, to see that performance being put together, but I'd even missed the boat there as well.

I realised that you could learn a lot from watching your fellow actors. Night after night I would watch Jeremy Brett as Mirabell and Maggie Smith as Millament in *The Way of the World*, one of those unbelievably complicated Restoration plays which for me defied comprehension. I found their performances mesmerising. But what really held me in awe was the knowledge that, whilst onstage those two people were portraying a romancing couple, offstage these old friends weren't even talking. The reason for their animosity was their relationship with Robert Stephens. After divorcing Robert, Maggie had started a new life with a new husband, Beverley Cross, and was happy to put Robert to the back of her mind. Jeremy adored Robert and felt huge loyalty to him. I suppose the resulting tension increased the element of danger in their playing: those two amazing actors circled each other like leopards in a mating ritual. Whatever it was, those two together were unforgettable.

I, however, in my role as Waitwell, Mirabell's servant and accomplice in deception, was totally forgettable. I got to play a big scene with Jessica Tandy, but although it should have been a real show-stopper, I just was not ready for it. Our scene opened the second act and I had to come on stage towards the end of the interval dressed in the most outrageous costume, disguised as a wealthy country squire, and pretty much do whatever I wanted to get the audience going. It was a golden opportunity for me to make my mark, but it was an opportunity that was completely squandered. I couldn't even get the audience to stop talking on most nights.

A Midsummer Night's Dream was a different kettle of fish entirely. I was playing Tom Snout the Tinker, AKA 'The Wall'. I had the stupidest, goony West Country accent imaginable, and without fail when I got to Tom's big speech in the play within the play, it stopped the bloody show. When it happened on the first night I didn't know what to do. Later Hume Cronyn – who was himself setting the stage on fire as Bottom – put me wise. 'Larry,' he said, 'it's something that comes from an audience. It's a situation where something that the performance generates leads them to take control of the show momentarily. You just have to ride it.' And ride it I did.

In a way, I rode it all the way back to New York City, but unfortunately once more I'd bitten off more than I could chew. Again I was out of my depth. I felt like a reasonably talented amateur suddenly finding himself on the pitch playing in the Premiership. The acting business – I was just beginning to realise – is lethally competitive. I'm not sure how I could have been blind to that fact for so long until then. I was now in a number one Broadway show, hired by one of America's foremost directors. I was in a company of actors picked from the finest that New York could offer – and yet I just wasn't cutting the mustard.

Years after the show had closed, I spoke to Jeff De Munn,

one of my fellow actors in the cast. 'Larry, it was just so sad to see what happened with you back then in *Comedians*,' he said. 'On that first day at the read-through, you absolutely were George McBrain. You were wonderful. But little by little, over those weeks of rehearsal, I watched that character piss right out through the toes of your boots.'

That really did sum up for me the way it had all gone. I'd been so supercharged by the audition and getting the part that by the time I got to that read-through I was riding on the crest of a wave. That was just a read-through, though: I had to prove my mettle. And right from the start it went wrong.

On the Friday afternoon of our first week in the Minskoff, Broadway's Rolls-Royce of rehearsal rooms, Paul Rodgers, the senior actor and a man with years of experience who had been brought over from London to head the cast, walked the length of the set, flapping his arms like a bird, and saying very seriously to Mike Nichols that 'if we don't get things sorted out . . .'

I hadn't really understood what he meant, but I certainly did when I arrived for rehearsals the next morning. He'd gone back to London. He had been my only real ally. Right from the first day he'd been a reassuring presence. On day one, I'd had a wobble about not being old enough, and I had suggested to him that I grow a moustache, but he calmed me down by saying, 'Larry, you *are* George McBrain. Just do it the way you're doing it now!' Once he had disappeared, I was on my own.

I got further and further out of my depth. Mike Nichols spent one whole day making me do my first entrance over and over again. In the end I was so despondent I stood on the stage and called out, 'Mike! Please just come up here and show me what you want and I'll copy you. Please!' But it didn't work and the torture continued.

Unlike Broadway we weren't trying *Comedians* out in a city like Boston or Philadelphia first. 'There's no point,' Mike had said, 'the show will be difficult enough for a New York audience to follow.' Instead we previewed for three weeks right there on Broadway. We played eight shows a week to packed houses. At that point it was very much a work in progress. We were given changes after every show. It was a nightmare! Jokes were switched around between the actors and I had thirty-seven to do on my first preview. I came off after that performance to find the writer, Trevor, sitting by the dressing rooms, his downturned head clasped between his hands.

'What's the matter, Trev?' I asked.

'What's the matter?' He looked up at me with such a look of pain. 'The second act took an hour and a half; the fucking audience will have forgotten they came to see a play!!'

There was another big problem too. The New York audience were having trouble with Gethin Price, Jonathan Pryce's role. He appeared to be some sort of sadomasochist to them, whereas to a British audience he was obviously a way-out punk. That caused a lot of sleepless nights for the production team and suddenly one day the rehearsals were being directed by Richard Eyre, the show's original director, who had been flown over from London to try and alleviate the situation. Between Mike and Richard they somehow sorted it out and we were open. Thankfully it was acclaimed as a huge success and I managed to be get mentioned as one of a 'gifted ensemble'.

I was sharing a dressing room with David Margulies, a real New York actor, and we became buddies. We'd go out after the show together to bars like Jimmy Ray's. He knew everybody. We were walking back to the theatre from a cocktail party one evening when he turned to me and said, 'I saw you having a great time talking to Arthur.'

'Arthur who?' I asked.

'Larry, are you kidding me? The big guy you were having the very intense conversation with. That was Arthur Miller.'

★

Stratford followed me down to Broadway. Maggie Smith and Beverley came to see the shows and then took me out to dinner at Joe Allen's. Then one evening we were alerted to the fact that Lauren Bacall was in the audience and when I got to the stage door, Joey the ancient stage doorman asked me, 'Did you see Miss Bacall? I senner ova' to your dressing room.' I ran back, not completely convinced that this wasn't some kind of a gag. But when I arrived, there she stood, wrapped in a million dollars' worth of mink. She was on the arm of Brian Bedford, the leading man from Stratford during my first season. He'd brought her to meet me.

'What a wonderful performance,' she drawled, 'and a marvellous show!'

I stood there, speechless. Even I knew who this was. Lauren Bacall – Hollywood royalty.

The show ran right through Christmas 1976 and, in true New York style, we played two shows on 25 December and had our Christmas dinner in the theatre basement. As the New Year wore on, the show gradually came towards a closing date. This of course meant decision time – what was I going to do? Should I go back to Stratford? I'd been asked back but the parts weren't any better than I'd already done. Or perhaps I should stay on in New York and try to make it there.

I'd always had a thing for imitating accents, and most of the time I was pretty good, but perfecting a standard American speech style was something I knew I'd have to do if I was going to avoid becoming a professional Englishman in New York. So I'd asked John Lithgow who was in the cast and he immediately replied, 'Larry, you have to get in touch with

Robert Neff Williams, the dialect coach. He's the best man in America. I'll get you his number.'

Mr Williams's office up at Columbia University was lined floor to ceiling with books, and he was every bit the figure John had described. Tall, grey-haired, patrician, old East Coast Establishment, he was a true gentleman. 'I don't really do this sort of thing any more, Larry,' he'd started, 'but your accent fascinates me. It's a real hotchpotch so I suppose I'll have to make an exception.'

Well, the work paid off and I started to go for auditions posing as an American. After the show one evening I went for a drink with David and into the bar trooped a gang of people I'd met that morning. It was the director and the entire production team; I'd spent about half an hour trying to convince them that I was American. They all knew David and we all sat down at a table together. *What can I do here?* I thought to myself. *Carry on with the ruse?* In the end I came clean and it turned out that they had been more or less convinced but not completely.

Finally, on a Sunday afternoon in April 1977, we gave our closing performance. I'd occasionally been good over that six-month run, sometimes very good, but that last show just didn't come together for me. I was so sad not to end on an upbeat note. Mike Nichols watched the show and as I tried to explain to him just how much I'd wanted to impress him on this, the last opportunity, I burst into tears and wept like a baby. It all came flooding out, all the pent-up emotion of my six-month baptism of fire. Nichols gave me a hug. 'Don't worry, Larry,' he whispered. 'It'll never be this hard again.'

25

Exodus

David Margulies, the actor I shared a double dressing room with at the Music Box Theatre, was taking me on a bit of a tour around the lower end of Manhattan. As we were walking, I spotted Mott Street: the name from that song, 'Manhattan', came ringing through my mind. I'd sung along with Uncle Terry and Ella Fitzgerald so many times as a young boy! Just to think what Terry would feel if he knew where I was and what I was doing . . .

David was a wonderful guide, a native New Yorker, and he shared his city with me. 'Bobby De Niro used to run around these streets as a kid; his father, Robert, was an artist.' We were walking through Little Italy. In those days it was a warren of streets, all decked out with tiny Italian flags. We'd eat crabs in Chinatown and Japanese food in tiny two-table restaurants midtown. He'd guide me past whorehouse hustlers touting their wares, 'a suck or a fuck for ten bucks!', and he even took me along to the Actors' Studio where we sat in on some of the sessions. He took me under his wing.

At the time I was having a bit of a fling with a Texan camerawoman who was at the beginning of a big career in cinema. Her name was Sandi Sissel and she was stunning. Her accent sounded like a cowgirl's to me and I spent hours just bathing in those long-drawn-out vowels, 'Hey Larry, the gahs ohn mah crew say ah gotta naksent? Djew thank Ah hayve?' She was something else.

It was tough for a woman to get work in the very male-dominated world of cinema, so Sandi was cutting her teeth filming news stories for the ABC network. She and her crew were on standby for twelve-hour shifts and they often got the tip-off on stories even before the police did. They had to race through the city, day or night, and get to the scene: fire, murder, accident, no matter what it was.

I'd met her through friends and the friends knew that Sharon was waiting patiently up in Stratford, Ontario, being a good girl. They threatened to tell her that I was running around with someone else, someone they'd introduced me to, so I called her and told her myself. It seemed the only fair thing to do. She took it in the way she took everything: steadfastly and silently.

And then a couple of nights later she phoned. 'Larry' – I guessed what this was going to be – 'after you called and told me what you'd been up to, I arranged to meet Joe after work yesterday. We had a couple of drinks and then I brought him back here, to our apartment. Is there anything you'd like to ask me, Larry?'

It wasn't easy to swallow but what right did I have to get away with it? We'd had a pretty honest relationship up until then. Let's just say we'd had a few minor sexual adventures but this was a major slip. It fractured the relationship in a way it never really recovered from. I think what I took away from this was that it was OK for both of us to do what we wanted. After all, once you know that the other one has done it with someone else, what's the point getting uptight about it? Unfortunately the relationship gradually fell apart. Yet another of my regrets.

★

New York was stunning – just to experience how upfront the women were, apart from anything else. I was riding the subway home after the show one night when I noticed one of them looking at me. In fact she was quite boldly staring. I could see she was holding a theatre programme and she flipped it around so that I could see it was from our show.

She smiled and made her way across the carriage towards me. 'I just saw you, didn't I? In *Comedians*?'

'Yes,' I smiled. Boy, this was something, she was lovely. She had really short, cropped, almost boyish hair. 'Did you like the show?'

'Oh you're British . . .' And that was just about it. She took me home with her, used me and abused me and pushed me out of her door the next morning. Blimey!

But all the fun of New York had to come to an end. Janet Roberts, my agent, called, 'I want you to come down to the house tomorrow afternoon, Larry. Come and have a cup of tea. I'd like you to meet a friend of mine and Jeremy's.'

Sheila Pickles was the sort of Englishwoman I'd never met before. She was just about my age, really sexy and a very successful businesswoman. She spoke beautifully – she was obviously from way up the ladder compared to me – and had been working for Franco Zeffirelli for years as his Girl Friday. Franco was the connection between Janet and Sheila; Janet was Franco's literary agent and Sheila was about to launch a new company in London that Franco was helping her to start. We hit it off immediately.

'So what are you going to do when the show closes?' she asked.

'That's a good question,' I said. 'I'm having trouble making up my mind. I don't know whether to go back to Canada or stay here. I've been working on my American accent because if I am going to stay here, I've got to go native or all I'll be doing is hanging around waiting for parts as Englishmen.'

'Well,' Janet walked back in from the kitchen, 'I don't think that's such a good idea, Larry. You'll just lose your identity. I was talking to Jeremy the other evening about just what you might do, and we both agree, you should go back to London.'

I thought it over for perhaps a day and then bought myself a one-way ticket to Heathrow.

26

London

I'd left London aged twenty to go and sell encyclopedias and now, almost thirty, I was back in this city that I didn't really know but now an actor. An actor with a bit of a track record and a patron in the shape of Jeremy Brett. Sharon and I had become friends with him in Ontario and he was insistent on repaying the courtesy.

'Larry, darling, you have to meet Larry and Joany.' I just about knew who he meant. Actually being seated at Sir Laurence Olivier's side at the great long dinner table in Jeremy's dining room at Ness Cottage was so daunting that I found myself saying, 'My name is Lawrence as well. Is yours spelt with "au" or a "w"?' What a klutz. His sidelong glance was enough to tell me I was blundering, but his grace hauled me out of the mire of my gaucheness.

Jeremy had me puzzled when he told me, 'We're going to the National to see Johnny G.' I had no idea who he meant by 'Johnny G', but a few weeks later there I was, being introduced to Sir John Gielgud in his dressing room after the show! I was starstruck and I couldn't really find a word. I let Jeremy do all the talking.

I became more accustomed to Jeremy's impressive list of contacts over time. Lynn Sackler, a Los Angeles friend of Jeremy's who'd come to stay, introduced me to Sir Ralph Richardson. 'What sort of work do you do, Larry?' I was backstage in the West End again. In Sir Ralph's dressing room, him in a big towelling bathrobe as his dresser served us enormous whiskys.

'I'm an actor,' I said.

He twinkled. 'Are you a good actor?'

'Well, Sir Ralph, I'm learning.'

Learning I was. But I needed to get some kind of income going. I'd already made contact with Sheila Pickles, Jeremy's English friend, who I'd met in New York at Janet Roberts's. Pretty soon she gave me a job in her brand-new perfume shop in the newly evolving Covent Garden. Wes and I stacked the first ever boxes of scents and lotions and potions on to the newly finished shelves in the basement of Penhaligon's.

I'd developed a big crush on Sheila. She took me to see her friend Franco Zeffirelli because she, a terribly classy Yorkshire woman, loved me reciting that old North Country party-piece of mine – the one she'd found out had got me into the theatre. On a cold winter's night, she and I sat with the great man on the outsized bed in his sumptuous suite at The Carlton whilst I ran through 'Albert and the Lion'. And in just the way Sheila had predicted, he loved it. In his exquisitely phrased English, he looked at me, weighed me up, and turning to Sheila said, 'Yes darling, he could play the plumber!'

I was in my first West End show, just like that. I had auditioned there and then. Sheila hadn't told me that Franco was in London casting *Filumena* when she took me to see him. *Filumena* was an Italian classic and starred Joan Plowright and Colin Blakely. It was a huge success and ran for two years at the Lyric, on Shaftesbury Avenue. Joan was triumphant, as was Colin, and, as well as getting me on the map, it proved a very sound platform for the young Trevor Eve and, after I had left, a not insignificant step up the ladder for Pierce Brosnan too.

Janet Roberts had alerted the London office of William Morris, so I now had an agent in the UK. Pretty soon, I had my first film work. Ironic really that I had left the US because it wasn't considered wise to hide myself beneath an American cover, and now I was playing a news editor at *The Daily Planet* in *Superman*. Mary Selway, one of the 'grandes dames' of the casting world, had passed me a script and said, 'Convince me you're an American. If you can you can be in the film.'

It turned out that I'd be in two films: they were filming *Superman I* and *II* out at Pinewood and a lot of the background action in those office sequences was used in both films, so it was really two jobs in one. And about six years or so later – having met Christopher Reeve – I was in *Superman III* as well, playing a West Virginian coalminer. This time, unlike in the first two, where you blink and you'll miss me completely, in the third film I got to play a scene with Christopher and Richard Pryor. These 'little' jobs can be very important: scenes in movies can make a career but in my case they stayed just that – scenes in movies.

★

Jeremy's friend Lynn Sackler introduced me to one of the most successful TV producers of her era, Verity Lambert. Lynn and Verity had worked together as young women and stayed friends over the years. Verity sent a fellow producer called Barry Hanson to see me in *Filumena* some weeks later. I was in my dressing room at the Lyric talking to him. He was a tough-looking, wiry Yorkshire man. He told me, 'I'm producing a series called *Out*. It stars Tom Bell and I want you to come and meet the writer, Trevor Preston, and the director, Jimmy Goddard.'

Out didn't happen for me, I was tied into *Filumena* and a lot of the filming for *Out* was to be done at night when I needed to be onstage. But in the way things go in showbiz, the meeting for one job turned into a role in another. Written, directed and produced by the same team, *Fox* was the saga of a London family. I was given the part of Joey, the ne'er-do-well middle son of the 'Fox' clan. And so the long line of Jeremy's patronage had landed me a starring role in what was to be a major TV drama. I was fortunate to work with a fantastic cast: Elizabeth Spriggs, Peter Vaughan, Bernard Hill, Derrick O'Connor, Eamon Boland and the young star we all knew was in the making, Ray Winstone. He always shone out and there was no doubt where he was headed!

Fox was in ITV's prime Monday-night slot but, as was the way back in those days, the BBC trumped us with *Yes, Minister* and so instead of pulling massive viewing figures, we never really got much above three million. Our competition became the legend that it is still to this day. Fox had made its mark, though, and I could see why when I watched it again recently. Filmed on the streets, it still stands as an amazing document recording life in London just as it was thirty years ago.

27

Mr Cassidy's Palace

Hollywood Road and the area around what was then St Stephen's Hospital in Chelsea was already very fashionable in 1978, although it was still a long way from the highly commercialised and very trendy quarter that it's become over the intervening years.

There were restaurants and several wine bars which were all enjoying a period of popularity, but drinking still meant pubs to a lot of people back then. Just along the Fulham Road was Finch's, still hanging on to its old spit and sawdust image. I wasn't a regular there, but now and then I would drop in just to get the feel of being in a real old boozer.

I'd noticed that right next door to the pub there was a yard closed off to the pavement by a farm-style five-bar gate, which I found a little strange in the middle of London. Up above the gate was a big 'TO LET' sign which had obviously been there for some time because the board itself was really weathered and some of the letters were fading away. All that could be seen of what was at the back of this yard was what appeared to be a boarded-up shop window, above which 'Humpherson's Plumbers' Merchants' was still legible on an ancient green wooden board. The 'TO LET' sign said there was 11,000 square foot of combined showroom, office and storage space available, so it was obvious there was more to be seen behind this façade. I really wanted to know what was there. I am inquisitive – nosy even – by nature, and this tired-looking gap in the frontage along this busy section of the Fulham Road just didn't make sense.

As I walked past the pub one afternoon, I saw my opportunity to get a look over the gate come walking across the yard. Mr Cassidy was the potman in Finch's. Everybody knew him; he was a real old local character, and his drink-battered features and greasy old trilby hat were a feature of the neighbourhood.

'Is this something to do with you?' I asked him.

'Well,' he said, his croaky old Irish accent still there after years in London, 'the people who're selling the place let me and my dog kip here in return for keeping an eye on it.'

'Well,' I said, 'if I gave you a drink, would you let me have a little look inside?' I'd already palmed a ten-bob note and, before he had a chance to refuse, I'd placed my hand in his and slipped it to him.

'Climb over. I'll show you round, but be quick.'

He took me through the main door and into what had been the front office and through the wide-open space where presumably the showroom had been – all long since abandoned.

Upstairs were further open spaces, and on the second floor there were offices and various other rooms. There was a full basement under the whole building with a really high ceiling, and out of a side door there was an archway that led to an inner yard with stables and an old hayloft. My mind was whirring. 'How long has it been empty?' I asked Mr C.

'Oh, I don't know,' he said. 'Ages and ages.'

'What are all those mattresses for?' I asked.

'I have a lot of friends and it's nice to have a big house so they can stay a night or two.'

I realised the place had even more potential than I'd imagined. 'I've got a friend, a businessman, who might be interested in this,' I said. 'If I give you another drink, can I bring him along to see it?'

'No problem,' he said, and started to walk into the pub.

I knew it had huge potential because the location was just phenomenal, but what sort of establishment would best be located there? That was the question. I began to list all the different possibilities in my mind and in the end, knowing that as a penniless actor I wouldn't be able to do anything with the place, I phoned Dougie Hayward and asked him if he would give me some advice. I trusted Dougie. He was a strictly no-nonsense businessman who had worked his way up from very humble beginnings to be one of the most successful bespoke tailors in the world.

Mr Cassidy was delighted with another ten-bob tip and gave Dougie and me another tour of the building, pushing open doors like the proud steward of a stately home.

'I've had this idea that perhaps it will make a wonderful drinking and dining club. What do you think?' I said.

Dougie was never one to say anything without considering his response first. 'Yes,' he said, 'I think you're right, but you're talking a minimum of half a million quid.'

Well, that sort of finished me right there. He might as well have said ten million – both figures were far beyond my means. 'But whatever you do here, it is a wonderful location, and you should keep on trying to get something going with it. Whenever you get it set up, make sure you get yourself a percentage.' And with that he climbed into a taxi and headed back to Mount Street, leaving me to ponder the future of what I was now thinking of as Mr Cassidy's Palace.

I ran into Barry Hanson a couple of weeks later and happened to ask him if he had been to the West Side Club, the gym we both belonged to on Kensington High Street. 'No,' he said, 'I haven't, and as a matter of fact I'm involved with a group of businessmen, all members there, who have decided to find a place to start their own.' Well, a big bell rang right then and there. Twenty-four hours and another ten-bob note later, Barry and I were standing back outside that gate saying goodbye to Mr Cassidy and his dog, discussing what to do next.

Things accelerated from then on; over the course of the next few days I saw a lot of Mr Cassidy, and he thought his ship had come in. At ten bob a visit he was making more than he'd ever set eyes on.

A man called Alan Fisher, a South African businessman, was the key player in the group that Barry was part of. He and a man called Bill Farragher, who owned an engineering company in Willesden, were not only fitness fanatics but very successful in their respective businesses. They were sold on the place as soon as they set eyes on it.

The very next Monday morning, I went with them to the offices of Daniel Watney & Co., the old established firm of estate agents who were handling the property. Alan and Bill made a proposal on behalf of the group and a deal was made to take a 100-year lease on 188A Fulham Road with the intention of turning it into a members' only health spa. Where did I fit into all of this, though? It was all very well for Dougie to tell me to get myself some sort of percentage as a finder's fee, but I was far too embarrassed to be asking for that. I think I was so excited to be involved in the project I assumed I would somehow or other be looked after. Everyone was full of praise and gratitude for me having found the place and it would have seemed rather churlish to ask for money. I guess it turned out to be a lesson learned. They did want me to be involved, they liked the idea of an actor having a hand in the future of the business, and so they suggested I could buy myself a directorship and a shareholding in the owning company by putting £5,000 into the kitty.

A dear friend came to the rescue and loaned me the money (I have to say someone I later treated appallingly, someone who never did me anything but good). 'Pay me back when you sell your shares for a fortune,' she said. So all of a sudden I had a business interest and, little by little, bit by bit, I helped to turn Mr Cassidy's Palace into a construction site. Mr Cassidy himself hung on in there as long as he could, but once the contractors were installed there wasn't any chance that a poor old Irish potman and his dog could stay in residence.

The building work was proceeding well and the damp, dark old building began to take on a whole new aura. It was going to be *the* club to belong to. It was exciting to be involved in the decision-making process. Alan and Bill were overjoyed to report to the board that they had managed to persuade the trainer from the West Side Club to jump ship and come to work for us on the Fulham Road. Attila was Turkish by descent but had lived in England for many years, and his army-style circuit-training exercise sessions were guaranteed to keep businessmen in tip-top physical condition. It was at this same meeting that Alan announced that he and Bill were proposing to find a female equivalent to Attila for the ladies' section, and had decided that they wanted to call the club 'Attila and Athena's Health Spa'. I was stunned by the second-rate style of name they'd hit on for what would be, in my mind, a really high-class establishment. I waited for the right moment. 'Alan, haven't you noticed that by some strange anomaly this little property, which in theory sits at 188A Fulham Road, actually has its own officially designated street sign up on the wall above the gate? Don't you think we should call our club Holmes Place?' The gathered members of the board turned and looked at me as though I were Moses handing them the Commandments, and that was it, that's where it all started. That's where the name came from, straight off the wall and those brilliant business heads hadn't even noticed!

Needless to say, when I married Linda and she learned about the source of my £5,000 investment, she fronted up the money so that I could pay it back. That was a load off my mind, guilt-ridden as I was. In fact, both Linda and myself took over the running of the club in the early days. We hung onto those shares for years but finally, during a very lean patch when our incomings were far exceeded by our outgoings, we had to sell the shares back to the board for their face value.

By the time the Holmes Place empire was up to 100 branches, someone who was a member told me that he had been reading in the club's advertising material about how the place had been discovered originally by an enterprising young actor called Larry Lamb. I managed to get Alan Fisher on the phone a few days later and, bearing in mind that the club was still essentially using my name to promote itself, I asked if it might be possible to let me have my shares back. He was full of regret but told me that the club was structured differently now and that big changes were afoot. Instead all he could perhaps offer me was a membership.

Richard Branson's Virgin Company bought Holmes Place for a sum reported to be around £200 million. I wonder how Mr Cassidy would have felt about that. He who laughs last, eh?

————— 28 —————

Lover Boy

I don't ever remember feeling any great desire to procreate and have a family. For me, my relationships with women were all about love. Love. How that word had taunted me. I thought I understood it but it fluttered before me like a dragonfly – always so attractive, always so elusive. I wanted to have it, and often before I had felt as if I had grasped it, but then all too quickly it seemed to go.

I was so desperate to be in love. I wanted to recreate the love and warmth I'd lost when my mum had gone. I hadn't been able to run to her or turn to her or to feel her love around me, and so I spent much of my life trying to find something, someone, to replace what I'd missed out on.

I'd loved my parents but their inability to sort their problems out had deprived me of my mum and my mum of me. For a long time, I blamed her for it. My father was so bitter about the way his life had turned out after he met my mum that he spent years turning me against her – and he succeeded. But I learned something else from my dad too. He had made me into something of a lover boy.

A lover boy really does hook on to women and for that second, minute or hour that he is with a woman, he loves her, really loves her, and she knows it. In that moment, I found myself generating the love that I'd been denied, but for it to really last it had to be with the right woman, and that was someone I had yet to find.

★

In 1978, I got an unusual television job. It was an episode of *The Racing Game,* a television adaptation of the successful novels written by the ex-royal-jockey Dick Francis. The series was being produced for ITV by Yorkshire Television who, back then, were a big burgeoning TV company. The episode that I was doing involved the kidnapping of the racehorse Red Rum, played by the horse itself.

The filming started up in Leeds at YTV's studios and then the entire production team decamped to London for a week. During that week it was the birthday of one of the crew and I got an invite to the party, which was being held at the Tara Hotel, just behind Kensington High Street, where the crew were staying.

The party gradually petered out as everyone had an early start, but I had no call for the morning. I was wandering through the lobby area, contemplating going home, when I picked up the muffled strains of some kind of music. Downstairs there was a disco going on and a lot of people were dancing. This is how I'd lived my life, it all flashed back to me. After all my years on the road it felt so familiar and comfortable now just to walk in and find myself a place at the bar. I surveyed the scene and 'checked out the talent'. It all came back so readily. All those nights on the prowl.

The place wasn't heaving but it was comfortably full, with a good, easy-going crowd. Two or three tables back from the dance floor, just twenty-five feet away from me, was a face that grabbed my attention. There was just no mistaking that instant feeling I got.

I can't quite catch her eye so I let a couple of dances go by. I cut free from my stool and weave my way towards her, trying to look as cool as I can. I say those familiar words again, 'Would you like to dance?' She puts out her hand and I take it and I know I have found her. I've found the one I've been looking for.

I'd hit the jackpot. That sense of warmth and joy that I'd craved took over me. I'd finally found that love that I thought was irreplaceable.

Linda and I ran like fools for three months. I was totally and utterly besotted. We did crazy things together and once she came down to London from Glasgow, just for the evening. We toured every corner of her native Scotland and we went everywhere. We got married on 13 January 1979, about eleven weeks after we'd met. And at about ten o'clock on the morning of 19 December, things started to move into gear. We were having a baby.

29

Georgie Boy

Nine months we'd waited for this day to come, for this momentous event, but when it actually started to happen, nothing went the way we'd been told it would. After all those antenatal classes, books, brochures, pamphlets and preparation, everything went very wrong.

Linda was suddenly hit with a huge onslaught of pain in her lower back; it doubled her up and she just keeled over. She knew the baby was coming but this was nothing like what she'd been told to expect.

I phoned the hospital and told them we were on our way. We had our little bag at the ready and I led Linda on a slow and painful journey down the long staircase to the street below. Nobody said anything as we made our way through the shoppers and into our little old Morris Minor Clubman. There were no wisecracks and comments from the stallholders. It was too obvious that Linda was in excruciating pain.

We were in Queen Charlotte's Hospital in about a quarter of an hour, and Linda was taken straight to the pre-delivery area. I was left to find a phone and alert our families. A nurse came out and told me I could come and see her but that she was in such pain that they had had to put her on a drip. She was already asleep. When I walked in she was linked up to tubes, wires and monitors. I stood by her side and held her hand but she was out for the count. I felt completely lost. This wasn't how it was supposed to be.

I looked across the bed at the nurse who was now adjusting one of her drips. 'Where is the doctor? Can I have a word with him?' I asked.

'I'll go and ask Sister,' she said, and hurried out of the room. The whole place felt so cold and impersonal; this was all so unlike the way the previous nine months had been as we had excitedly prepared for the birth.

Linda was 32 when she first became pregnant and back then she was considered an older first-time mother. Consequently we'd been looked after by a big-shot professor and we'd been made to feel extremely confident about the whole thing. Now it was the morning of 19 December; the big-shot professor was off skiing in the Alps with his family and we were high and dry in Hammersmith.

A young doctor came in and introduced himself and told me that what had happened to Linda was extremely uncommon, but that by sedating her they could monitor her progress without her pain upsetting the baby. From what I gathered, the baby was somehow or other pressing against a nerve from the inside. 'Don't worry, Mr Lamb, your wife and baby are both fine and, by handling it this way, we will be able to ensure both of them have a less traumatic delivery. You can watch what's going on here.' The young man seemed very confident and showed me the screens that displayed Linda's and the baby's heartbeats. They seemed to be good and steady. All I had to do was wait.

I sat by the bed watching those monitors right through the day, with nurses coming in from time to time to check the machines and Linda's progress. During the afternoon, the sister checked again, 'Your wife seems to be dilating at a steady rate, Mr Lamb, but I think perhaps the doctor will have to break her waters.'

'Is that normal?' I asked, feeling slightly alarmed.

'Oh yes,' she smiled, 'perfectly normal. It happens all the time.'

The doctor came in. 'Hello again, Mr Lamb. We are going to break your wife's waters now; it's a perfectly normal procedure. You can stay here while we do it.'

I wasn't altogether convinced by his tone; he was several years younger than me, which didn't help. I let him and the nurse go about their business down at the other end of the bed whilst I sat holding Linda's hand, stroking it – I'm sure in an effort to calm myself as much as Linda. Watching the screen over Linda's shoulder I could track her contractions. There was no big response as there would normally be; the drugs took away the pain, but the screen registered the deep movement going on inside her and I could follow each one of them.

I heard a lot of liquid pouring on to the floor and turned to see the doctor who was now standing between Linda's upraised knees staring straight at me like a boy caught with his hands in the biscuit tin. 'Mr Lamb, would you mind waiting outside for a few minutes?' He was bluffing! I knew it. What could I do? He was turning as white as a sheet and when I looked down at Linda's face I could see the colour draining from her too. I looked at the nurse standing by the doctor and made the decision to do as they wanted. This was obviously not good, but what could I do?

I went out of the room, the polished parquet squeaking under my trainers. I was completely lost. I waited for what seemed an eternity, my heart in my mouth. Suddenly a middle-aged man came running down the corridor, putting his white coat on as he ran straight into Linda's room. The nurse came out and walked directly away from me – she didn't acknowledge me at all. I felt totally isolated, helpless – a little lost boy.

The middle-aged man came out. My heart was in the back of my throat. 'Mr Lamb, I am the registrar. We've managed to stabilise your wife but she's lost quite a lot of blood, so we've put her on another drip. She and the baby are both fine.'

Linda looked like death. She was white as a sheet. I sat holding her hand, watching those screens for hours.

By about 10 o'clock that night we had a new team around us. The midwife hustled about the room, setting up pieces of equipment, and at about midnight they took Linda off the drug.

'She is going to have to be awake to help push the baby out, Mr Lamb. She will be a bit groggy but we need her to push.' The midwife gradually patted and cajoled her back to consciousness: 'Come on, sweetheart, baby is ready to come, you'll have to help, come on, push.'

My baby boy was born at about 1 a.m. but he took one breath and that was it, he couldn't expel the air because his lungs were blocked. My world stood still. The midwife put her fingers down his throat and plunged a needle into his thigh and said, 'Come on little man, come on!' and she literally brought him back to life. He breathed out; I was so relieved. 'Good boy,' she said. 'Good boy!'

She reached over to the monitor, pressed a button, and out reeled a slip of paper like a till receipt. She looked it over and handed it to me. 'Just inside the wire,' she said, 'he'll be fine!' It turned out that another two seconds and that boy's life – and ours – would have been so different. It had come that close.

Linda had taken in so much of the drug they were sedating her with that George had been affected by it too and his diaphragm had just seized up. He could breath in but not out.

Linda held him for a few minutes and then slid off into a coma-like sleep, and so I sat for hours holding that wee man in my arms, chatting to him and welcoming him to his new world. My son, our Georgie Boy.

30

Southampton Station

Recently, I was talking to my father's second ex-wife, Janet, who I had grown close to, and we hit upon the topic of tantrums.

I laughed. 'I certainly had a good trainer in that field, didn't I, Janet?'

'Yes,' she giggled, just the way she always did. 'You certainly did Larry. It was a lesson in performance art, really.' I said. 'Dear old Ron.'

'You know,' I paused as I told her a story. 'I remember so vividly the look on Linda's face as we stood late at night on the platform of Southampton Station. We'd only been married a month or so. I had a tweed fishing hat on and Linda was wrapped in her beautiful mink jacket. I ripped the hat from my head, throwing it to the floor in front of me. In full public view, I started jumping up and down on it, as though I was trying to drive it into the concrete. I'm sure the reason for the stunt touched on something as trivial as punctuality, not one of Linda's strong points, but certainly it was nothing important. Linda fixed me with those fathomless eyes and, once she'd assured herself that I was for real, she said, "Larry, you know unless you stop behaving this way, I don't think it's going to work out with us." I knew she meant it. I was nuts.'

'Yes, you Lamb boys could certainly misbehave!' laughed Janet.

There was no reasoning with me; I was possessed. It was

jealousy, agonising jealousy, and I couldn't deal with her not being right there with me every second.

I'd met Linda the night she'd been hired for a huge new job down in London. She was a buyer of ladies' clothes and whilst this big job with the large salary to match was fantastic for her, it was a big pain for me. It meant something else was going to be getting her attention and, worst of all, her bosses were men, which was something I couldn't handle.

In the end I told her she had to make an excuse and leave the job. She told them she had to go with me on a job in America, but they were so impressed with her that they offered to pay for her to commute out there every week to see me. She still quit anyway, just as I wanted her to. In doing so she lost a career.

We reasoned that it didn't matter because she was able to mother our boy, and I suppose his arrival would have caused problems for her workwise anyway; but no matter how you dressed it up or explained it away, letting my possessiveness take over our lives to that extent was just ridiculous. It wasn't just that aspect of things that meant it wasn't going to work, though. The arguments began.

'Larry, you don't put milk bottles on the table,' she'd say in her beautiful Scots accent. I should have got some sort of inkling that things had to be done properly when her mum first served me sandwiches on plate complete with a doily, but I didn't assume that her daughter would do things the same way.

'So what do you do with it?' I roared back.

'You take it from the fridge, Larry,' she went through the motions as she spoke, 'and you pour it into a jug. The jug goes on the table and the bottle goes back in the fridge.'

I was speechless. 'So what if you don't have a jug?'

'You put the milk into the cups and put . . .' She paused and started again, 'Why would you not have a jug?' She looked as bemused as me.

This was nuts. How could we be finding all this out about one another now as newlyweds? Well, that's what happens when you rush into it all without really knowing each other – I knew that much from what happened to my parents.

We'd have such stupid rows over seemingly nothing. Everything was wrong, but in spite of it all we did adore each other – she really was the one for me. Gradually, gradually, though, we came to the realisation that we just couldn't stand living with each other. We both drove each other absolutely mad. There was very little I could do that in some way didn't upset her and it was the same the other way around too.

So in the end, in 1982, when George was a toddler, we went through with buying a little house we'd planned to move into together. It was just around the corner from the flat we were in, but I never moved in with them. Linda and Georgie moved around the corner leaving me in the flat. The deal was that George kept the room he'd always had, so he never really moved as far as he was concerned; he just had a room in both homes.

That was the way our lives went from then on. If we had a row, we had it over the phone and never involved George or let him see us at each other's throats. We told him that 'his mum and dad love each other dearly but when they live in the same house they have arguments.' From that point on, we lived around the corner to each other and brought George up between us under a flag of truce instead of in a state of war. It was hard but it worked.

A few months into that truce, I had the biggest favour done for me I think a person ever had. The three of us drove around Richmond Park and pulled into one of the parking areas. George was having a bit of a tantrum, the kind of thing all toddlers do; he was just being normal but I'd had enough. I pulled him from the back seat and held him in the air with one hand and swung him 360 degrees around me. He was hanging petrified at the end of my arm.

'Larry!' Linda yelled at me as she grabbed him and held him to her. 'If you want your relationship with this boy to be the same as the one you have with your dad, you just keep behaving like this. But I don't think you do.'

A great big alarm bell went off in my head and, more importantly, I listened. I listened for the first time in my life I think.

From that moment forward I never once tried in any way to dominate my son and I never once said anything negative to him about his mum. I might have been ready to cleave her head in two with an axe at times, but I did my best to make sure that George was never party to any of my feelings.

That day in Richmond Park set the tone for my relationship with George. It could easily have gone so wrong, I could have followed my dad's example and passed on the same poison he'd been doled out. But that amazing woman, his mother, saved me and gave me my boy.

—— 31 ——

On Stage

By the beginning of 1980 I was doing quite well with TV work, but I'd not been on stage since finishing *Filumena* and television gets you television work, it doesn't breed theatre jobs.

Somebody had mentioned that I could do a few passable American accents to a young director who was about to cast a play by the legendary American playwright Sam Shepard. Its title was *Seduced* and it was loosely based on the reclusive Howard Hughes. Hughes was reputed to have lived in a hermetically sealed-off hospital room with a nurse/manservant who attended to his every need – well, not quite every need: young women were brought in to provide services of an erotic nature.

Ian McDiarmid, years before he'd become known to millions around the world as Palpatine, was playing the central character known as Henry Hackamore, and I landed the part of Raul, the manservant. Spicing things up on the girls' side were a super sexy Celia Imrie and Kate Fahy. The play had been a big success in New York and we had a very popular hit on our hands upstairs at the Royal Court. It was my first piece of noncommercial theatre and gave me a chance – so sought after – to work at what was probably back in those days the number one arthouse theatre in London. It was a really big break for me.

About a month after the show had closed, I picked up the

phone one afternoon and someone said, 'Hello, is that Larry Lamb?'

'Yes,' I said, desperately trying to fit a face to this voice.

'I hope you don't mind but I got your number from the Royal Court. I saw you in *Seduced* and, well, I've written a play and I'm trying to organise a rehearsed reading of it. I was wondering if you might consider looking at it with a view to reading one of the parts?'

'What's it about?' I said.

I listened to the young man and when he'd finished I said, 'I don't need to see it, I'll do the reading, just let me have a copy of the play.'

About a month later we read the play in a room over a pub in Hampstead, The Three Horseshoes, I think it was. Every important theatre in London sent someone along to hear it read: the National, the Royal Court, Hampstead, the Bush; they were all interested. It worked like a dream: just four actors in four chairs, no props, no lights, no movement. We just sat there and read it. And every one of those theatres loved it, they all wanted it. The play was *Insignificance* and it launched a major playwright in the shape of a young ex-actor, Terry Johnson.

It took over a year to get it produced but finally, in the summer of 1982, *Insignificance* came to the main stage of the Royal Court. Judy Davis flew over from Australia to play the actress. Ian McDiarmid played the professor; Bill Hootkins, a Texan actor resident in London but sadly no longer with us, was the senator, and I got to play the ball-player, the part I'd read originally.

We were a huge success. It worked in exactly the same way it had on that first reading in the room over the pub. The audiences were spellbound; it was profound, hilarious and deeply moving. Judy was truly magnificent – she became Marilyn Monroe night after night – and for the first time in my still very early career I played opposite a real genius. My inexperience led to a near catastrophe on one occasion. I didn't quite manage to stop the door that Judy slammed in my face as I made my entrance. I was supposed to make it look as though she had almost broken my nose, but on one particular night she very nearly did. I got it completely wrong and sat on stage with real blood running down my face, but there was no way around it, I just had to see it through.

And of course a play that is the talk of the town draws all kinds of people in. Judy called me up to her dressing room one night after the show to introduce me to a colleague of hers. I actually stood and bathed in the aura of one of the all-time greats of the cinema: Ingrid Bergman. She was just as serene and kind as her image made her out to be; she was a true goddess of the screen. And what do you do in a situation like that? You make pleasant chitchat and count another of your blessings.

Six years later I was back at the Court, this time in a truly bizarre play by Howard Brenton called *Greenland*. Once again I found myself in really august company: Jane Lapotaire, Sheila Hancock, Janet McTeer, Lesley Sharp, Ron Cook, David Haig, Ben Onwukwe and me – what a cast. The press were very strongly against it, though, and hardly anyone came. I had a bit of a row with the legendary Max Stafford-Clark, the Court's then artistic director, before a sad Saturday afternoon matinee.

'Max, we're going on stage at the end of each show, making an appeal to the audience to contribute to the repair of the theatre's roof. Don't you think you could do something about getting us a bloody audience? We've got thirty-eight people in this afternoon. It's embarrassing.'

The event that really marks that show in my memory was the death of my beloved father-in-law, George Martin,

Linda's dad. He was one of the greatest men I've ever known and some of his innate wit and strength lives on in my son, so I've managed to keep a bit of George Martin – he's still with me.

Mr P of Kensington

It was 1982. Linda and I were still married on paper but I was now living as a bachelor in the flat above the market on the North End Road. I was in a spin and I didn't know where I was or which way was up. Linda was the only solid thing in my life but, as far as I was concerned, I'd blown that relationship, and she and George were now living around the corner in Mendora Road.

'So why have you come here, Larry?'

Good question, I thought. 'Well . . . a friend, someone who knows you, recommended that perhaps a period of psycho-analysis might help me sort myself out, so here I am.'

Mr P, the wise, older man that he was, smiled and nodded sagely. I warmed to him immediately. He was like the father figure I badly lacked. He was tall and rugged and whilst probably twice my age, he was very fit.

'What I want you to do is draw me out a family tree,' he said, his Austro-American accent very distinct. I found him totally captivating. 'You see, Larry, I imagine we will be talking about various members of your family quite a lot and I have found that if I have the characters laid out in front of me, it will save us a lot of time. I can just pick out the name and see the relationships: who they are to you and each other, rather than you using the time to explain.'

It took a couple of sessions in the tiny consulting room at

the back of his townhouse just off Gloucester Road until we touched on alcohol. 'So Larry, you say you drink wine every evening? How much? A glass, two glasses?'

'A little more than that,' I ventured. 'Nearer a bottle, sometimes more.'

'How much more?' He started to make notes in a file that sat on his knees.

'Well . . .' I pondered. There was no point trying to pull the wool over this man's eyes: who would I be kidding if I did? Only myself. 'Erm, I suppose at least a bottle every night and sometimes I open another one. I might have a beer beforehand and sometimes a little shot of Armagnac.'

'How little?'

'Well certainly not more than a normal double measure.'

He stopped making notes and put the pen down. He looked at me, his head tilted slightly to one side.

'It would appear to me, Larry, that perhaps you drink a little too much. Wouldn't you say so?' He paused and let me answer. Amongst the company that I kept I'd only really figured myself as an average drinker. I certainly drank regularly, but I wasn't what I considered a drunk. But then I was here for help and this was someone who in theory could provide it.

'Yes, I suppose you could say that,' I conceded.

In one of our earlier sessions we had discussed the character of Stanley Kowalski in *A Streetcar Named Desire*, a play I'd narrowly missed doing. 'Don't you think that perhaps the two are related? That perhaps all that anger that the "Stanley" in you feels has something to do with the drink? That perhaps like your grandfather . . .' He reached for his family-tree paper on the floor by the side of his chair. 'Albert,' I said. 'Yes, that's it, Albert. And also perhaps like your father when he was younger. Don't you think you should try to drink a little less?'

I took a breath and nodded. He had to be right. I knew only

too well that the drink did have a tendency to fire me up, not to the point of physical violence, but certainly until my temper became very short-fused. And, as I knew from experience, well-aimed verbal violence can do every bit as much damage as the physical. I'd trained at the knee of a master, my father.

'So what do you think, Larry? What will you do about it – that is of course if you want to?'

'Well, I certainly do want to, that's for sure, so I suppose it's obvious really, I have to stop drinking, don't I?'

'Well, Larry, that's perhaps a little radical, there's nothing wrong with a glass of wine with a meal, perhaps even a little more than a glass, but a bottle?' He shook his head in a way that said, 'Oh no, we both know that's far too much, don't we?'

'What you should do, Larry, is before you open the bottle of wine, drink a big glass of water to quench your thirst, then when you've opened the bottle and you're letting the wine breathe, you drink another glass of water. Have a little sip of the wine to see if it's ready to drink and when you're sure that it's OK, you have another glass of water.'

'Well,' I laughed. 'If I drink all that water . . .'

'Exactly, Larry! If you drink all that water you naturally won't want so much wine. What sort of wine do you buy? Do you buy good wine?'

'Well I like to get value for my money,' I said.

'How much do you pay for a bottle?'

'Perhaps two pounds for a litre bottle.'

'Well I think it would perhaps be a good idea to pay four pounds – or maybe even five pounds – for a normal-size bottle rather than a litre bottle. Drink a better quality of wine, one with less additional materials. I think that could be a good idea, don't you? After all, if you only have one or maybe two glasses with your dinner, it will actually mean that you're spending less than you are now! Oh, and perhaps instead of the beer beforehand, just have the water, and instead of the

Armagnac afterwards, maybe a nice cup of coffee, what do you think?'

'I think you're right, Mr P. In fact I'm sure you are. I'll start tonight.'

He had this little system where he never really took money from his clients – not physically, hand to hand. He had a straightforward private arrangement: there were no letters, no appointment secretaries and no monthly bills. He asked me on my first visit how much I could afford and I explained to him that that would vary according to the work I had at the time. 'So at the moment, fifteen pounds per hour, would that be OK?'

He nodded. 'Yes, that will be fine. You just make a cheque out to me and put it right over there.' He pointed to a little glass jug on the corner of the mantelpiece. There were already two or three cheques sitting there.

I added mine and he walked me down the passageway, past his big stately gentleman's touring cycle, and shook my hand warmly as he bade me goodbye. 'See you next week, Larry, same time.' And so it went on, week after week, for the best part of three years. I took his advice to heart and started to do things the way he'd said: better wine and less of it, and certainly nothing before or after. And each time, as I rode my bike away from his little mews house, without fail, no matter how wound up I'd been when I'd arrived, the same thing happened: I would start to laugh and I'd laugh all the way home!

---— 33 ——

A Nautical Episode

The BBC called me in. 'Larry, we're going to make a television series on board a North Sea Ferry and I'd like you to play Matt Taylor.'

It was Bill Sellars who had called me. He was a big-shot producer who had brought *All Creatures Great and Small* to the screen. He was offering me the romantic lead in this, the BBC's first go at taking new lightweight cameras out on location to film drama. I would be playing opposite Kate O'Mara and Michael Craig, with Joan Greenwood and George Baker added in for good measure. It was too good to believe. Bill had seen me in *Fox*. 'I thought you were very good, Larry, and I know you're going to be great in this.'

And so, once again thanks to Jeremy pushing the boat out, I was getting another big chance.

Triangle was a logistical nightmare for the production team. We were filming onboard a ship full of passengers and then we had to race ashore to record more material, which meant unloading and then reloading all the kit. Everything was done with old-fashioned BBC military-style precision.

There were such storms too. Michael Craig was a seasoned sailor; he'd served for years in the merchant navy. The ship could be standing on its head and he wouldn't bat an eyelid; he'd just sit and puff on his pipe while I popped seasickness pills like Smarties. Nothing fazed him; he'd done it all before. It didn't seem to affect Kate O'Mara either. 'I just don't think about it, darling! I just get on with it.' Besides, the storms were the stars. They were truly awesome. We sat in the middle of one with force ten gales for twenty-two hours. And we carried on filming. Waves were crashing right over us. Walls of water would just rise up and smash against the armoured-glass windows. It was terrifying. We were forty feet above the water level.

The North Sea is renowned for its winter storms and we were going backwards and forwards through them all the time. The only relief came in the couple of hours we spent in port every day. The filming on land was easier, although not without its own dramas. Michael and I missed the ferry one night in Holland and had an extraordinary 'follow that ship' episode in an Amsterdam taxi as we chased it out of the city on its way along the giant canal that cuts its way through the polders and dykes. We finally caught it up in one of the locks and climbed aboard with the pilot.

And in another episode, this time onshore, in a swimming pool, the contents of my nasal passages poured all over Kate's face as I grasped her in an aquatic embrace. It was so embarrassing; it was as though half my brain had run out of my nostrils. Kate, the old trouper, didn't even register it.

The series ran for three years and during that time we did get a trip to sunnier climes as well. The shipping line we worked with had a route from Italy to Greece. But after a wonderful run ashore in Crete, we got caught up in an Adriatic storm – and if you're prone to seasickness like I was, who cares what sea you're on? They're all as bad as each other.

Nineteen eighty-three saw me back on board ship, this time on a life-sized reconstruction of the *Santa Maria*. I was now a conquistador, off to discover the western route to China with Gabriel Byrne as Christopher Columbus. Sailing a man-made sea in Malta, high up in the rocks over the Mediterranean where the horizon of the tank we were in matched up with the true horizon, making us appear to be in the middle of the Atlantic, it was movie magic.

We were in that place for three months, day after endless day. As November turned into December and even Malta's weather turned cold, we spent a week of nights filming the storm that almost finished off Columbus's tiny fleet. With the engines and propellers from World War II fighter planes whipping up the wind, and mast-top water sprays creating a huge downpour, we lashed ourselves to the ships and waited for the final onslaught. All around us stood what looked like giant steel water slides; at the top of each one was a big tank that would empty down a chute on to us. When two tons of water hit us it was almost more scary than being back on the Triangle line.

Oliver Reed was playing Martin Pinzón, the captain of one of the sister ships. At one point he stopped the filming and demanded vodka for his crew. He'd grabbed a megaphone from the assistant director. 'Send us vodka!' he'd bellowed. '*Vodka.*' I remember thinking that surely rum was more appropriate, but he was adamant they had to have vodka. So sure enough, two of the safety frogmen had to make their way in a rubber speed boat to his ship with a case of the stuff!

The filming turned a bit ugly at one point. A young Maltese extra who hadn't lashed himself to the mast was literally blasted through a section of the ship with the force of one of those man-made waves and finished up with a serious set of broken bones.

Christopher Columbus had marked a change in my work pattern. Although the casting was in London, the project wasn't. It meant dropping out of the scene in England for eight months. Of course it would represent a shot at the American market, but it meant falling out of the work loop at home – but it seemed the right thing to do. Hollywood was still beckoning.

That eight-month job began a whole new series of chapters that didn't really do too much for my career, but it introduced me to Europe and that was absolutely what I needed. Christopher Columbus was really a huge Italian travelling roadshow. Four months in Malta, two months in Spain and another two in Dominican Republic. I started to pick up Italian and Spanish – they came fairly easily and there was ample opportunity to speak them both as apart from the actors everybody spoke one or both languages.

I also made a lifelong friend: my Italian brother Brizio Montinaro. Our communication – a real hotch potch of French, Italian and Spanish – worked then and has continued to do so for almost twenty-three years.

34

From Atocha to Chamartin

The door of my compartment closed with a well-oiled click and I slid between the crisp linen sheets on my bed on the overnight sleeper that ran up from Granada to Madrid. I was on my way to discover a city and I really didn't know why; I just knew something was pulling me in the direction of a place that seemed to have some as yet unknown significance for me.

Atocha Station's huge glass canopy was – just like its English counterparts – blackened and crusted with the grime of years. The station serves Madrid for trains coming up from the south. And at seven o'clock on a chilly March morning, I stepped out onto the platform. A porter took me to the taxi rank. 'Hotel Zurbano, *por favor*,' I said to the taxi driver once they'd loaded my bags.

'*Si señor*,' and we were off.

Just as Edward Duke had said, it was clean, comfortable and just off the beaten track. I left my bags in the room and walked out on to the Calle Zurbano and started walking back downtown. Zurbano Street ran right through the city like a once very important but now superseded artery and, as I walked, the city came to life. Neighbourhood led into neighbourhood and the shops and places of business opened their doors: there were fish shops with fantastic displays, just being laid out for the day, of sharks, porpoises, tuna, huge piles of shellfish and creatures I'd never seen.

The markets were bursting with food from every corner of the country.

I wandered on and on; the architecture and the people, all speaking Spanish, were all so different, so new to me, and my newly acquired Spanish was bursting to be used. I walked past grocery shops, ironmongers and haberdashers – all these relics of Victorian Spain still opening up in 1984 for the day's trade and me!

Around 10.30 I found myself in a dusty square, no traffic to speak of, and one end of it was taken up by a huge, ornately castellated hotel, the Hotel Gran Victoria, and at the opposite end, adorned with the names of Spain's great playwrights, a theatre. From what I could make out it was part of the National Theatre of Spain – Teatro Español – and there, right across from it was an old Spanish pub, its long brown name board announcing 'Cervecería Alemana', or 'The German beer house'. Five minutes later I was eating serrano ham (that I was by now addicted to) and drinking a glass of fino with *'una ración'* of sparkling olives and I'm chatting up a storm with my first ever Madrileño – Madrid local: the waiter, well into his fifties, who treated me like he'd known me a lifetime. Oh, what bliss.

And, just as Edward had told me to, I spent that night at the ultra-chic bar of the Miguel Angel Hotel, just across from the Zurbano, chatting to a couple who introduced me to a friend of theirs, an air hostess for Iberia Airways, who it turns out – when we get back to her apartment as dawn is breaking – has a big thing about owls. She's got hundreds of them! In glass, ceramic, wood, wool – every form of the creatures in any spot they would fit. It was there that I had a wonderful introduction to Spanish womanhood. Forget the owls.

'I'm going to take you somewhere,' she said over coffee in her 'owly' kitchen. 'Let's just finish breakfast and I'll show you a part of Madrid I think you'll like.'

An hour later I was standing back in that square. 'There you are, Larry. The Plaza Santa Ana.'

★

A year later I was there again, and this time I was working in the city on a crazy 'Euro-pudding' of a film called *Americonga*. It was a nightmare but the pay was good and I was living back in that wonderful city that I'd so enjoyed the year before. Within a week of starting, all the actors, production staff and electricians – people from France, Spain, Chile and England – knew it was a dog of a film, but with all of them introduced to the corner of Madrid I'd discovered, no one cared. Every night we partied.

On one such evening, I found myself sitting at the dinner table between two sisters. They both spoke four or five languages and were back living in the city they'd grown up in. They'd both become fascinated with 'La Corrida'; having had a complete disdain for bullfights as girls, now they were grown up they were set on really understanding it.

It wouldn't be fair to reveal their names but they were two beauties. One was an artist and one was a banker and they lived in a lovely old studio at the top of a small apartment block owned by their family. I was besotted with the artist, but over the weeks of that roasting summer I grew more determined to bed them both.

Every Sunday we went to the bullfights. And then, as the real aficionados do, we went to the bars where the sports journalists go and sat and discussed the afternoon's outcome with them. I wasn't active in the discussions but as a passive participant my Spanish was certainly keeping apace – thanks to my two teachers. More than anything they taught me about their country. They had such style and such grace and I would sit between them as they cooled us with their fans.

I was staying in the glorious old hotel on the Plaza and like the *cerverceria* across the square, it was steeped in bullfight history, and it was one of the hotels where by tradition matadors would dress for the corrida. Up in my room overlooking the square, I finally bedded the banker. The artist left us to it.

'What do you think she's going to do?' I asked.

'I don't know, Lorenzo, I really don't know.' The banker shook her head in disbelief as she drove us through the city back to the studio the morning after that extraordinary night.

We walked up the four or five flights of steps and into their home. I thought it would be better to leave them alone so I took the early morning sun on the terrace. I listened intently. There were no raised voices, just their normal whispered tones and then, to my sheer amazement and relief, I heard laughter – not raucous laughter, but it was gentle and real. I wandered in and looked at them both – what amazing women.

Half an hour later we were across the road outside a restaurant having a light lunch before the afternoon's trip to the bullring.

The three of us lived together all that summer. I was their man and they shared me, but strictly on their terms and to their timetable. We made love in the afternoons, each in their separate room. And then, as the heat of the day retreated and darkness took over the city, we would pull mattresses out on to that terrace like three little kids and with me between them, we would giggle ourselves to sleep.

The interminable turkey of a film finally ended and it was time for me to go. I was leaving the city in the way I'd arrived that first time: on a sleeper train. This time, however, I was going north to Paris from Chamartin. The three of us stood on the platform waiting for the moment to say goodbye. 'This,' I said, 'has been the most unbelievable time of my life.' The artist smiled and looked at the banker, then they both turned their glorious dark eyes on me and almost exactly in unison said: 'Yes, Lorenzo, for us too.'

═══ 35 ═══

The French Connection

I'd been edged towards picking up French at the age of ten by Miss Smith at my junior school and I soon began to understand about places in the world that were totally different to where I lived during my time at grammar school. My next French teacher was Miss Pagan, a woman who instantly held me in thrall, and for whom I would gladly have died. She taught her students songs and poems and she gave us the spirit of what was still then the old France. In me, she managed to engender the joy of communicating in a foreign language. France, and the French language, would remain special to me. Years later, when I spent time in Canada and heard people from Montreal speaking Joual, as their dialect is called, I heard those extraordinary sounds and it was like jazz going freeform. I found it a joy that I had enough of a command of the language to be able to differentiate between accents.

Nineteen eighty-five was an amazing year in many ways, but it really started what was to become a lifelong relationship with France. It all began with that job in Spain, with the Franco-Chilean co-production. The film actually never saw the light of day – which was perhaps just as well. But it put me in touch with the French, and the real pay-off to doing the job was another little film that sprang from it as a consequence.

Along with thirteen Frenchmen and -women and one Portuguese, I went up into the Sierra Nevada mountains in the south of Spain and made the second half of an unfinished feature film, *Ubac.* The best way to make friends with a bunch of French people is to tell them that they need never speak English. I spent two weeks immersing myself in their language. We worked all day and night and I spoke nothing but French. At dinner one evening towards the end of the second week I realised that I was actually party to everything that was being said at that table. By the end of the film, Alain Chocquart, the lighting cameraman, and Philippe Deneau, the gaffer, or chief electrician, became two of my new brothers. I was accepted into their world as one of them, in their language and on their terms.

I'd seen the property market in Madrid go insane during my time there, and missed a golden opportunity to get in on it, so when I learned that prices in France were ridiculously low, I asked Alain about it. He told me about the two big national property magazines – they were a treasure trove.

For the next three years I spent a lot of time in France with the boys – and became addicted to those two magazines – and on a beautiful August Sunday evening Rachel, my then partner and I, rolled into Livarot, a famous Norman cheese town. We met up with Philippe and his girlfriend Beatrice and their friends, Bernard and Doris, and by the strangest fluke, as we walked in the country near Livarot, I stumbled on 'La Cour'.

I saw a 'FOR SALE' sign just as everybody else had turned back for lunch at the hotel. I stood staring down the driveway; I knew this was the place I was looking for. I started to walk away then looked back to see a man and a boy driving a cow through its gateway.

The man was Albert Boisjoly, mayor of the tiny commune of St-Michel-de-Livet.

'*Bonjour m'sieur. Je m'appelle Lamb. J'ai vu les afficies . . .*'

I was about to go into an explanation about the signs on the gate and ask him if he were the owner of the property.

But Albert ran his all-seeing eyes over and through me and within half an hour I was running back down the hill after the others.

'There's a place up there, it's unbelievable. It's an old cheese business. There's a main farmhouse, all oak beams and amazing barns and . . .' I was breathless as I tried to explain everything that I had learned. 'We can go back and look at it at the end of the day.'

After lunch we spent about three hours with the local estate agent being shown around places that paled into insignificance. By tea time we were all climbing over every inch of what I already knew was my new home. On Monday morning Rachel and I walked into the notary's office and bought 'La Cour'.

FOR SALE

Old family cheese-maturing business '*fromagerie Legendre*'
sits in 3 acres of rural Normandy.
The principal house is in traditional 'Colombage style'
with ten rooms, an original art deco conservatory, boiler
room, two kitchens, large chimney piece and a featured
exterior chimney to the rear.
One double hangar-type barn and two other farm buildings:
one with potential to convert into three-bedroomed house;
one with chimney piece – could make caretaker's cottage.
The property has small springs rising to the rear
that could be developed into a water feature.
Price £30,000, negotiable.

That's how La Cour sounded on paper back then in 1988. There was no mention of the dilapidated state that the whole place had descended into over the forty years that Madame Louise Legendre had lived there following the death of her husband Maurice in 1948.

They'd been given the property in 1920 by Maurice's parents as a wedding gift. They'd built it up into an extremely successful business over the following twenty years or so, buying cheeses from the local peasants and processing and maturing them. They marketed their distinctive 'Livarot' at Les Halles in Paris.

When the war came, Maurice was the mayor of the tiny commune of St-Michel-de-Livet, where the house sits, which is 200 or 300 feet above the thriving town that gives its name to this distinctive, rather strong-smelling cheese. Livarot, Camembert and Pont L'Évêque were the three kings of the cheese platter back then.

La Cour, as the property is titled, was originally some kind of ecclesiastical residence but, as with all the local housing stock, the deeds and original documents were destroyed when the City of Caen was virtually razed to the ground by the Allies during the reinvasion, and the district records office went up in flames.

Everything I learned about the property was passed on to me by Maurice Legendre's eldest daughter – herself a very sprightly eighty or so by the time she wandered in to have a look at her old family home. Between her and the older neighbours I soon realised that Rachel and I were now the proprietors of a little piece of local history.

The daughter, one of the five beneficiaries who'd been involved in a feud that was fuelled by the selling of the place, was absolutely delighted to find that it was now owned by an English couple.

'My mother would have been pleased,' she laughed. 'When the Germans arrived here, Livarot, because of its railway station, became an arms dump. Munitions were stored there and carried by train up to the big guns on the coast. The officers used to come up to the house on a Sunday afternoon and have tea and gateaux on the lawn in front of the house.

I'll show you photographs. My mother was a great admirer of National Socialism.'

'And what happened when the Germans left?' I asked.

'Ah well, then things changed. My father, in his capacity as mayor, had to deal with the local commanding officer. When the Germans stopped coming for tea, the English, Canadian and American officers were made welcome in their stead!'

'What was the feeling amongst the local people?' I asked.

The old lady shrugged. 'There was only one choice for the mayor. He either worked with the Germans or he was stood up against the wall. It was very difficult. As a matter of fact, at the time the Germans were leaving, a staff car broke down and was rolled into the front fields. It sat there for years; nobody would come and take it away.'

It was wonderful to get all the inside information on the place, but it didn't really do much to change the fact that it was literally crumbling back into the Normandy soil from which it had sprung. The main body of the house, the 17th-century farmhouse, was constructed from flintstone, oak timbers and mud mixed with straw and manure. The only non-local material was the slate roof, but originally that would have been a reed thatch. Everything had come out of the ground it sat on.

One of my neighbours, Pierre sur Dives, a tough little retired lorry driver, never without a yellow-papered cigarette burning between his gnarled old hands, told me how, when he was a young lad back in 1938, he'd helped his dad, a local mason, to build the extension that makes up the southwestern end of the house. 'I carried the buckets of plaster in to him as he finished the walls and ceiling,' he said. 'And you see there?' He was pointing at one of the fabulous sculpted log-planters that dressed up Madame Legendre's *jardin anglais*, the delightful creation at the front of the house. 'He made those out of cement himself.'

It turned out that Madame Legendre was quite a character. '*Une vrai garce*,' was the term the local doctor used when I told him where I lived. It wasn't at all what I expected to hear, but perhaps she'd been a bit troublesome in later years when he would have been dealing with her. Still, 'a real cow', from the doctor?

For forty years she'd lived on in that house and little by little it had fallen into rack and ruin. Nothing had been spent on repairs. Bits of wood were nailed in to replace broken window-panes, moss and weeds were growing in the mud-based filler between the beams, the gutters were rotten, whole sections of lower wall had turned into a kind of soup. It seemed that parts of it shouldn't have been standing at all. But, as they say in all those television property programmes, it's all in the location. And sitting where it does in the lee of a big plateau, that's exactly what it has: a perfect setting. Perfect.

36

Life at La Cour

It wasn't just the new house and all the promise of the home I'd always dreamt of, it was everything that went with it. I was drawn to the added spice of 'foreignness'. I wasn't involved in the English way of life here and I could become my own version of a Frenchman. I already had my French friends and my relationship with all of them was conducted in their language. I didn't depend on their speaking mine. Now I could have a life in France in my very own little bit of it. I could enjoy all the aspects of what was back then still the last remnants of Old Norman France.

In 1988 my part of Normandy was filled with grass farms – and to some extent it still is today: that's what they grow. They feed it to the animals in the form of hay and silage in the winter; for the rest of the year the animals graze the endless green pastures. It grows in great abundance. In Normandy it rains a lot; sometimes it's as though it will never stop and everything is waterlogged for weeks, and then all of a sudden it changes and the sun shines on and on.

The land I live on has been pasture for generations. The only thing that they actively cultivate, other than vegetables for the table in a household potager, or veg garden, are apples and pears. My house is in the Calvados département, number 14: a good steady number, just like the place. The apples make the cider, the pears, pomeau, and of course Calvados, the eau de vie or spirit that gives the region its name, is drunk throughout France. It's their equivalent of whisky, and the finer, well-aged varieties are considered by the experts to be as palatable as a first-rate malt. Of course you can get the 'rough stuff' too: 55 per cent proof and always sold with the entreaty to cut it 50/50 with pure water. Not a warning to be ignored, I should point out. I once stumbled into the *cabinet* or surgery of our wonderful local medico, and he took one look at me. 'You've been drinking the local cider?'

'Yes,' I nodded.

'And some farm Calvados?' He shook his head. 'You English, why do you do this? You don't seem to understand that the apple turns to sulphuric acid in your stomach.'

I spent the next three days in total agony, groaning like a wounded bull. Medications he'd prescribed did their work, only too slowly. I had what he called colic; I already thought I was going to die. It was without doubt the most pain I'd ever suffered. Beware!

But of course there were lots of pluses. I enjoyed the Monday morning market at St-Pierre-sur-Dives in the truly colossal 14th-century market hall, the size of a football field, with the most higgledy-piggledy cobbled floor imaginable. It was the only place to be on the first morning of every week of the year. Christmas and New Year no exception and, for me, back then at the beginning of my love affair with France, it was impossible to miss.

The European health Gestapo hadn't seized control of markets in the late 1980s and early 1990s, so this was a modern version of a real country market. Farmers' wives would sit behind a picnic table (with a well-pressed tablecloth) and sell a couple of chickens and a rabbit or two together with some of the eggs they didn't need. You could buy more or less anything you wanted to eat in the way of fowl – alive and kicking – and to watch the locals poking and stroking geese and turkey and capons around Christmas time was just fascinating. No self-respecting housewife would buy the Christmas dinner in any other way.

Geese and ducks were wrapped in brown paper and placed upright in a cardboard box, with string tied around and then knotted into a handle. The bird would sit, turning its head from side to side like some comic handbag. The turkeys were always carried upside down, and with their longer necks managed to get their heads into an upright mode, their black beady eyes and red-skinned throats jerking from side to side, completely bemused.

But much of that's gone now. There are no more live animals in the market hall. They have all been banished to the open air and, needless to say, in the twenty years or so that I've been there, fewer and fewer people buy their food alive. There are still young rabbits and all the various types of poultry on sale for people to fatten up at home, but the throng of hundreds of people in that hall; the squawking and quacking and honking that accompanied the calls of various vendors; the chatter, the banter, the greetings and kissing on cheeks: it all seems so much tamer now.

And of course having the house sitting slap-bang in the middle of a working dairy farm did put one directly in touch with agriculture. I'd worked in rural areas a lot, back before I'd started acting in Nova Scotia, and in the US much of the work had been in regions far from any city, but now I was actually living with animals all around me, and that was an altogether new experience.

At the very beginning, the house was uninhabitable, and Rachel and I borrowed a camper van to sleep in while we stripped it out. We'd park under the roof of the big old hangar and make a fire outside to cook on. One night, as we sat in the tomb-like dark, the fire crackling and spitting, a cow coughed in the next field and I almost jumped out of my wellies. Rachel, herself a countrywoman, almost wet herself laughing – but how was I to know it was a cow?! It sounded like some sort of giant clearing his throat! I was mocked mercilessly for weeks. Townie!

Albert had been such a dream of a neighbour that I'd made him promise that, whenever he needed me, no matter for what, he must call me. We'd had the phone on almost from the beginning, even before we had a proper electric supply; it didn't take long before it rang in the middle of the night. It was Noel, Albert's wife. 'Albert is down in the barn. He needs someone to help him.'

The calf was a breech birth and when I got down there – stumbling across tyre- and hoof-rutted fields in the pitch dark – I found Albert stripped to his vest with his arm right up to the shoulder in the cow's birth canal. 'I'm trying to get this cord around its hoofs,' he said. 'It's difficult to tell what's what.'

He finally got a loop around the hooves but, just as he pulled out his arm, now steaming in the dank barn air, the mother-to-be lost control of her bowels and gave him a full chocolate coating from his eyes to his belly button. It really wasn't the time to laugh – I knew I could leave that to Noel – but later, and rubbing himself as clean as a handful of straw would permit, he handed me one end of the rope and told me to 'Pull steadily . . . it will take some pulling but we have to be careful not to tear its hooves off.'

That was a bit daunting – how would you judge? – but I just watched him on his end and gradually I felt the thing start to move; and then gently, gently, out it came. Albert took hold of its front legs and finished the job, and out it flopped – all mucus and blood and steam – and after a quick rub-down with another handful of straw, it was pulled across to its mother's feet and that was that: I had helped deliver my first calf. We both retired for the night – just another one for Albert, but a big one for me.

And of course that had sort of put the seal of approval on me. I was accepted as one of the community. I could be depended on. I have to say it did slightly go to my head. I felt so much a part of things that I found myself chasing a bull across a field with Albert – it had been misbehaving and as far as Albert was concerned he wasn't having it. He had a big stick (and I have to say Albert even without a stick is frightening) and the bull was running towards the barn – to take cover presumably – and I just joined in: what if it had turned around and gone for me? It never occurred to me, fired up as I was with my new-found role as 'a man of the land'.

For me the most enjoyable time of the year was without doubt haymaking. I suppose like all town-bred boys that image of haystacks and tractors and men in shirtsleeves wielding pitchforks was lodged somewhere in my mind, but in our little community that's just how it happened. Albert was the key player – he was the full-time farmer with the tractors, the bailer and the trailers. All the other haymaking hands had small areas of hay to get in – not enough to warrant investing in machinery – so for about six weeks or so from perhaps as early as late May until some time well into July, depending on the weather, every afternoon the gang would gather to bring in *les foins*: the key crop of the year. The crop became the focus of the community.

When the weather was right and the sun was shining regularly, Albert could cut in the morning then 'fan' the previous day's cut into lines. Then he would tow the empty trailers to the field to be worked on, and then after lunch he would start to bale. Running up and down the regimented lines of cut hay, the machine he towed behind the tractor would gather up and compress thirty-pound bales, each one about three feet long by about a foot and a half square, tightly bound with nylon string; the machine would spit them out every few yards or so up and down the field.

Gerard worked for EDF, the power company, Jean was a manager at a local factory, old Jean was a retired farm labourer, Pierre was a retired lorry driver. Jack, Albert's oldest son, Laurent, his giant of a young one, and Michel – another neighbour – were pretty much the regular crew, with various others called on from time to time when the weather threatened to turn ugly.

We would gather in the appointed field and gradually the work would start. Albert would usually have the baling done by 5 o'clock or so and the first thing would be to pick a pitchfork – *la fourche*, a three-pronged variety with tines or prongs about a foot long – and walk the lines of bales, setting them in rows ready to be loaded on to the trailer and, if Albert was still in baling mode, make sure the lines of fanned, cut hay were pulled as neatly together as possible in preparation for them to be gobbled up by the old clonking 'Klaas' baler.

Then the real work would begin. Jean or little Pierre, the older guys, got to drive the tractors that pulled the big thirty-foot-long trailers and then, with a couple of stackers – usually Gerard and Michel who knew how to knit the layers of bales together into an unslippable load – the crop would start its way from field to barn.

The key to the operation was the speed of it all: that's why you need a steady old driver who will just keep that tractor rolling along at no more than a walking pace – backwards and forwards, up and down those ranks of bales. They needed to be steady by the time the bales were reaching twelve or fourteen layers deep above the trailer floor. The stackers had to feel confident they wouldn't be bounced off – they would be a good fifteen feet from the ground, and if you're tossing a thirty-pound bale on the end of a five-foot-long pitchfork, you need to know the point you're aiming it at will be where it should be.

It's quite a knack using a *fourche* – you've got to stick it into the bale in just the right way in just the right spot and then, with the right amount of force applied and the right swinging motion, up it goes in a long sweeping arc and hopefully you land it right in front of the stacker, who in theory is ready to grip the two binding strings and slot it into its place in the Rubik's-cube-like bale puzzle.

Two, three, four trailer-loads would be gathered and loaded up and then back to whatever barn they were designated for, and Albert had them in different corners of his well-spread-out farm. Most of them would be stacked in the big open-sided hangar next to his cow shed, but quite a few trailer-loads would be consigned to ancient buildings hidden away in fields invisible from any road.

And the stacking in the barn is hot, dusty, sweaty and repetitive work, especially when you're already cooked by the late afternoon sun, but it all has to be put away – crammed into every nook and cranny, literally right up into the very last corner under the eaves. And there it will sit, until perhaps the last knocking of another long, cold, wet Normandy winter.

But of course there was a payoff to the evening's work. Once it was all offloaded and we'd guzzled handfuls of cherries straight from the tree in the farmyard, everyone would grab a chair at Albert's table and out would come the pastis, the cold beer and cider, the peanuts and cocktail biscuits. Now we were in Albert's wife Noel's hands: she and Jeannine, Pierre's wife, would serve us dinner: fabulous tomato and tuna tart – my favourite – followed by the meat – duck, chicken, veal or pork – all reared right there. There would be potatoes sautéed in butter, piles of bread, as much wine as you wanted, and the Camembert made from the milk that Noel worked – morning and night, seven days of every week – to produce from her eighteen cows. Then a chocolate Charlotte, or the *pièce de résistance* – the measure of any Normandy farmer's wife's culinary skills – *tarte aux pommes*, apple tart, absolutely busting with butter from those same cows that'd be eating the hay we'd just stacked.

And the ceremony, the work, the bottles of cider from Albert's bottomless cellar cooling, the picnic box by the side of the field – under the same tree it had cooled beneath since long before plastic had been invented – has all disappeared now, all finished, in that corner of Normandy anyway. All that fun, all that sense of family and community has ended.

Somebody – some brilliant engineering mind – invented a baling machine that rolls the hay into great big round bales, each weighing about half a ton: far too big for a man to toss on a pitchfork. And so with a tractor fitted with a forklift device, one man can do the whole operation. How brilliant. How efficient. How sad.

And I saw it all disappear – a tradition gobbled up by progress. And that community has disappeared with it. That coming together in a common effort, that celebration of the land and being a part of it that those people took for granted, is no longer there to be enjoyed.

Albert gave up dairy farming because the European health regulations regarding the cleanliness of milking parlours became impossible for him to adhere to. So, after spending all her working life as a farmer's wife who milked morning and nights, Noel only had the house to run and the chickens and rabbits to feed, and never a gang of raucous, ravenous men back from the fields, the way it had been for centuries.

What a thing to have been part of; what a thing to have learned! So sad to see it all gone – what price progress?

37

Getting the House Together

Albert and his glorious, funny wife Noel invited Rachel and me into their already large extended family and looked after us as we set about trying to get the house into shape. We'd bought it entirely on a whim and it was in a hell of a state. The local plumber stood at the back of the house staring up at it; he'd told me it would need a completely new system installed. And that there was nothing worth keeping.

In some ways that was pretty straightforward; there actually wasn't much anyway – there was no bathroom and the lavatory was outside – but the twenty-two iron radiators and all the steel pipework, what seemed like three miles of the stuff, had all frozen and split. The old oil boiler that fired it all up had completely imploded during an ice storm a year before. Electrically it was a museum piece, the entire rear façade was fast sinking into the Normandy soil and would have to be underpinned, and there were serious damp problems too. All in all it was a bit of a handful. I still have, on a page of my old Filofax, a list of tools that I had to buy, with their French names.

Slowly but surely, visit by visit, month by month, the place began to be brought back into line. We had various friends who helped us along the way. An English friend, Pete, gutted the place, a French friend of Philippe's installed a complete central heating system, and Albert turned up with Gerard Bliault, a local power-company employee who helped me install all the wiring. Albert and his tractor-mounted concrete mixer – and his smiling patience – saved me thousands, and my brother-in-law, Neil, got stuck in too. We worked like miners, digging, wheelbarrowing shovelling and pouring, section by section, until the whole house was securely underpinned. We worked tirelessly to expose the original beams, stripping back layer after layer of plaster; we brought the place to life in a way it hadn't been for years.

The one thing I knew I had to do, that I couldn't wait to do when all the other practical things were taken care of, was to make my little lake, my swimming hole, just the way they had them on the farms I'd worked around back in the States.

At the back of the house was a swampy pond or '*une mare*' as they call it. It was big, about eighty feet long by twenty-five feet or so across. Water ran in one end from little springs and out of the other down the valley, into the River Vie and off to the sea. The swamp sat in a natural clay basin and it was the basin that would enable my dream to come true.

I had to wait until the freezing winter of 1989–90, till early January when the ground was solid, before we could start digging and empty the swamp of about 2,000 tons of black, oily slop. I then had to build a dam. No one could help me at the time so I literally built the whole thing myself. I was determined to do a good job and I ended up building something far bigger than I would ever need, but I built the bloody thing. Little by little the lake began to fill and, in the middle of spring, in beautiful sunny weather, I lay basking in the water. It was only just deep enough to cover my body, but to me it felt as if I was on some glorious Caribbean island. I had created it.

By November the water reached the top of the dam and passed through the overflow pipe. I now actually had a little lake to swim in. I was beside myself. However, on my first visit back in the following spring, I noticed water coming out of the ground on the dry side of the dam. The bastard was leaking. I hadn't dug my foundations deeply enough and, as water does, it had found its way under the structure and up the other side. I built another dam a bit further down the ditch, but a year later that bugger was leaking as well. In the end there was nothing for it but to build it all up with soil, which did the job. It held the water back, and so, since then, the locals and I have had a great place to swim.

★

I used to ride a bike back in those days. I'd got back into it when George was a baby and he rode everywhere with me. I was out for a ride one afternoon, in desperate need of stretching my legs after a hard day of labour in the house. I met a local man who turned out to live opposite the entrance to my house. I extended my right hand to him as we rolled down an empty lane.

'*Je m'appelle* LARRY,' I said clearly.

'Gabriel.' He smiled as he shook my hand.

I became a part of the Mesnils, his family. I would go on my own and eat lunch with Gabriel and his wife, Bichette (a nickname which meant 'little doe'; her real name was Germaine but was rarely used by any of the many who loved her). They'd been together since the Germans had been kicked out. She was thirty when they got together and she had a baby boy in tow; Gabriel was a sparkly nineteen-year-old farm labourer with a heart as big as an elephant's.

Those lunchtimes were such an unimaginable treat to me. All I had to do was pick up the phone and say, 'Bichette?'

'*Midi-trente*, Larry,' she'd say. 'Twelve thirty and don't be late.'

As I got to know them better, I gradually learned of the great sadness they shared. After their marriage, they'd been blessed with two more sons and now there was only Jean-Claude, the middle one. The eldest, who'd come with Bichette, and the youngest, had both been killed in accidents at work.

They had buried their tragedy and their loss and only occasionally would they allow it back out into the open. Gabriel and Bichette lived on and enjoyed the joys their lives brought them.

I met Gabriel's mum, old Grandma Mesnil. She was ninety-four and had been operated on eight times for cancer. *Le pneu Michelin* or 'The Michelin tyre'. She called herself *increvable* – she was indeed indestructible in many ways. The mother of thirteen kids, she'd had them in the days when the government gave mothers medals for breeding children. She told me how her husband would come home drunk. *'Et voilà enceinte encore'* – she would be pregnant once more.

In the end her husband had hung himself from a beam in the barn and, at ninety-four, with knobbly, work-worn fingers, she still ran that tiny one-up, one-down cottage where she had raised those thirteen award-winning children. She was still the force to be reckoned with in the Mesnil family. At the mention of her great-granddaughter having a crush on a boy, old Grandmère raised her gnarled fist and with a profound twinkle in her eye said, *'Attention le boudin blanc.'* She had me rolling on her kitchen floor: 'Watch out for the white sausage!' A ninety-four-year-old lady!

Rachel and I spent as much time in France as our work would allow, and Gabriel gradually became the unofficial guardian of La Cour. He kept an eye on it and whenever we were back there – and the mood and the type of work suited him – he would help me. He taught me how to reuse and recycle things from the house and how to repair slated roofs and guttering. We argued like brothers. 'You know best!' he would shout, and off he would storm.

He could make a fire and keep it burning until every bit of bush and cuttings and garden rubbish was reduced to a fine ash. Fencing: how to set the posts, how to straighten barbed wire; all that knowledge he passed to me.

We built the deck I'd always planned – along the entire length of the rear of the house, overlooking my lake – day after hot summer day, until finally Bichette and Grandmère did us the honour of coming over and sitting on it. '*Plus que mille tire-fonds,*' he said proudly. 'More than a thousand coach bolts!'

And when it came to the realisation that I would have to build a second dam, we dug the footings, made the shuttering, mixed and poured the concrete – everything side by side.

'*C'est pete encore,*' he said as we both gazed at the little spring down at the foot of the dam number two. I couldn't believe it, it was leaking again. He lifted his old cap, scratched his head and made another of his profound statements. '*C'est difficile, l'eau. C'est difficile.*' Water was indeed difficult.

I came back after months away on a job to find that Gabriel's beloved Bichette had died. He said he hadn't let me know because he knew I was busy.

'Ah, *mon* Larry. *Elle a laissé un grand trou,*' he told me, 'She's left a great big hole in my life.' He told me that he just wandered around that empty house. We both wept. And then we laughed and wept when we placed a little memorial from Rachel and me on Bichette's grave. '*Une vrai copine*', it said. She really was just that: a real mate.

But about a year or so after she'd gone, Gabriel got himself a girlfriend.

Indeed I felt I knew the lady already. Jacqueline, Gabriel's new squeeze, had lived at the bottom of our hill as the wife of a serious old drunk, and I'd passed her hundreds of times on the way in and out of the town. So when he finally presented me to her, we both recognised each other.

The drunk had succumbed to '*le pinard*' – plonk – and Jacqueline was now a free woman. She and Gabriel met in the street one afternoon. They were two poor old tired-out and lonely widowed folk. They stopped and did the four kisses each thing and got into a 'comparing loneliness' chat.

Gabriel being Gabriel, the knight in shining armour, he suggested they should go and have a coffee and she couldn't offer up any reasonable excuse as to why she shouldn't. So she took him up on it. Within a few months, they were sharing each other's lives. Each kept their own house, but they only ever slept in one, and I'd see them roaring around the countryside on their matching mopeds and their matching black jackets and crash hats like two crazy kids.

*

My almost-finished barn was the perfect setting for the local Bastille Day meal. Jacqueline was there with Gabriel and about fifty or sixty of us commemorated the glorious revolution.

I'd become a part of a French community. And I enjoyed the fact that they had absolutely no idea about my life in England and all that had happened to me as I was growing up. They didn't know anything of my acting career. They were just tickled by the fact I was *un comedien* – actors there are a curiosity to the average person, but the profession enjoys a level of respect that unfortunately is not part of our society. To them, I was someone who helped to get the hay in or to pull calves from cows' rear ends, or cleared the tables after the annual fete and lent a hand when I could. As far as they were concerned, I should be inducted into one of their local committees. 'Oops, sorry. Brakes on. Not interested in that. Thank you but no thank you.' (And by now all in reasonable French.) 'Didn't come here for that, dear!'

The following morning, I was in the kitchen looking out towards the front of the property when I saw Jean-Claude, his wife, Eliane, and Gabriel's grandsons, Patrick and Roman, walking down the drive towards the house. I opened the door to them to find them all crying. I didn't know what could have brought them to me in that state. Gradually I managed to piece together what had happened.

Traditionally, I'd driven Gabriel – and in the old days Bichette – to their savings bank twenty-five kilometres away in their home village. We would take the long way there; the trip had become a part of our lives and I always drove them slowly, like in the old days when they'd ridden in the 'charabanc'. The morning after the celebrations, Gabriel hadn't wanted to bother me about doing the honours, but he had to go to the bank to draw money to pay for Jacqueline's upcoming birthday party. However, as he'd just presented his beloved granddaughter Emily with a new car, she'd offered to take him instead. Jacqueline went with them too, sitting in the back. They didn't take our longer route, they went the normal way, and as they came round a long curve in the road, a newly retired Brit in his brand-new Porsche was driving the same bend on the wrong side of the road. Gabriel took the full force of the impact and was killed instantly. Jacqueline was badly battered but she and Emily escaped major injury.

The funeral was held in the beautiful church in the middle of St-Michel and it was fit for a king. People from miles around filled it, spilling out into the graveyard and on to the roadside. I sat with the family and wept.

About a month after he died, I was looking across the front field when I saw a puff of smoke from the spot by the gate where he'd always made his fires. He was dead, for sure, and certainly nobody had lit a fire there after him, but that smoke was there and I smiled as I thought of my dear old friend.

The house in France meant so much to me. I would sit on the little jetty that I'd built sticking out into the lake and I thought back to the jetty on the riverbank at Roydon that I saw from the train every day of my journey to school. It had belonged to some rich person whose grand house bordered the river and I always used to promise myself that one day I would have something like that too. Something of a marker, I suppose, that I would have made it in life. I looked at my house and across the lake that I'd created and I felt happy and content. At night I would sit out there in the pitch black, the house lit up like a twinkling ship. All of this gave me a hugely satisfying sense of purpose. I'd brought this piece of France back to life and made myself a permanent camp, a place that really was my home. I knew every nook and cranny, every door, every corner; every room was something that I had made happen. It was my home, more of a home than anywhere else had ever been. But my old mate was gone.

38

The Mid-eighties

Ubac, my little French film which we'd shot in the Sierra Nevada, was turning into a ticket to France. My new family of French film-makers lived just outside Paris in Noisy-le-Grand, a little surburban town with its own character, built along the banks of the River Marne. It was a world away from Paris but only twenty minutes by road. I was backwards and forwards there at least once a month.

Ubac was selected for the Cannes Film Festival. It was only in a special low-budget category, but it was there and so was I. I wasn't in a fancy-dancy hotel with the paparazzi snapping at my heels though – no, I was in a tiny room in a minute hotel, somewhere way to the back of the town.

Richard Bohringer, our 'star name', assured the film an audience, and so I got my first taste of the madness and hype that the festival generates, albeit from a third-class seat. But thanks to my friend Lady Colin (Georgia) Campbell and her friend Claire Pennock, I didn't have to slum it all the time down in the town. They were staying in a fabulous villa, which Claire's family owned, up in Grasse, and visiting them there did get me a sniff of the high life.

Ubac was also invited to a little film festival at a ski resort up in the mountains near Grenoble, so I took George for a trip to the mountains and he learned to ski with his own personal instructor. I, however, did things the hard way and very nearly killed myself. I got on the wrong lift, finishing up on a really advanced slope and decided to give it a go. I zigzagged my way down, crashing into the snow banks time after time, until I finally came to the big straight run that led down to the finish, at which point I threw caution to the winds and went for it. About a quarter of a mile from the end I flew out of my skis and crashed in a bloody pile right in the middle of the run. I had to be helped off to the medical centre for stitches in my nose. I was lucky, though – it could have been so much worse.

A few weeks later I was in Bristol with Rupert Everett, Ian Dury, Richie Havens and Ronnie Woods acting in *Hearts of Fire,* a rock-and-roll film starring Bob Dylan. Dylan was playing an ageing rock star coming out of retirement and I was playing his manager.

After waiting around for hours I was finally ushered into his presence. The director, a lovely man called Richard Marquand, introduced me.

'Bob, this is Larry Lamb. He's playing Jack, your manager.' Bob was tuning his guitar, a still-burning cigarette jammed under the strings up by the tuning knobs. His curly hair was creeping out from under his battered old hat.

'Hey Larry, good to meet you!' And that was it, I was actually acting with Bob Dylan – a bit slowly, he didn't follow the script too tightly, but it didn't really matter: he was basically being himself.

We had a great afternoon. He was talking at one point about fame. 'Man, I took a trip out to Africa, I wanted to get some peace. I drove for two days over dirt roads, another day in a dugout canoe cruising way up a river, and finally we came to a tiny village, really deep in the jungle. I stepped out of the canoe and a guy steps out of a hut, walks towards me and says "BOB DYLAN!"'

He was a delight to be around and after work one evening he said, 'What are you doing tonight, Larry?'

I still can't believe how stupid I was. I said, 'I'm going home.' Just like that. I'd turned down the chance to go and have a beer with him. Where was my head?

Back in Paris with the boys, I got a call from Luca Morsella, one of the production staff I'd worked with on *Christopher Columbus*.

'Larry, do you think you could come to Rome? Alberto Lattuada is directing a mini-series for Berlusconi's TV company and he thinks you could play one of the leads. It's called *Due Fratelli* – Two Brothers. One of them runs a big hospital in the north of Italy and is being investigated for corruption by his brother who is a public prosecutor from the south. Do you think you'd be interested in playing the Doctor?'

That evening I was seated at the dinner table, in Rome, having supper with Alberto and my two co-stars: Massimo Ghini, an Italian TV star about a year or so younger than me, very good looking, who spoke English about as well as I spoke Italian, and Cyrielle Clair, a French actress who spoke good English and reasonable Italian. We had a lovely meal and everybody hit it off. Alberto made the decision to film the whole thing in English and then dub it into Italian and various other languages for the export market.

We met up three weeks later to start shooting. We were going to work at night as the temperature in Rome in August was way up in the nineties. Since that dinner, though, Albert had changed his mind: we would work in our own languages. To an English way of thinking that is an impossible situation, but in Italy most of the TV dramas are dubbed in post-production anyway, so it was nothing unusual.

I have to say it was an amazing challenge and at times really nerve-wracking: I was pretty much OK on the French but following it all simultaneously in Italian? It certainly kept me on my toes!

There was a particularly dramatic scene between the three of us where the doctor I was playing is exposed as a crook. All three of us were going at it hammer and tongs: never a pause, never a missed cue, rattling away in three languages. When Fabrizio Castellani, the first assistant yelled, 'Cut!', the whole crew broke into spontaneous applause. It was a terrific compliment, it doesn't usually happen and we were thrilled. What a team, such an achievement.

We had to film in Verona, which certainly wasn't a tough call. It's such a beautiful city and we had a sequence of scenes to do in the opera house. I got chatting to Bruno, the chief stagehand. He was making sure our crew had everything we needed. My Italian was getting plenty of exercise and it was improving a little every day. He and I were hitting it off. I'd noticed that Pavarotti was going to be performing there soon – billboards announcing the great man's appearance were everywhere. I asked Bruno if he could arrange tickets and he made me a wonderful offer. 'Come to the stage door tonight and ask for Bruno. You can come and listen with me backstage and you'll get to meet him. He's a wonderful man.'

So what did I do? I spent the entire evening in a fruitless attempt to get Cyrielle Clair between the sheets. She was having none of it. So not only did I miss out on that French beauty, but I also missed standing a few metres from the Maestro and listening to him sing. That's one to add to my list of big-time regrets.

My fruitless pursuit of Cyrielle Clair might have had something to do with the fact that Linda and George were in America. Linda had met a gambler from Reno, Nevada, whom she'd been introduced to by Ilse, the woman who'd bought the house on Mendora Road and whom I'd become romantically involved with.

In a nutshell I was jealous of Linda's new man, but I'd figured she needed to be free to start out again so I paid for their trip. This guy, Glen, was showing her and George around America. The jealousy I was feeling was really more a fear that they could both finish up moving out there. We'd spoken on the phone a couple of times and George was loving the States. I was terrified he was going to stay there.

It didn't end that way though. They spent about six weeks in America but in the end they did come back to my great relief.

Around that time I got a call from Michael Foster, my agent in London: 'Larry, Phil Collins is starring in a film about Buster Edwards, the Great Train Robber. The director is a guy called David Green and he wants you to fly back and do a test for the part of Bruce Reynolds.'

'Do they know I've already played Ronnie Biggs?' I laughed.

'Do they need to know?' countered Michael, always the consummate deal-maker.

'No, I suppose not,' I said.

I flew back to London twice in the end, once to do a screen test and then a week or so later to act a couple of scenes with Phil. After that, I got the gig.

It was about two months later during a break in a night shoot, as we filmed the actual robbery, that I met Rachel, the woman with whom I would spend almost the next ten years of my life.

We spent a couple of weeks in Acapulco filming the scenes of Buster on the run, and then Rachel and I flew on to Los Angeles to get things organised for my big assault on Hollywood. After all, I'd sidestepped the opportunity to go for gold at the time when *Christopher Columbus* was released. Maybe it would be second time lucky?

39

1989

It wasn't to be. LA to London just like that. I was back with a bump. I can still remember the smile on George's face when he saw me. It was a good move but there was lots to sort out. It had been an expensive operation and, together with ongoing work on the house in Normandy, I had to get moving and get some work, so I took on a role in *Pursuit*, a mini-series for NBC and Harlech TV.

It only took the flight in and out of what we used to call Yugoslavia on a clapped-out Soviet jet to know I never wanted to do that again. I was playing a Jewish freedom-fighter struggling to set up a new homeland in Palestine. Zadar, a city on the Adriatic in Croatia, was standing in for the Holy Land. Lots of TV and cinema was being shot out there whenever they needed to do anything that was set in a warm location – it was the flavour of the moment.

Veronica Hamel and Ben Cross were the starts of *Pursuit* and Ian Sharp was the director. Ian had pulled together a cast that included Jon Glover, Nickolas Grace, Simon MacCorkindale, Ian Richardson and an as yet unknown Sarah Jessica Parker. It was supposed to involve three round-trip flights to Zagreb and the first one had been hard enough, three wasn't funny. In the end, the production manager gave me the two other round-trip fares in cash and Rachel and I put the car on the train at Boulogne and, after an easy overnight sleeper, drove down from Milan and all the way to the seaside location. It also meant that once my next bit of filming was done, we had a week or so to explore that beautiful coast. There was little more than a dirt road that ran the length of the country all the way to the Albanian border.

My time there was just prior to the Iron Curtain being finally pulled down, so we were experiencing the dying moments of the old Soviet system. People were so poor that there were rooms to rent for pennies, which made it a tourists' paradise. The sea, the beaches and the old Venetian port towns that we passed along the way were all in a rather sad state, but they were beautiful to wander around and savour.

Back in London, Michael Foster, got me in to see an American director called Robert Allan Ackerman to talk about being in a brand-new play he was directing called *A Madhouse in Goa*. It's really two plays in one and all the cast play different characters in both parts. To my surprise and delight I got the job. The play was written by Martin Sherman and he really gave all the characters a good crack of the whip. My two were so completely different: one was Nikko, a macho Greek restaurateur, and the other, Oliver, was a very camp old gentleman's companion with a sideline in acupuncture. It was a joy to do.

I was on stage with Vanessa Redgrave and I made a new friend too in Rupert Graves. The three of us were in the middle of a scene one evening, with the audience at the Apollo on Shaftesbury Avenue hanging on our every word, when suddenly our leading lady disappeared, leaving Rupert and me just staring at each other with not a word passing between us. Neither he nor I could understand what was going on when suddenly she was there again and she just carried on from where we'd left off. The three of us were on the verge of a giggling fit but somehow or other we pushed on through to the end.

We waited for Vanessa to take her final bow and as she came offstage we both cornered her. 'What happened back then?'

'The elastic in my knickers broke,' she told us. 'They were

around my knees; there was nothing I could do but get them off!'

When I finished that job, I had some more luck on the work front: this time it was a job back in the States. *Frederick Forsyth Presents* was a series of television films based on his short stories and I was cast as a flying squad detective sent to a make-believe British island in the Caribbean. The whole thing was going to be filmed in Florida and Bimini, one of the tiny islands in the Bahamas where Hemingway used to go fishing. I was off on the road again.

I'd never heard of Chris Cooper before I met him – this was a long time before he'd won an Academy award – and we hit it off immediately. He's very much like the characters he plays: he thinks things out before he speaks, he's a taciturn type, a great guy. We were handling the murder of the islands' British governor and Chris's Miami-based detective character was teamed up with me, his Scotland Yard counterpart. There's no business like show business.

Jimmy Cellan-Jones, our wonderfully eccentric director, was real old-school BBC but with a glorious devil-may-care attitude. He was a man who would literally turn up in a dinner suit, shod in sandals with no socks, and he didn't give a damn. On our first day, he knocked on my dressing-room trailer. 'Larry, old sport, I think you should come and meet Lauren. She's in her trailer.'

So for the second time in my life I was going to be meeting Miss Bacall.

I decided I wasn't going to remind her of the first time I'd run into her back at the Music Box Theatre. If she'd forgotten, which was very likely, it could be a little embarrassing.

'Well hello,' she smiled. 'How lovely to meet you, Larry. Jimmy has told me all about you.'

'Well hello to you too,' I ventured. 'Erm, I'm a bit confused as to what to call you.'

'You call me what you goddamn-well please!' And we all roared with laughter, but I thought as a new boy I'd stick to Lauren – Betty was perhaps a bit too familiar. All the American crew called her Miss Bacall.

'Larry, when you get a little spare time I would love it if you'd run through those great big goddamn speeches I have. You're so lucky I've got all the words and I'm having a hell of a job remembering them.'

So there in a TV film called 'A Little Piece of Sunshine', you can see me playing opposite the real queen of the silver screen, Lauren Bacall.

One of my favourite moments happened as we filmed yet another take of a really difficult scene, when James, our director, in his glorious plummy tones, yelled out, 'Would somebody tell me why we've flown three thousand fucking miles to boil our balls off in a concrete bunker on a Florida beach?!'

Just before the filming came to an end, the director organised a dinner so we could all listen to Lauren Bacall's fascinating stories of life with Bogie. 'He wouldn't let me out of his sight. If I went on location he came too!' she told us. Rather than some fancy-dancy restaurant, we all took her to a big, easy-going place and, bathing in her glorious, funny banter, we all had burgers with 'Betty'.

40

A Time Bomb in Teddington

I was playing a northeasterner in the BBC saga *Our Friends in the North*. I always feel a bit uncomfortable doing that sort of thing on telly: playing someone from a different part of Britain. Sure, I can usually get together a workable imitation of an accent – sometimes more than passable – but when it means that actors who are the genuine article go without the job, it somehow gets to me. Anyway, I did feel slightly less conspicuous in this case as I was working with an actress from the northeast who was playing a southerner, so we were able to help and encourage each other and it was a great plus.

As happens on big, long, complicated television series, hold-ups and hiccups occur and hours get spent sitting in caravans up and down the country waiting to go on and do your bit. Those hours are often filled with extraordinarily wide-ranging discussions on life, art and just about anything.

My partner Rachel was going to be away working over the whole of a bank holiday weekend and, as Ron and his second wife Janet had finally broken up after twenty-eight years, I'd decided to invite him to come and spend the three days with me. We'd spoken on the phone about his break-up, but it made much more sense to get him to come to Teddington.

I'd mentioned this to my colleague and it had led us to compare the problems we'd both suffered, her with her mother and me with my dad. There were lots of similarities in the things we found them responsible for, and the talk had gone on over the few days leading up to the weekend, when we were due to have a break in the filming schedule. There was only one difference in our parental problem scenarios – a major one: her mum was dead. We said our goodbyes on the Friday evening and – like the rest of the cast and crew – headed back to our real lives for the three-day break.

This was not going to be at all easy. I couldn't remember the last time I'd even slept under the same roof as Ron, let alone spent three days with him, but he was feeling pretty upset about Janet having left him, so in an effort to help him and perhaps to do a little repair work on our relationship, I thought it might just be worth making an effort. I was pushing fifty and had hardly seen him over the past few years. As my new colleague and I had agreed, perhaps it was a good idea to try and mend some bridges.

The Friday evening passed easily; we had our evening meal and then both fell asleep in front of the television. Rachel phoned, which woke us both, and we spent the rest of the time before we turned in chatting about nothing in particular, just catching up on people and events we'd missed in each other's lives. But of course inevitably it came around to the situation he'd found himself in for the second time in his life. He'd been abandoned – dumped I suppose one could call it – and it didn't sit well with him. What I couldn't tell him – as much as I was tempted to – was that I'd been speaking to Janet on the phone. She'd told me what she felt she had to do to survive and, finally, just like my mum before her, she'd taken the bull by the horns and run. Perhaps I should have told him what she'd said: that love him though she obviously did, he'd become impossible for her to live with and there was nothing she could do but leave. I didn't, though, which meant he assumed that I would be as amazed as he was about her going. He simply couldn't understand how she could break up what he plainly saw as a warm, loving relationship.

The conversation gradually tailed off – we were both tired – but it wasn't finished, that was clear. We drank a couple of cups of tea together and finally turned in for the night. This was proving to be harder than I'd imagined; he was so convinced he was the 'wronged' man. He was so bitter and hurt, it was an exact replay of the way he'd been throughout my teens. This was the Ron I'd known back then, still full of anger and bile. How could this woman have left him after all he'd done for her? It didn't bode well for the morning, but I was too tired to let it deprive me of a night's sleep. I had to get some rest.

I fixed him a big breakfast and left him pottering around in the garden. It was a beautiful sunny day and he preferred to entertain himself while I went out to run a few Saturday errands. I got back to the house in time to make us a light lunch, but our conversation started to get a bit stilted. We were both skirting round topics that we disagreed about. He was determined to get me to see Janet as the wrongdoer. It was the same old scenario I'd lived through before: all that old 'blood is thicker than water' Victorian nonsense, and I was having none of it. As far as I was concerned, Janet had taken twenty-eight years with him, nineteen more than Mum and about eleven or so more than I'd been able to stomach. He started to tell me how I was still disloyal. He asked me why didn't I listen to him – then I would understand, he suggested. I felt my pulse rate starting to rise; he was getting to me.

'Ron,' I said, trying not to shout or sound aggressive. 'If you want to start playing the truth game with me, I would be very careful. I've got forty years bubbling up inside of me and I don't think you're ready to deal with it.'

'What are you talking about when you say "truth game"? What do you mean?'

'I mean, Ron, that you don't seem to recognise the fact that I am a grown-up. I'm a father myself now. You are not telling me how to think. I know Janet and truly respect her and if she decides after twenty-eight years that she can't live with you any more, I figure she's given it enough of a go. If she feels the only way to deal with the situation is to leave, to break her life up – not just yours – then she's perfectly entitled to do that and neither you nor anyone else will ever make me feel differently. Frankly I'm amazed she stood you that long!' As I made the last rejoinder, I knew I should have kept it back.

'What do you mean "stood me"?' He stared me right in the eye. But before he could say anything more, the phone rang.

'Hello?' It was Linda. 'Larry, is everything all right?' She could read the tone of my voice and – knowing that I was spending the weekend alone with Ron – she sensed something was up.

'Yes, it's fine,' I said, not giving anything away.

'Larry—' she started again.

'Don't worry, darling, everything's fine. I'll give you a call later on. Bye.'

'Are you sure? Larry darling, please be careful.'

'Everything's fine,' I said. 'I'll call you later.'

And with that I put down the phone.

Ron was straight in. 'So what did you mean by that last dig? "Stood you that long"?'

'Ron, I just said to you, I've got forty years boiling up inside me. This is not the time to start playing the truth game.'

He wouldn't let it go. 'What do you mean about a bloody truth game? What are you talking about?'

That was it. I knew now it had gone far enough – too far, in fact. I walked to the kitchen and closed the window and then the one in the utility room and another that I remembered was open upstairs on to the back garden. As I walked to each one I could feel the anger pounding up inside me. This was it, the moment of truth, the moment I'd waited all those years for: here it was.

I yelled at him: 'Shut your fucking mouth you horrible, horrible old man!'

I don't know what the decibel level was: I didn't care. I'd done my best to save sleepy suburban Teddington from my coming tirade by shutting the windows. If they heard through the double glazing, then best they withdrew to a decent distance. I'd waited forty years to say this and, as Ron had taught me, if you want to frighten someone, then lay on the volume. He'd certainly been a master of that.

'What do—?' He started to shout me down but I wasn't giving an inch.

'Shut up! You fucking little monster!' I was now roaring right in his face, just like he'd roared at my mum all those years ago. 'I'll tell you what I mean by the truth game. Do you remember when I was a little boy in Trinity Lane and you tore the carpet out of the stairs? Do you remember that? Do you?! You nasty, nasty, bullying old man. Do you remember? Well I do, just like it happened yesterday. I remember how you crouched there, stark bollock naked, scaring the shit out of me. You were roaring like a wounded bear.'

'What are—?' he tried interrupting again. I was giving no quarter. I stood right over him and drove every word right into his face.

'And what about when you poured the teapot over Mum's head. Do you remember that? DO YOU? She stood there weeping as the tea trickled down her face. Have you forgotten that lovely stunt, you disgusting little bully? Shut up. I haven't finished! All your years of threatening me, all those things you said you would do to me, have you forgotten that as well? Have you?'

He started to say something again but again I yelled with all the force I could muster right into his eyes. 'All those lives you fucked up. Me, Wesley, Penny: all of us completely fucked up. We're emotional cripples, all thanks to you, you fucking shit.

And my mum – the things you called her in front of me and the way you tried to turn me against her. You weren't even satisfied with that, though, you went to work on poor little Kay. When she and Janet came into your life she was a bubbly little toddler and you've managed to work your magic on her as well.

'And you have the audacity to expect me to be shocked and upset that Janet has left you! Are you totally fucking mad? I'm amazed she's put up with you for twenty-eight fucking years!!!'

He started to say something else but I was on a roll. 'Shut up! Do you understand now? There's nothing you can say. You're a nasty poisonous bullying shit and I've waited forty years to tell you . . .' And that was it. 'Don't you dare try and shout me down.'

His face had gone as white and lifeless as his wispy old beard.

I flopped down on the bottom of the stairs, completely exhausted. I felt drained and my whole body was palpitating. He turned and walked through the house, opened the back door and went into the garden.

I had to lie down. I literally crawled up the stairs to my bed and lay there for a few minutes trying to calm myself, but there was no controlling the state I was in. All I could do was to breathe deeply. A few minutes went by and I dragged myself to the back window. I could see him sitting at the far end of the garden in a chair by the old brick shed.

I went and lay down again.

Another few minutes passed by and I was beginning to get myself under control. I heard the back door click open and after a minute or two the front door opened and closed.

I caught up with him a few minutes later, walking down the road with his little suitcase. I pulled alongside him in the car and lowered the window.

'Ron, you don't have to walk to the station. If you're going, I can take you there.'

'Fuck off,' he spat out at me.

'You know, Ron,' I said, 'that's your trouble. You can give it but you can't take it.'

I didn't realise it at the time, but that was the end of our relationship and we never ever spoke again.

'How was your weekend, Larry?' my colleague asked me the next morning in the make up bus. 'Did you have a good time with your dad?'

'Not exactly,' I said. 'I sort of let him have it with both barrels. I got it all out, maybe went a bit too far.'

'Well,' she smiled, 'at least you didn't have to do it the way I did – standing at the edge of a six-foot hole yelling down at her in a box!'

41

Working my Way Through the Nineties

Another phone call from my agent had got the nineties really going. I had to meet a director at the Old Vic and his name was Steven Pimlott.

'Are you sure you've got the right Larry Lamb?' I laughed.

'Oh yes,' he said with a flash of his rather cherubic smile. He wasn't that tall but he exuded both peace and power and I liked him immediately.

'I thought I knew your work from seeing you on the telly, but then I saw you give that speech at the end of Martin Sherman's play. What was it called?'

'*A Madhouse in Goa*,' I told him.

'Yes, that's it. Well when I saw that I realised that I didn't know so much about you, so here we are.' He laughed.

We actually talked for over an hour and the two casting agents Pippa Ailion and Irene Cotton were beginning to get twitchy: this was going to upset their day's interviews, but on and on we went.

'Let's read a bit,' Steven finally said. 'Do you know the *Dream*?'

'Well yes,' I said. 'I was in it at Stratford Ontario. I played Tom Snout the Tinker.'

'Marvellous,' he said. 'Well let's hear you read some of Oberon.'

We worked on the script for about half an hour and that was it, we hugged each other like old friends and off I went.

The following morning he offered me the job, or rather jobs
– this was a double production of *A Midsummer Night's Dream*
and the contempary German version by Botho Strauss, *The
Park*. To play Oberon in both plays opposite Frances de la
Tour's Titania and Peter Wight's Bottom.

The rehearsals were fantastic. We were a company of twenty-
five actors, all with a six-month contract and everybody hand-
picked by Steven. It was a joy. By the third week we were starting to piece the original together with a plan to start looking
at *The Park* on the Monday of the fourth week. On the Friday
morning, the whole company was gathered in the beautiful old
rehearsal room that sits way up beneath the roof of that glorious old theatre. We were all set to start our daily physical and
vocal warm-ups when Steven came in and asked us all to sit.

'I've just been told that I'm not supposed to tell you this
but . . .' He paused and turned his head and pointed to the wall
behind him. 'Behind that wall, in the office, we are all being
sacked – all of us! Me, the casting department, the design
department, costumes, everybody. Seemingly the management have decided that the project is far too costly and in the
light of the losses already sustained they are pulling the plug
on the show.'

So that was that. We were chucked out.

There was a lot of talk about staging a sit-in but there was
nothing we could do. The management was going to pay
us half our money – which was actually far more than they
needed to – and we were theatre history, a show that never
was.

We all gathered together at my old flat on the North End
Road – and indeed we continued to do so every day for a week
– in a sort of last-ditch attempt to salvage something of the
wreckage, but in the end it all fizzled out. We'd been destroyed
as a company and returned damaged to our individual states:
twenty-five actors and a director looking for work.

So much for a good start to the nineties.

But relief was at hand. *Broke*, a BBC comedy drama written by Stephen Bill, which was to star Timothy Spall, Susie Wooldridge, Sheila Kelly and me, came swooping out of the clouds of gloom. I had been rescued. And I got a lifetime friendship with Stephen as a bonus, to say nothing of Leo his son!

Soon after *Broke* came *Get Back*, which saw Ray Winstone and me playing brothers again and John Bardon, who would soon become the beloved 'Jim' to millions of *EastEnders* fans, played our Dad.

The fabulous young actress who played one of Ray's daughters gave John and me a real laugh one afternoon. We were standing in the corridor chatting when the young lady in question passed by. John called out to her – he said something about being sure to get her homework done that night (she was still doing her A levels) – she turned her head and looked back at us then ran off down the corridor lifting her skirt and flashing her bright red panties. That was the young and as yet unknown Kate Winslet: how much would we have to pay for that now?

We did the show for two years but it never quite took off, and then, right at the point when I thought my career was coming to an end, another phone call came from my agent's office – the 'cavalry' was perhaps going to save me again.

'Jonathan Powell, the head of Carlton Television, wants to talk to you about taking over from Kevin Whately in *Peak Practice*. I think this could be very lucrative if it comes off.'

I walked out of Carlton's headquarters not knowing what to think. Mr Powell had come down to the lobby to meet me, walked me into his grand suite of offices and basically talked to his assembled production staff as though I'd already got the job. You never know, though, in this business.

My lovely agent, Lindy King, phoned as I walked back into the house.

'Sit down, Larry,' Lindy told me. *Oh no!* I thought. *I've blown it. What did I do wrong?*

'Tell me the worst, Lindy.' I was sick with a sudden burst of panic, remorse and self-loathing, a lovely cocktail.

'They want to hire you. Ten episodes in the first year at twenty-five thousand pounds per episode. With thirty per cent increments over three years, that's a million-pound deal.'

My life changed from that moment.

I had to find a house up in the Peak District where the series was filmed because I was going to be there for the best part of six months.

I found myself in the milking parlour of Cyril Hudson's farm, way up high in the beautiful, wild Derbyshire hills. 'What do you work at?' he asked, his old flat cap jammed down on his head and a big brown apron wrapped right around his body.

'I work in television.' I smiled.

'Well,' he said, his rich local accent curling itself around the vowels that are unique to that corner of the country. 'If you rent this 'ouse, first thing you can doo is get a ladda an get oop on that roof and fix that bloody aerial.'

I'd fallen on my feet. I had a home on a dairy farm with a lovely old couple who were puzzled at my willingness to muck in with the work but who were happy to include me in their lives. By the time I'd been there a couple of months, Cyril and Mary, and Brian and Cyril, their sons, had made me feel part of the place.

Of course there was still the series to film, but my character's story was being built up very gently. My character had a wife played by Jane Wymark and he had been a naval doctor before coming to the practice but it seemed to be taking a very long time to get me into the story.

Then, on a Monday morning, as we were starting the fourth episode, word came through from London that all work was to stop. Richard Handford, the producer, had gone.

It had been common knowledge that there had been tensions between our producer and the bosses up at Carlton. The Monday meetings had been getting more heated and now he was gone.

Everyone was in limbo and no word came as to when we would restart with a new boss.

On the Friday I took the train down to London because I had some post-production recording to do on *Our Friends in the North*. In the studio I met my *Peak Practice* co-star Saskia Wickham, who by coincidence had been in that show too. We talked about all the drama going on in *Peak Practice* and she told me that in fact she'd heard that virtually the whole production team had got the axe.

I had some friends up from London for the weekend and was back in the old farmhouse by nine or so that evening, fixing dinner, when the phone rang. I assumed it would be Rachel because she was driving up straight after work.

It was Jonathan Powell. 'Hello Jonathan,' I laughed. 'I don't ever remember being called by the head of a TV network before. What about all these sackings I'm hearing about? I was beginning to think . . .' The penny finally dropped. There was a huge, deafening silence.

'I'm sorry, Larry, I've had to make an executive decision. I have to let you go.'

The bottom fell out of my world. Crash and burn. Chucked out again.

But in the end, thanks to Lindy's brilliant work, I got paid a quarter of a million pounds to *not* be in *Peak Practice*.

here did you get that hat? Filming *Christopher Columbus* with Oliver Reed in the Dominican Republic in 1984.

Brizio Montinaro, my Italian brother, on the set of *Christopher Columbus* in Malta in 1983.

Playing opposite a Hollywood legend with Lauren Bacall in *A Little Piece of Sunshine*.

With my screen dad, John Bardon, and playing my brother for the second time, Ray Winstone, in *Get Back*.

A superstar-to-be playing my niece and Ray's daughter, the very young Kate Winslet in 1993.

On stage with an icon. Me with Warren Mitchell (second from left), Des MacAleer and Sian Thomas (right) in *The Price* by Arthur Miller.

The Sisters Rosensweig with Maureen Lipman, Lynda Bellingham, Janet Suzman and Brian Protheroe at The Old Vic 1994.

Playing the old man – it happens to us all boys! In Sam Shepard's *Fool for Love* at the Apollo Theatre with Juliette Lewis, Martin Henderson and Joe Duttine.

Deck building with Gabriel and Pete at the house in France.

Constructing the dam in Normandy.

La Cour, my spiritual home for twenty years.

A rare night out on the town with Clare at the wedding of Samantha Janus who played my onscreen daughter Ronnie Mitchell in *Eastenders*.

Eloise's first trip to the seaside in Swanage.

My daughters Eloise and Eva-Mathilde.

Eloise with Auntie Celia.

Two little French schoolgirls, Eloise and Eva-Mathilde on the way to Eva's first day.

Peak Practice, the show I never appeared in.

With a very young, pre-*True Blood* Stephen Moyer in *Deadlines* in Tunis in 2004.

With James Corden – one of my boys!

Who dunnit par excellence. On the bar room floor of the Queen Vic.

The happy couple. At the alter with another icon, the beloved Barbara Windsor.

That bank holiday on Barry Beach with my *Gavin and Stacey* family.

Meet the Shipmans with Alison Steadman and Mathew Horne.

Daddy's Boy.
Me and George.

42

After Peak Practice

It took me months to come to terms with getting the boot from what would doubtlessly have been a life-changing job. I'd grown to love my funny old house 'up on the tops' in Derbyshire. Cyril Hudson and Mary his wife were absolutely flabbergasted to hear what had happened, I'd become almost one of the family. But of course, despite the major setback for me, life on the farm – over a thousand feet above sea level; usually shrouded in freezing mist and regularly dressed in snow – went on all that winter. I'd rented the house through until the following March and, as I was being well compensated financially, I didn't have to go looking for work. I needed to think it through and get used to what had happened, so I just stayed there, mostly on my own. Rachel was working on a film and would come up and join me at weekends. I needed the solitude – and the hard physical energy-drain that tramping those moors demanded.

I enjoyed the country pursuits too – I'd always wanted to learn to drive a horse and trap so I did that with a local horseman, and at least once a week I would go to one of the local livestock markets with Cyril. Of course, back then absolutely nobody knew who I was, so I could wander round looking at the animals, watching the farmers and herdsmen assessing the beasts. I would have warm mugs of tea and sausage sandwiches in the snack bar and generally soak up that little world, which was so far removed from life in London.

Standing in the auction barn hearing the auctioneer at work and listening in on muffled conversations between tight-lipped countrymen didn't make up for what had happened, but it gave me plenty to think about when I could easily have become totally self-obsessed. I'd bought moleskin plus fours and waistcoats from a country gentleman's clothier in Bakewell and a brand-new pair of walking boots and I just hung on in there and got on with it. It was a way of burying the whole thing and leaving it all back there where it had happened. 'L.L.P.P.R.I.P.'

I got a call from Richard Handford, the man who'd been the first to go in the putsch that I'd also fallen victim to. 'Larry, I've got a new project I think you might be interested in. You're not working yet, are you?'

'Not yet, Richard,' I laughed. 'I'm still the walking wounded!'

'Well, do you think you could come and meet me at my new office one evening this week?'

'Yes,' I said. Despite the sudden healthy bank balance situation, it was obvious I would have to get back into the saddle sooner or later, and Richard was someone I'd taken to instinctively. 'How would Thursday suit?'

'That'll be fine.'

Ardent Television was an independent TV production company headed by none other than Prince Edward. Channel 4 had commissioned a ten-part series called *Annie's Bar*, which was supposed to cast a satirical, topical eye on the goings-on behind the scenes at the Houses of Parliament. Richard offered me the part of Terry Dunning, a tough, no-nonsense government whip.

'Obviously we can't pay you what you were getting in *Peak Practice*, but we can pay reasonable fees.' He couldn't have been fairer than that and, like it or not, I needed a job. The scripts were to be kept as up to the moment as possible and the original idea was to have an actual real-life politician appear in the series from time to time. It was all very avant-garde and great if it were to work. 'It's going to be wonderful, Larry. A sure-fire hit.'

They had hired two directors to cover the ten episodes: Baz Taylor, a man with years of TV directing under his belt, and Sarah Harding, an equally experienced pair of hands. The acting company was very diverse and highly talented and, right from the morning when we read through the opening episode, everyone felt sure we were on to a winner. I certainly did; I'm an eternal optimist.

The idea was to work in the old TV style: rehearse an episode for four or five days and then film it in a studio over the weekend. The art department had located an ideal 'stand-in' for the interiors of Westminster in an old country pile out in Berkshire. We would go there for one day each week to do everything that took place in the lobbies, the corridors and in the chamber. The mock-ups that Dave Ferris, the designer who would later work his magic on *Gavin and Stacey*, and his crew had built were phenomenal and really did feel like the real thing. Obviously we weren't going to be filming in the 'palace', although they did let us in for a guided snoop-around, just to get the flavour of it.

A young actor called Dominic Taylor was cast as the central character, David Dashwood, a rather naive young MP, and with Jonathan Coy, Paul Brooke, the late Tom Watson, Eamon Boland (my younger brother from *Fox*), Elizabeth Bennett and Simon Chandler, it was altogether a cast of first-rate actors and actresses and we were ready to make TV history – or so we thought.

The problem was keeping the thing up to date and getting the scripts written in time to meet the deadline, coupled with the difficulty of getting real MPs to look real in a TV drama. It all seemed so simple, so straightforward. The first couple of episodes went smoothly, but gradually trying to make the hastily written scenes come to life, even with experienced artists working on them, got too difficult, and sadly the whole thing finished up a bit of a wet firework. Despite all the efforts that all the talents applied to it, *Annie's Bar* fizzled out and was dumped. There was no way the network could justify going for a second series.

Everyone agreed that with the right amount of work and radical changes to the overall form it could work, and indeed work well, but Channel 4 just couldn't afford to go through with that. It became a one-series wonder.

But 'it's an ill wind', as the saying goes, and I certainly got some 'good' blown my way. Dominic Taylor and I became real friends. He was raising two young boys alone and playing the lead in the show – I was full of admiration. We used to be driven out to the Houses of Parliament location every week in the same car, and every week we would pass a big set of gates to a very substantial property as we drove though Henley. Every driver who took us would always say the same thing: 'You know who lives there, don't you?' It became a bit of a joke for us because Dominic already did know who lived there. It was his godfather, but he never actually said that in the car, he only ever admitted it once we'd arrived at the first location on the very first episode. Week by week we drove past those gates and every week I would say 'No' and every different driver would let us in on the secret.

On about the eighth week, Dominic just couldn't resist it. When the inevitable question came he said, 'Yes! As a matter of fact I do, and when you drive us back this afternoon we're going to stop there for tea. He's my godfather.'

The driver almost crashed the car trying to turn around and take in what he'd heard. At the end of the day's shooting we drove back along our normal route and finally we pulled up in front of those much-discussed gates. Dominic called through on his mobile phone: 'Yes, it's us. We're here now.'

The gates swung back and we drove into the most stunning gardens I'd ever seen. There were streams and little lakes and grottos and cabins; it was a truly magical world.

And there, working with his gang of gardeners, unloading some new trees 'just in from Germany' was the man we'd come to see.

And for the next hour Dominic and I sat in the kitchen of a house that was every bit the match of the gardens, talking about anything and everything and having tea and biscuits with George Harrison of The Beatles. He was just the most normal, gentle, easy-going man, just another regular guy. What an amazing pay-off to that job. Unforgettable.

There was more good news to come. I'd been trying to sell an idea for a series of dramas set in the Tower of London that had come to me about five years or so before. It was very straightforward, very simple, and every producer I'd put it in front of was immediately interested. Brenda Reid, who was at the time head of drama at Anglian, had actually taken an option on it, but in the end for whatever reason decided she couldn't go ahead with it. So, as *Annie's Bar* came to a close, I realised that Ardent, with its royal connection, was the obvious company to present it to.

I spoke to Eben Foggitt, Prince Edward's head of production, and he jumped at it. 'I'll put it in front of Edward tomorrow! I'm sure he'll love it.'

He did, and a couple of days later I was in HRH's office in Charlotte Street sorting out a deal. Indeed I finally got a credit as an executive producer on a series called *Tales from the Tower*, which Ardent produced for the Discovery Channel. And as a matter of fact it went to a second series.

About a year later, while Ardent's offices were being rehoused away from the West End, I went to Buckingham

Palace (twice) for production meetings. Albeit in a very plain and simple receiving room, I was served tea and biscuits by a footman. My grandfather turned in his grave, I've no doubt, but jolly nice it was too.

43

Treading the Boards Again

As well as the sackings, the nineties were pretty eventful in terms of theatre as well as television.

I worked for the first time at the Almeida, which was already considered one of the classiest London theatres. It was being run by Jonathan Kent and my old colleague from the Royal Court, Ian McDiarmid. Ian was directing Frank Wedekind's Lulu plays (*Earth Spirit* and *Pandora's Box*) and had managed to get Joanne Whalley-Kilmer to come back to London from Hollywood to play the title role. She was playing opposite the young Michael Grandage but unfortunately the production got terribly behind in terms of rehearsal and we were totally unprepared by the time we did open in front of the press.

We were also totally unprepared for their response: they hated it; they all attacked us like a pack of hungry wolves falling on a flock of fine fat sheep. I'd only suffered an onslaught like that once before, at the Royal Court, in Howard Brenton's *Greenland*, and it's not at all a pleasant experience.

Joanne took it personally, which was sad because with a bit more time it could have been great, but she felt responsible. Anyway, fate interfered in the most extraordinary way.

We were using the under-stage area of the theatre a lot for entrances and exits, and at one point Joanne and Mr Grandage had to slide down a chute fashioned from a huge curtain. It supposedly looked magical from the auditorium, but from down where we were standing in the darkened bowels of that old place, it had a slightly comedic value. On the night of our eleventh performance, as the two of them finished their slide and hit the tower floor, we all heard a very noticeable 'click', and something told me that it was bone-related.

Indeed it was. Joanne made it through to the end of the show, but once we'd taken our bows she was rushed off to hospital in a taxi and we never went on again. She was in such pain, she couldn't even contemplate carrying on. And that was it; they had to close the show. Sad as we all were, there was a definite sigh of relief from more than one or two of us as we came in and got our pay a week or so later. It was as if it had been jinxed.

The 1990s were busy with a lot of TV jobs. There were two series of *Get Back* for Laurence Marks and Maurice Gran, and *The Wimbledon Poisoner*, which was the first time I'd worked with Ali Steadman. I managed to do more theatre too, though. Michael Rudman, who I'd always really rated as a director, called me in to talk about playing Jane Asher's husband in a play by James Saunders called *Making It Better*. Michael, an all-American boy – a Texan to boot – took a real swing on me.

'What about the accent, Larry? This guy is a real middle-class BBC World Service producer. You think you can manage that?'

'Absolutely no problem at all,' I said.

'Of course you can,' he nodded, 'and just to make sure, we'll get Julia Wilson Dixon in to coach you.'

He hired me on the spot, just like that. He didn't even get me to read to him. It was the only time that's ever happened to me! It was also the first time I'd played someone 'up the ladder' from me.

Jane was phenomenal: she somehow managed to juggle her acting career and her commercial life in a seamless, effortless way – and she had a family to look after too. She amazed me. David De Keyser was the most senior member of the cast. He and I hit it off immediately. Together we would watch the youngest member of our foursome, Rufus Sewell, creating a performance that was to put him well and truly on the map. On about the second day of rehearsal, when Rufus and Jane were working on a scene, David leaned across and whispered in my ear, 'I think you and I might as well pack up and go home, don't you?' I nodded in total agreement. Rufus was awesome.

The play was yet another big success for the Hampstead Theatre Club, as it was back then, run by Jenny Topper. After a bit of a delay, we transferred to the West End, with Eddie Kulukundis as producer, and reopened the newly refurbished Criterion Theatre. But we'd waited too long for the theatre to be ready and lost all the momentum that the initial surge of popularity had generated. Within six weeks the show closed.

I found myself back in Hampstead within a year, this time with the incredible Harriet Walter. It was just the two of us in Marguerite Duras's play *La Musica*. It was one of the most difficult jobs I've ever undertaken. There were pauses in true French-movie style that were two or three minutes long, and by the time one got to the end of some of them you'd forgotten what the bloody play was! But Harriet has to be one of the greatest actresses of her generation. So for me it was such a pleasure and I have to say an honour.

The roles kept on coming, and there was a very quirky, other-worldly play by Phyllis Nagy back at the Almeida. This time it was being directed by Steven Pimlott, so at last we'd got the chance to work together, four years after the Old Vic debacle. It also got me on stage with one of the finest actors I've ever worked with, a man who had completely blown my mind in my early days back in London. I'd seen him at the National

Theatre in *The Madras House*, and there was a moment in the play where he calmly, meticulously rolled a cigarette with such beauty and precision that it made me understand there and then just how far I had to go. The actor was Oliver Cotton, a true master of the actor's art – and I was working with him! Or at least I was trying to, because as well as being a brilliant actor, he is without doubt one of the funniest men on earth. We would stand around backstage – both not really having the best time of our lives – in absolute hysterics. He would be doing his Terry-Thomas impersonations whilst I was swearing I was never going to work in theatre again.

But of course I did, and within about three or four months I was out in Greenwich with Maureen Lipman, Janet Suzman and Lynda Bellingham in the big Broadway hit *The Sisters Rosensweig*. I was playing a Jewish furrier, Merv Kantlovitz. Brian Protheroe was in it and we would play brothers years later in *The Price*. Altogether we were a really happy group of actors. It did go a bit adrift one evening when the entire theatre was emptied out on to the street due to a bomb scare, but, undaunted, Maureen walked out amongst the audience and shouted, 'OK folks, let's all adjourn to the park next door and we'll carry on from where we were so rudely interrupted!' The audience were thrilled: a bomb scare and an alfresco show, what a bonus. Fortunately the security people gave us the all-clear before I had to make my first entrance. I wasn't too sure about theatre in the park: it wasn't quite my style!

Big hit that we were, there were no theatres available in the West End, so I finally got to work at the Old Vic. We transferred there and did wonderful business. There was a bit of a security fuss going on one evening and it was all being kept hush-hush, but it turned out that Tony and Cherie Blair were in that night and Maureen invited us all to her dressing room to join them for a glass of champagne. This was just when he was becoming increasingly well known. I was so impressed with both of them then that I wrote to him at the House of Commons the next day to wish him luck and to say how I'd found both of them really open and approachable – the sort of people I'd love to see running the country. I suppose you'd call it a fan letter. About a day or two later I got a handwritten reply. It was a really lovely note and I was thrilled.

It was after that that the whole *Peak Practice* thing happened and all the *Annie's Bar* aftermath began. Life was about to take me on a big detour.

I knew I wanted to move on. I wanted to have more children and, after almost nine years of trying, it was pretty obvious that it wasn't meant to happen with Rachel and me. It was so sad a situation to be in. I began to avoid being around people with young children and I actually found myself resenting their happiness because all I wanted, more than anything, was to be a father again. Nine years of trying to make a baby and then along came *Nine*.

I'd dropped in on Lesley Duff (back in the days when she was still an actress) and her husband (back in the days when we were friends), Miles Anderson. Miles had been into the West End to get a copy of the cast recording from the Broadway production of *Nine*. Lesley was auditioning for a part in the upcoming Donmar production and wanted to listen to the song she'd have to sing. In that production, Raul Julia had played the role of Guido Contini, the Italian film director modelled along the lines of Federico Fellini in what is really a beautiful musical homage to his film *8 1/2*, which delves into his unbelievably complicated personal life. More specifically, it is about the women – from his mother onwards – who inhabit his mind and his life. As I listened to him sing those songs it really was a case of 'I can do that!'

Miles was really keen for me to try out for the part. 'You could sing those songs, man! I'd be in there like a shot if I had half your voice.' By the time I left, I had a cassette with a copy of two or three of Guido's main numbers and I was all set to try and get an audition. I worked on two of the numbers all Saturday evening and for most of Sunday, but by the time I went to bed that night I'd given up on the idea.

On Tuesday morning I phoned Miles. 'Are we still going for that walk we talked about?' I asked him, and an hour later we were in Bushy Park.

'Did you phone your agent about *Nine*?' he asked.

'No, I—' I couldn't think of a sensible reason but Miles cut in anyway.

'Here, use my phone. Call your agent now.'

He was very forceful. I think it was what I needed to push me out of my comfort zone and into the terrifying world of musical theatre.

'Lindy, what do you know about *Nine* at the Donmar? Have they cast the man?'

'Well, I do know that the world and his brother are after it: everbody from Kevin Klein down, but David Leveaux is directing it and he's got very definite ideas about who he doesn't want. Why? Can you sing?'

'Well, Miles Anderson is telling me I should have a crack.'

I looked at Miles who was laughing to himself.

'Give me a minute,' Lindy said. 'I'll call you back.'

She was back on the line almost immediately. 'They want to see you tomorrow morning at eleven. They had no idea you could sing. I told them I hadn't either. David will be there and Gareth Valentine, the MD. Just ask for Anne McNulty, head of casting. You're a dark horse! That would be wonderful to get, wouldn't it? Best of luck, and call me and tell me how you get on.'

I sang those two songs all that night and woke up singing them on Wednesday morning.

David Leveaux, the director, is very trim and ultra-chic in his style, his black mop of hair contrasting with his pale complexion. 'Thanks Larry,' he said as I finished the second of my two songs, 'that was great. I'd like you to come back in a couple of days' time and perhaps do one of the other numbers. I'd like you to run through a couple of scenes, too. I'll get someone in to read with you. Thanks, lovely to meet you!'

A minute or two later, having given me a copy of the script, Anne McNulty saw me to the stairs. 'Well done, Larry, that was terrific. We'll call you and tell you what scenes David wants you to work on and we'll let Lindy know the time.'

That was pretty terrifying, I said to myself as I walked down Neal Street, *but I suppose I must be in with a chance.*

And indeed I was. I called Lindy as soon as I got home. 'They loved you,' she said. She told me that they had called her straight away with information on what they wanted me to look at.

The Friday audition was even more of a freak-out. This time Sam Mendes was there in his role of artistic director. It made me more nervous, but the scenes I had to do went well and the singing seemed to please all concerned. On the following Monday afternoon, Lindy called to say I'd got the job.

I was going to be playing the lead in a West End musical. The jump from singing 'Li'l Abner' on an army base in Germany during the summer of 1970 to playing Guido Contini at the Donmar in 1996 was too much to contemplate but, as my old nan used to quote to me: 'You make your bed and then you've got to lie in it.'

Lie in it I did, and in a funny way I'm still lying in it. I met Clare Burt; she was playing Guido's lover Carla and art imitated life. Fourteen years later we're still together, with our two glorious daughters Eloise and Eva-Mathilde. During the run of *Nine* I got another mating call. I had to follow it up. It was such a terrible long-drawn-out process to extricate myself from the life that Rachel and I had set up, but I had to do it. I had to move on again. I knew I wanted those children – and Clare wanted them too. I had to break away and start all over again.

44

King's Head to Denver

In reality my incursion into the world of musical theatre turned out to be a failure. It started and ended right there at the Donmar. Now I was back on a run of theatre work. It tends to go that way for me: producers and casting agents see you in a play and suddenly the television work seems to dry up and it's back on the boards again.

Nine had been such a nerve-wracking experience in every way that I'd sworn – not for the first time – to avoid the theatre at all costs, but temptation arrived in a brown manila envelope biked over from dear old Dan Crawford at the King's Head. He'd always talked about getting me to work there, and he had suddenly come up with a project. I have to say that, to my shame, I'd never even heard of *Inherit the Wind* – Spencer Tracy's film of the play had been done a bit too early for me – but it literally took a couple of minutes' reading to know I had to take Dan up on his offer. No money, no frills, but what a role!

I was a bit young to be playing the character based on the legendary lawyer Clarence Darrow, but this was a chance to say the words that had been lifted verbatim from the transcripts of the history-making 'Scopes' trial, where the state of Tennessee was prosecuting a young teacher for having taught his students Darwin's theory of evolution. The opportunity to play that great man of the law and speak the lines that his brilliant mind had created was just too much. I had to take it, regardless of the mortgage payments and the fact that I had a baby about to be born.

Playing that part was probably one of the most satisfying jobs I've ever had. I really became that old lawyer, night after night, taking the audience on an amazing journey, with everyone listening, completely carried along with the arguments. The play is to all intents and purposes impossible to stage in economic terms – there are too many characters – but somehow Dan had gathered together a company. A lot of supporting cast were commuting into London for nothing more than their travel costs, just to be in that play, at that theatre.

George Sewell and John Warnaby made the whole experience a complete and utter joy. I was thoroughly enjoying myself and, to cap the whole thing off, on a Sunday afternoon, just after our matinee performance, out popped the new girl in my life: Eloise Alexandra. My cup was overflowing.

It continued to do so, too. *Art* was *the* play in the West End that every actor wanted to be in. I hadn't even realised I was on the list: the actors changed every three months and I was asked to join cast number nine (that number again). A great deal of energy went into matching up each three-man team, and I found myself in the rehearsal room – once again up under the roof of the Old Vic – with Jack Dee and Tim Healy. Jack had done the play before; he'd enjoyed it so much he was back for a second helping. We all hit it off immediately and the three-week rehearsal period flew by.

The audiences were phenomenal. The play was already a huge hit and so everyone who bought a ticket knew that they were in for an extraordinary theatrical treat. Ninth company we might have been, but show after show we had the customers roaring with laughter. It was such a joy to perform. And the three months just wasn't long enough.

But early 2000 threw up another big surprise. My agent called me to tell me I had to go and meet Sir Peter Hall. He was casting a theatrical spectacular, a series of plays which would tell the story of the Trojan War, to be rehearsed and staged in Denver, Colorado, and then taken on a tour of Greece and then to England. As a final bonus it was due to be filmed for television in association with American Express.

I was in Peter's study, slightly bemused at being called in for a project like this.

'I haven't seen you on stage since the play you did with Vanessa,' he said.

'*A Madhouse in Goa*,' I smiled.

'Yes,' he said. His rather tired, sad eyes lit up momentarily.

'I've been talking to one or two people whose opinion I set great store by, and they've convinced me that you could be the man to play the three kings in *The Tantalus*.'

'So, erm yes. That's what my agent said. This would be to play Agamemnon, Menelaus and Priam? That's . . . er . . . quite a line-up.'

'Yes, it is, but I'm assured that you might well be the man for the job.'

We spent the next two hours working on the scripts. John Barton, the great Shakespearean scholar who had written the plays over twelve years, had managed to make them absolutely accessible to anyone who could read English: his style of a sort of modern-classical language was so easy to speak and instantly comprehensible. I had a great time going over the scenes, with Peter showing me how he wanted them performed, and finally he closed the text he was holding, looked at me and said: 'Well, I'm very interested. What do you think of it?'

'I think I can make a really good job of this, Peter, I find it so accessible, not at all what I expected.'

'Right,' he said, 'the next thing we need to do is get the plays delivered to you so that you can read them all. I shall get them sent to you later this afternoon. You read through them – take your time, but read them thoroughly, then call me back and tell me what you think.'

I read them all and finally got to bed about four the following morning.

'Peter, this is just wonderful material. As I said to you yesterday, I feel I can do you a very good job with this.'

'Larry, I'm delighted. The next thing we need to do is to meet with John. I'll try to arrange a time for this afternoon.'

John Barton is a tall, bearded, rangy and altogether gentle man. He is someone who, through his love of the classics, his knowledge of the theatre and his great affection for actors, has become a living legend in world theatre. His London home is a fabulous old apartment in the heart of Fitzrovia. I rode up to his floor in one of those old open-sided, steel-grilled elevators. Boy, this was going to be some second audition.

There I was with these two great gods of the theatre, working my way through a series of plays that they had been labouring over for years. It was a truly humbling experience, but the more they put me through my paces, the more I knew I was ready for the job.

They both directed me in scenes and they both read with me, on and on for another two-hour marathon. We were trying all different aspects of those three fabulous roles. One would have been a gift, but the complete trio? Manna from heaven. All three parts were so beautifully observed and so straightforward to read.

I'd sort of expected them to give me their verdict on the spot, but obviously they needed to discuss their feelings about me, so it wasn't until I finally turned in at about midnight that I faced the fact that I must have blown it. I did feel I'd given it my best shot, which was a small consolation – rather that than knowing you could have done it better.

'Larry, I'm sorry, I know what it's like for an actor in this situation. John is absolutely convinced you are the man for the job – a hundred per cent – but I, I just need to see you again.'

This message greeted me first thing the next morning, and by 2.30 p.m. I was back in Sir Peter's Chelsea town house, sitting down in his basement study. 'Larry, there's something I didn't get from the work we did together. Agamemnon is a great orator, a man who instinctively communicates directly face to face with his people. Reading the plays just didn't allow me to see that in you.'

'Peter,' I said, knowing that this was absolutely now hanging in the balance. It was make or break, and decisive action was the only way to walk out of the office with the job. 'I just played the Clarence Darrow character in *Inherit the Wind*. It's still fresh in my mind; let me give you the speech that for me sums up the soul of the man and what he stands for.'

And without taking a breath I switched into the rural Midwestern accent I'd used in the part and delivered the speech, just as I'd done it time after time at the King's Head.

He sat, the tips of his fingers pressed together, his eyes reading my face like a scanner piercing flesh.

I finished and he nodded. 'We're in business, Larry.'

It took a good six weeks to sort out all the formalities, to say nothing of making my own arrangements for Clare and Eloise – who by now was six months old – to leave London and set up home in Denver. George was going to take over the house. He and his friend Simon, who would eventually form the band Audiobullies, were beginning their careers in the club music business and we'd set up a recording studio downstairs for them to work in. So all was set for the coming ten months and I was going back to America. What a way to return it was, too!

The Denver Theater Center is really something that could only exist in America. Blessed with funds that stagger the mind, it produces world-class drama year-round, and draws in artists from all sectors of the performing arts, providing them with facilities and budgets undreamt of elsewhere. *Tantalus* was to be a 'magnum opus', not only for Sir Peter and John, but for an international team of designers, musicians, technicians – and an Anglo-American company of actors. It was such a project to be involved in, and everyone was made to feel a part of something extremely special.

Clare and Eloise followed me over a couple of weeks after I'd started and, within a few days of them settling in, we felt completely at home. The work was slowly progressing; we were reading through the plays and gradually formulating a plan of attack. We had six months to get the whole spectacle mounted. It was to have a running time of approximately ten hours, and the idea was that audiences would be able to see it in sections or in all-day marathons. There were voice classes, movement classes, sessions with musicians, and all of it was so exciting.

Peter would sit at the lectern placed in front of his chair and listen, listen, listen so intently to the rhythms each actor brought to the text. John meantime would work with us on interpretation and, as a lot of work needed to be done on the opening sequences involving the chorus, I spent hours with him working on the speeches my three characters would make.

I suddenly got the call to go through to Sir Peter. My big moment had arrived: Agamemnon's first big speech and I was ready for it. They even had the big gongs beating for my entrance. I gave it everything I had and, as I finished, the ultimate accolade: Sir Peter looked up from his lectern and gave me the thumbs-up. I was thrilled. I was well and truly on board.

As the assistant stage manager walked with me back along the corridor, she said, 'You must have got it right. I've never seen Sir Peter respond in that way!' What a buzz!

We finished the third week's rehearsals on a real high, and

on the Monday of week four we started work on the next of the plays in the series. We had a company meeting at five and the whole rehearsal room was alive with talk of how well it was all going.

'Larry, Sir Peter wants a quick word with you. Would you come through into the next room?' The stage manager led me through the melee of actors who were all in the middle of a game that we'd been playing – passing balls to one to another.

'Have a seat, Larry,' Sir Peter said.

I smiled and started to ask him how he was.

'Larry, I'm going to have to let you go. I'm afraid this is a mountain that you are not going to be able to climb.'

The world came crashing down around me.

I was sacked, dumped. My head caved in, every ounce of energy drained out of me.

There was no arguing or reasoning that he would allow. I walked back into the rehearsal room where the entire company were all standing, spread out across the vast space. The entire company, standing staring like totems. A ball rolled across the floor and bumped against the wall.

'I'm really sad to say this, I said, 'but I've been fired. It's been great, but that's it. I'm going home!'

45

Redemption

Getting the sack is such a bitter pill to swallow in any profession, but with the drama attached to getting an acting job, the amount of yourself you put into a role, the number of people you're up against, the level of competition, the fact that you know who else will be in the running for anything you're after, makes for a descent into the deepest, darkest depths of depression. This was the third time it had happened to me in ten years. That's not even including the time that I'd been replaced in a TV pilot episode for a series and everything I'd recorded had been re-shot with a different actor – and no one had had the decency to let me know; I only found out the night it was being transmitted! But hey, there's no business like show business.

This dismissal was a catastrophic blow there was no mistaking. My self-confidence was decimated. How the hell was I going to get over this?

Joyce Nettles, who had worked with Peter Hall for years casting countless productions for him, jumped into the breach. Luckily for me she had something coming up that I was the right casting for: an episode of *Midsomer Murders*. She phoned me as soon as she heard what had happened and, bless her, put me in touch with the director, David Tucker. He agreed with her that I would be right for the part and that was it: within a month of being washed up, high and dry on the rocky shores of Rejects Island, I was back into the swing of things. But that was a huge stroke of luck and it was a truly generous offer of help. And boy did I need that.

I got even luckier when an episode of *Kavanagh QC* with John Thaw came my way too. It was going to be directed by Jack Gold, who took pity on me, so the two jobs following on from the disaster not only helped to boost my confidence but also got the bank manager back on side. I have to say that I lived every day on the set of both programmes convinced that the producer would walk up and fire me, and nothing that anyone could do or say would relieve me of that fear. Slowly, though, I gathered strength and got back in charge.

One of the reasons I'd been so thrilled with the *Tantalus* job, besides the fact that it was such a prestigious thing to be involved in, was the fact that it meant I would be getting a chance to work in classical theatre. I'd done some Shakespeare back in my early days in Canada but, since then, all my theatre work had been contemporary. I knew that if I wanted to prove myself a serious actor, I would have to have a crack at 'The Bard' and John Barton's texts would be a perfect way to move into that world.

OK, so I'd worked at all the major theatres – other than the RSC and the National – and had done at least half a dozen shows in the West End, but the standards established in Britain are world class. Great works of the master play-wrights are focused on here, and that's why British actors are so widely acclaimed – and that one step up the ladder had been snatched away from me. I knew that sooner or later I was going to have to get back on the boards. It was great doing telly again, especially working on good material, but that for me is tightrope-walking with a safety net. I needed to get back on that wire with nothing underneath but a pool full of sharks. I needed to be performing live on the stage.

I was just on the verge of doing a play to be directed by Christopher Morahan. I was literally on the point of making the decision to agree to the terms of the contract over the phone with my agent when she said, 'Hang on, let me just hand you over to Michael. He's got the RSC on the line.'

'Hello Larry, Steven Pimlott is directing Sam West's *Hamlet* at the RSC. He wants to offer you the part of Claudius and Michael Attenborough is offering you a lovely role in the new David Edgar. What do you think?'

'What do I think? Are you kidding? Yes!'

So that was that, I was back in the saddle. The RSC. Just what I'd dreamt might happen. It was all back on course.

Claudius is a hell of a role and I was thrilled. The last time I'd been in the play, my first professional job, I was a minor player; now I was going to get to play the ultimate baddy at the RSC. I also had a part in David Edgar's new play, *The Prisoner's Dilemma*, as well, playing an American academic. To have two such great parts was an amazing stroke of luck. *Hamlet* was scheduled to open the 2001 season, and I was absolutely bound and determined to tear the part to pieces. I started to learn it immediately because I knew that I wanted to know it inside out and backwards before I set one foot on the floor of the rehearsal room. Nothing was going to stop me this time.

Steven Pimlott loved actors. One might hope that would be something you could say about all directors, but in fact unfortunately some of them don't. Working for Steven was a sheer delight; he made the whole rehearsal process a fascinating, all-inclusive joy of a journey. We spent the first week or so of our three months at the RSC's London base in Clapham talking, talking, talking. We explored every nook and cranny of the play. No stone was left unturned; every aspect of every line was opened up for general inspection. Everybody was expected to understand everything that was said, thought or done. There were no mysteries, no flimflam. It was everything I could have hoped for and more. It was a master class, overseen and encouraged by this loving gifted man.

Just as I'd planned, I never once walked on to that floor relying on the script. I knew it by heart from the very first time I gave Claudius's opening speech. It just made things so much easier for me. Armed to the teeth with the ammunition, all I had to do was concentrate on logistics: where I needed to be and in what state of mind. I loved every minute of every day.

I found a beautiful little converted barn to rent in the village of Snitterfield, about three or four miles from Stratford-upon-Avon: close enough for me to be able to walk to work but far enough to savour the joy of rural living. It was a fabulous home from home where Clare and Eloise could come and join me as and when it suited. Everything was just perfect.

Finally we were in the build-up to the opening of the new millennium season and *Hamlet* was the first to be launched into the public sphere. The whole place was jumping. The Memorial Theatre contained, as Steven put it, 'A bigger volume of air than the Royal Opera House.' It seats 1,300 people and on that Saturday night in April there was not one place unfilled. The audience that gather to see the first public performance of the season are the die-hards, the true aficionados.

The battlement scene opened the play and those 1,300 punters were locked into their seats, Steven's direction already drawing them deep into the soul of this incredible play. To the accompaniment of a great fanfare, I walked through the huge doors way at the back of the enormous stage, hand in hand with my glorious queen, my Gertrude, Marty Cruickshank, the pair of us immaculately dressed in beautifully hand-tailored business suits, every bit the modern monarchs. Lined across the stage in front of us, with their backs to the audience, were the members of the court, twenty-one besuited apparatchiks – courtiers and interns alike – evenly spaced a couple of metres apart right across that enormous stage.

At last the moment I'd been waiting for. I turned to my queen and, with a fond smile, let go of her hand and took my designated two paces forward.

> 'Though yet of Hamlet our dear brother's death
> The memory be green; and that it us befitted
> To bear our hearts in grief, and our whole kingdom
> To be contracted in one brow of woe . . .'

And that was it. Nothing more was coming. I'd dried absolutely stone dead.

Hamlet, opening play of the season, year 2001. It was the first public performance at Stratford-upon-Avon Festival Theatre. It was my first big Shakespearean role. I'm playing Claudius and I'm supposed at this moment to be giving my opening placatory speech to the people of Denmark.

But here I am, twenty-five years in the business, looking at my court of twenty-one actors, standing with their backs to the audience across that enormous stage, every single one of them desperately trying to think my words into my head for me, focusing, willing me to get it. But nothing is coming out. I'm frozen.

And the clock ticks.

I look to my right, to my queen, my Gertrude, Marty Cruickshank, an actress with a lifetime of theatre under her belt. She smiles a warm and encouraging smile. Instinctively she knows something is up, and she's right on the money.

Something is seriously up. My mind has gone into meltdown. My understudy Robert Jezek walks towards me and starts to speak the lines that he and I know so well. He's been shadowing me for thirteen weeks now and, as his contract demands, he is ready to take over the role at the drop of a hat, or in this case the death of an actor.

That is what is happening here. I am dying in front of the 1,300 paying customers who fill this massive auditorium, I'm dying in front of my friends and family. There's not an empty seat in the place and I'm dying.

And the clock is ticking.

My life is flashing across the screen of my mind. What on earth am I doing here? Whatever prompted me to break away from the sad existence with my crazy dad in that mud-pie island of a new town in the middle of Essex farmland? Please! Even Harlow would be better than the place I am in right now.

And my understudy may as well be speaking Chinese. I can't understand a word he's saying. The body language of my courtiers – still with their backs to the audience but now picking up with me the frisson of energy from the audience who are starting to suspect that this might not be part of the show – is piling on the pressure.

And the clock is ticking.

I look down. Big mistake. The stage starts to race away, down and down and down and I am falling after it. What in the name of fuck can I do? Nothing. There is nothing there. Why am I here? Why did I want to do this? What on earth ever made me think I could bluff my way into the theatre? How had I got away with it for this long? Now I was paying the price. I was being exposed as a fraud.

And the clock is ticking.

My heart is pounding and my throat is tightening and I walk, I pace across the stage to my left and back to my right as if some movement might dislodge something, anything. Please help me, get me out of here, away anywhere. I just shouldn't be here, I should have realised that this was something that you don't dare yourself into.

And the clock is ticking.

The panic, the panic, the panic is taking me over; there is no getting out of this. The shame, the disgrace, the humiliation! Bang, bang, bang my brain is pounding in my skull. That's what it is, that's what this is all about, that's what's killing you. Peter Hall has finally got you. It's him . . . it's him . . . it's him . . . he cut your balls off and now he's got you . . . !

And the clock is ticking.

And I realise I've walked down stage right. I'm all alone in that semi-lit corner – as far away from the stage manager with the script, all ready to prompt me, as I could possibly be, because instinctively I have realised deep down in my subconscious that this is far more than just forgetting my lines, and that having them read to me will only confuse things more. I'm lost, but now I know what is wrong – now I know that getting fired by Peter Hall in Denver is what this is all about.

And the clock ticks.

This problem I am facing is all about me but that isn't what I'm here for, I am here to tell a story.

You are here because Steven Pimlott, that wonderful, generous man, has given you the chance to show you can do this and, more importantly, so that you can prove to yourself that you can do this. So you'd better get out there and give everyone back their show.

I walked back across that stage to the twenty-one actors now all standing like Easter Island monoliths with jaws dropped and eyes wide open in absolute disbelief at what they are witnessing.

And the clock ticked.

And Marty, my Gertrude, stretched out her hand and, with a tiny inclination of her head, she smiled that regal smile of hers, as if welcoming me back to the earth, to the world, to our kingdom. I took her hand and looked out to those 1,300 theatregoers and carried on with my speech.

And the clock stopped.

Meanwhile, about eighty-five feet away, up in the front row of the royal circle, George, my son, realised that although he'd just aged thirty years and probably sprouted his first grey hairs, he had made the right decision not to dive off the balcony to create a diversion.

Backstage I stood at the fountain, pouring cup after cup of ice cold water on to the molten core of my innards. This had been just the first of Claudius's many scenes, so I had to try and get back some element of mental tranquillity. There were still three hours to go and I'd already been floored in the first round.

As my fellow actors passed me they petted and stroked me and did their best to calm and soothe me and make it all better. The sense of support that this amazing company gave me was unforgettable.

Hattie Morahan, fresh from drama school, the youngest member of the company, stood and stroked my back.

'You know,' I said, 'as I finally gave the speech I was convinced I was playing Claudius as Minnie Mouse.'

'No, not at all,' she said. 'You came back on like a raging bull.'

God, I thought, where had I been?

But their trust and confidence helped me through. I went on and gave a fault-free performance that night.

But then of course I'd have to do it again the next night and the next; indeed I was contracted to play in *Hamlet* for fifteen months.

Pimlott – God bless him, wherever he is – was backstage seconds after I got to my dressing room. 'Well,' he said, 'that was drama. I'm thinking of keeping it in.'

Fortunately he didn't, but he did restage the scene, and from the following night onward the courtiers still stood in a line right across the stage, but now they faced out and Claudius and Gertrude passed between them and stood right on the apron, right on the very lip, as close as possible to the audience, with the courtiers behind them.

'I'm going to put the house lights on so you will be able to see every single person in the auditorium,' Steven told me, 'and when you speak that speech, I'm going to be out there amongst them, and if I don't believe that you are talking to every single one of us, I'm going to be heckling you!'

That's how we did that scene night after night, and my confidence grew and grew, just as the wonderful man knew it would.

46

Mr P of Hampstead

Michael Raeburn, my Zimbabwean film-maker friend, invited me to a dinner party. He was living in Paris with Heidi Draper, an American documentary maker. They were sharing her fabulous boat moored right at the foot of the Eiffel Tower. It's one of those beautiful river freighters you see as you drift along the Seine on a *bateau mouche* and you think to yourself: *Fancy living there!* Right in the heart of the world's most beautiful city, where could you find a better place to live in this, 'the city of light'? Heidi had made her home there and so, for quite a few years, did Michael.

The party was one of their periodic shindigs. There was no particular reason or occasion; it was just an excuse to get a bunch of people together and have some fun. That was the way Heidi and indeed Michael liked to do things, and between them they knew a lot of people. Heidi had left the States years before and had raised her two children in Paris. She'd started out married to their father but when things took a turn for the worse between them she decided to stay on and switch from being a corporate wife to living a more bohemian 'American in Paris' existence. The boat was her fantasy come to reality. She was living the dream, and into the dream walked Mr Raeburn.

Michael had come to Paris in the late 1960s to study film. He was an inherent, instinctive rebel. He'd been kicked out of what was then known as Southern Rhodesia by the Smith regime and remained a thorn in the side of the old British colony's administration. He'd produced a film that made no bones about the way he felt regarding the way his country was being run, and finished up *persona non grata*. By the time I got to know him in about 1981 or so, he had established himself as a sort of gypsy film-maker. He wrote scripts, raised the money and produced and directed films that touched on things that he felt needed to be understood. A truly heroic character, he was unfazed by any threat of coercion and harassment; he would just laugh and make the film, no matter what the danger.

He and Heidi made a great couple: she had an easy-going but canny and perceptive old East Coast American style, coupled with *Vogue* model looks; and Michael was tall and rather shambolic in a very Oxbridge, tweedy, English sort of way. They were great fun to be around and they lived a wonderfully cosmopolitan life. They were on a constant round of cinema- and theatre-going, dining out with friends from all corners of the globe on their way through the city and really enjoying everything in the way of the arts that Paris had to offer.

I was down in Normandy when Michael phoned me one afternoon. 'Larry, any chance you can come up to Paris tomorrow night? We're having a few people over for dinner, be lovely if you could join us.'

I'd been at the house for a few days on my own: it was during the first few months of living with Clare and on the rare occasions that I actually went to Normandy, it was always by myself, so an invitation to the big city was extremely welcome.

There were about twenty people at the boat, a real mix of Michael and Heidi's friends, and I found myself seated next to the wife of a world-famous physician who'd been friends with Michael for years. She was French, and by profession she was a psychiatrist. She and her husband were in Paris for a few days whilst he attended some kind of symposium or seminar and she visited friends and family.

Our conversation ranged over all sorts of topics; she was a fascinating woman who'd managed to ensure that her professional life was never eclipsed by her husband's. They had a family back in the USA, where they both currently worked, and each of them were enjoying the fruits of their equally successful careers.

I told her about my experiences with my first 'shrink', Mr P of Kensington, and explained to her that I was considering going into analysis again. My break-up with Rachel and the new relationship with Clare were causing me a lot of sleepless nights. I was riddled with guilt for what I'd done to Rachel and desperate to be absolutely sure that jumping ship yet again had been the right thing to do.

I kept asking her if this line of conversation wasn't becoming a busman's holiday, but she assured me it wasn't and we got into a really deep discussion about everything that was bothering me.

When the party gradually started to wind up and she and her husband were getting ready to go, she said, 'If you decide to go and see someone again, get Michael to give you my number. I can put you in touch with a lady in London who may well be able to help you find the right person.' We said our goodbyes and that was that.

I think it must have been about a year later that I made the call. I only managed to leave a message on her New York number, but in a day or two she called me back and gave me a number in London. She told me to call the number and mention her name.

The lady I went to meet – let's call her Mrs S – was beautiful and elegant. I would imagine she was perhaps Swiss or Austrian; she spoke exquisite English but chose not to lose her native accent in any way. She was, I would say, in her mid- to late sixties, and within a few minutes of sitting down in her beautifully appointed office she had me entranced.

I told her all about myself, everything she needed to know – my whole life parcelled up and labelled in about an hour and a half. She had lovely wavy, darkly grey hair, and was superbly dressed in a blue-grey cotton blouse and skirt. *Another mother figure to take care of me*, I thought.

'Well Larry,' she smiled. 'You would probably like me to take you on, wouldn't you? But' – she didn't let me answer – 'I don't actually do that. What I do is put people together. Finding an analyst that suits is not so straightforward. I will try and find the right person for you. Now, I don't think it's going to be a woman, do you?'

'No,' I said as I shook my head.

'No,' she agreed. 'Because you would, I'm sure, be inclined to fall in love with her – so no, that wouldn't do. And it's not going to be a younger man, is it? That would never work for you, would it?'

We both knew that that was right.

'I think that I might have the right person for you. It's a question of geography to begin with. Where in London do you live?'

'I'm in the north,' I said. 'Crouch End.'

She nodded. 'Good, that might work out. And what about the financial side?' she went on. 'These things are not cheap; you should expect to pay about forty pounds per hour. Is that feasible?'

I was in the cast of *Art* at the time, so it wasn't a problem. 'As a matter of fact,' I rather gleefully pointed out, 'I'm doing a play in the West End at the moment and it's very well paid, so not only do I have a fixed schedule, which will mean that I am actually in London for the next three months, but it also means that I can afford it.'

Obviously the more regularly one could attend, the faster the progress. So there was I, with the time and the money, and after my hour and half session with Mrs S I was itching to get started.

It took about ten days or so for her to get back to me. 'Larry, the person I thought would be right for you to meet has some space available. Let me give you his name and telephone number . . .'

It was another Mr P, this time in the north of London. It was an easy drive from home and not difficult from the West End.

'You phone him and arrange to go and meet him. If it works out, then very good, but if for any reason you have any misgivings, you phone me, not him. I will deal with any problems.'

A couple of days later I arrived at the designated location, a large red-brick house with a whole series of numbered buzzers to the side of the massive old black-painted front door. A rather muffled Scottish voice bade me come in and I took a seat in the waiting room.

I could see a staircase in the hallway through the open door and a man walked down the stairs. 'Mr Lamb,' he greeted me. I smiled and stood up. 'Mr P, good afternoon.' I stuck out my hand, which he rather reluctantly shook, firmly enough but with no real enthusiasm. 'Would you like to follow me upstairs?'

This was an altogether different type of character to his southwest London counterpart. He was very definitely Scottish, about medium height, over sixty, very fit and neatly dressed in a well-pressed open-neck shirt, a pullover and well-ironed slacks: altogether neat and trim. But as they would say up where he hailed from, 'very dour'.

We walked up a couple of flights of stairs and then down a longish corridor with two or three doors opening off it, and finally through his door and into a very modest study. There were no real adornments, just a desk, a big winged leather armchair in one corner and, believe it or not, a couch. He offered me a seat and sat himself down behind the desk.

'One thing I need to tell you, Mr Lamb.'

'Call me Larry, please!'

'Let's just leave it at Mr Lamb for the moment, shall we? An hour in terms of analysis is fifty minutes, just so you know.'

He was so what I didn't want. He had the same sort of demeanour that my grammar school teachers had specialised in: cold and very impersonal. This was already looking like a big mistake.

'So what do you want to do?' he asked, not even the slightest sign of any warmth or humour shining through the steely eyes set in his tough-looking face.

'Well,' I said, 'I want to try and sort myself out. I spent several years in analysis before and I'm ready to go on. I feel I'm at the point where I need to go deeper. I'm going through an extremely stressful emotional upheaval and I want to talk to someone about it.'

'OK, well off you go then.'

About forty-nine minutes later, as the big hand just about struck fifty minutes, I stopped for breath. He rearranged himself in his chair and said, 'So what do you want to do next?'

'Well, I really want to explore everything that I'm feeling. I really need to get going on this.'

'Right.' He picked up a diary from his desk and opened it up. 'What I suggest you do is come back at the same time next week and we'll take it from there.'

I walked back down the stairs with one thought on my mind. *Phone Mrs S and get her to find me someone else. This guy has had a quadruple humour bypass.*

But I didn't phone her, I don't know why. I thought of little else for the whole week but, even on the eve of the second visit, I still didn't make that call.

I found myself back there in the same waiting room, each time with people desperately trying not to make eye contact, trying to look as if they were anywhere but outside a shrink's office. I caught the eye of a young teenage boy, the shame of the whole experience was oozing from his poor sad pores, and I tried as best I could to give him a friendly smile.

'Would you like to follow me upstairs, Mr Lamb?' Mr P was suddenly there.

Not one additional ounce of charm, no glimmer of a smile; he was as cold and disinterested as a jailer. I followed him up those stairs thinking to myself, *Why didn't I phone her? Why have I set myself up with this again? I didn't call; I'm so stupid.*

But within ten minutes of sitting back down in that chair, I knew that saintly woman, Mrs S, had got it right. Dead right. She couldn't have possibly got it more right.

This was exactly what I needed: a tough, no-nonsense, no- flimflam man; no chit-chatty 'blokes in it together' relationship here. This man sat and he listened – to whatever I said. If you charge an actor forty quid to talk to you, you'd better believe he's going to get his money's worth. Boy did I talk, and once again, as the clock hit ten minutes to the hour, the session was drawn to a close and arrangements for the following day were made. I was on my way. I had exactly the person I needed; it all fitted like the finest bespoke suit.

Three months those visits went on for: three glorious months, five days a week and more than sixty sessions in total. On and on we went, deeper and deeper. I could talk and talk about whatever was bothering me and I would just follow on each day from wherever I'd left it the day before. I'd relate dreams I'd had overnight and explain what I was feeling about how my life was appearing that day. He'd just move his head slightly and shift in his seat. 'What was that you just said?' or,

'Just go back and tell me what you meant by that' and 'Just explain what you think you mean by that?'

That's how we went on, day after day, week after week. I remember spending days going into the whole relationship with my father, sometimes the emotion really affecting me physically, as though I was actually shaking him out of me and off me. 'You know, Mr P,' I said towards the end of a particularly powerful session on Ron, 'I'm not quite sure whether this is me talking or my father talking through me. It's almost like he's right there inside me, as if he's taken me over.'

He looked deep into my eyes and gave the slightest movement of his head and said, 'Mmmm,' not questioning, not asserting anything, not agreeing, just registering exactly what I'd said and encouraging me to carry on thinking and carry on probing.

Just as Mr P of Kensington had had a huge effect on me each time I left his sessions, the same thing happened every time I ran down the steps outside the big front door of Mr P's of Hampstead. I smiled, and I knew I'd cleared out another corner of my big untidy cupboards. Every time the same.

And then *Art* came to an end, and with it the regular job with the regular money. I returned to being an actor for hire, which meant I couldn't be sure of the times I could come, and £200 a week had to be thought about carefully, no matter how worthwhile it was.

I suggested dropping down to once a week, but we compromised at two. 'I don't think once a week is so interesting to me,' he'd smiled.

We did twice a week for some time and finally I told him, 'I'm ready to go now. I came to move on to the next level and I'm there.'

He stood up, put out his hand and said, 'Well, off you go, Larry.'

And that was it. I walked out and into a new stage of my life, one that had clicked into gear at that dinner table on that beautiful *péniche* at the foot of the Eiffel Tower.

Thanks to that incredible man Mr P. I now understood a whole lot more about me – and the only person who had taught me was myself. It was such an extraordinary feeling. I had an overall sense of being cleansed, unburdened, released.

47

Onstage with an Icon

The RSC contract finished in spring 2002 and it seemed I'd never work again. I went for an audition at the BBC to be in *Spooks*. Everything went well; the producer and the director seemed to really like me. But then I got a call from my agent.

'Larry, there seems to be a bit of a problem. The producers want to book you, but there's someone blocking it.'

When he told me the name I said, 'I had a bit of a run-in with him years ago on another programme when he was an associate producer on it, I think.'

'Well, he's now very influential at the BBC with commissions from outside contractors, and he's told the producers of *Spooks* that they can't give you the job. He told them he wouldn't hire you if you were the last actor alive – or words to that effect.'

I took a very deep breath; this was not a situation that any actor wants to find himself in – work is scarce enough. That was a real blow.

'Erm, well, what do we do then?' I asked.

'Well, the producers are going to push as hard as they can, but there's not much they can do as he has to OK all casting. I can't really see any way around it. What happened? Did you hit him or something?'

'No, not at all. He was throwing his weight about and being particularly officious and I called him on it. He was treating the actors with real contempt; we had to go up to Scotland for a week and he was making a big thing about how all the actors had to fly on one of the new budget airlines and how he wouldn't be doing that himself, he'd be flying British Airways. I questioned his attitude and he didn't like it.'

'Well, he obviously has a long memory.'

'Yes, I guess he does.'

Apparently he finally moved on from that position and the producers came back and hired me to play another character in an episode from one of the later series, but even then my seemingly 'difficult' status was still registering somewhere. It made it hard for them to hire me, but I did a good job for them and my agent called me to say that the production company and the Beeb were delighted with the performance I'd turned in. Having gone out on a limb to use me, they felt entirely vindicated. What a bloody relief for me and my agent.

I found out that he had quite a lengthy 'blacklist', and evidently I was by no means an exception. He was someone who held grudges.

'Sean Holmes wants to talk to you about playing one of the brothers in *The Price*, the Arthur Miller play, do you know it?' My agent again. 'They're doing it at the Tricycle Theatre. Warren Mitchell is the name and Sean wants you to read it and meet him tomorrow. He said to look at both the brothers.'

I opened the script and read the stage directions. Miller's tone, even in the description of the set, was enough. I knew immediately I had to do this play. Sean Holmes had been one of the young up-and-coming trainee directors working at the RSC during my time there, and although I'd not worked with him, his name had come up several times in conversations amongst actors.

I was sitting across a desk from him the next morning. He's about six feet tall, dark complexion, extremely well educated and very definitely from a working-class background – and he doesn't try to hide it. I liked him immediately.

The whole rigmarole of meeting a director to talk about a job is so complicated. Both of you are sizing each other up, but of course the director holds the trump card: he's buying and you're selling.

'What do you think of it, Larry?'

'I absolutely love it,' I said. 'And I'm such a bloody philistine, I'd never even heard of it, let alone seen it before.'

'Well, you're not unique in that. It's not one that's done that often. What do you think about the brothers?'

Now this was the point I'd been very wary of right from the moment my agent had mentioned that he wanted me to look at both of the brothers. Sure enough, age-wise I was right for both of them, but the complications started to ring alarm bells. What if he, as the director, had already decided what role he was thinking of for me and I gave a different answer? It was very tricky; it all hung in the balance. How loaded was the question? This felt like the point of no return.

'Well . . .' I took a breath and decided to tell him exactly what I'd come to think about it overnight.

'You see, Sean, in life I am one of two brothers and, in my life, my role is that of Walter, the doctor. My brother Wesley is very definitely Victor the policeman. Now obviously I could play either of them, but I think that it would be far more interesting for me – and I think I can honestly say better for you – if I were to play my brother in this. I feel instinctively drawn to the character of Victor.'

Sean smiled and nodded, that's all; just smiled and nodded and the next day he hired me to play Victor.

Warren Mitchell is an icon. His Alf Garnett is one of the great characters in the pantheon of British comedy. And although I didn't know it when I met him at the rehearsal room upstairs at the Tricycle in Kilburn High Street, we were starting out on an adventure that would run on and off for the next two and half years. And indeed we formed a friendship that led to me becoming a sort of extra son to him – or perhaps a younger brother to him and Connie, his glorious wife. Whatever, I'm an associate member of the Mitchell Clan – the Highgate branch, that is; the Walford Mitchells in my life are another story!

Des McAleer played Walter brilliantly and Siân Thomas was breathtaking as Esther, Victor's long-suffering but adoring wife. Day by day this incredible play was coming together, and we all knew we were involved in something really special. Sean was proving every bit as great a director as we'd hoped.

We opened to amazing notices and played to full houses for our whole run; it was a resounding hit. After a tense period of waiting during the invasion of Iraq, when there was great fear of London coming under sustained terrorist attack and a lot of theatrical activity went on hold, we finally opened at the Apollo. My second time there on Shaftesbury Avenue. We played for about four months and Warren won the Olivier Award for Best Actor.

So well had the play done, in fact, that we took it out on a ten-week tour. Audiences in Oxford, Cambridge, Malvern, Bradford and Edinburgh absolutely loved it too. It was a total triumph.

Warren was in his element playing an ancient furniture dealer. 'The part is written for an eighty-nine-year-old actor,' he chuckled. 'I'm too young!'

We got into a real state one evening. At a certain point I had to sit on one of the old dining-room chairs he'd come to bid on. This was the real item sought out by the art department; it was in actual fact riddled with woodworm holes. On this particular night it broke, spectacularly – every leg crumbled and the whole upper part, with me on it, dropped about eight inches. The audience erupted in spontaneous laughter and applause; they were obviously convinced it was part of the show.

'I'll have to knock a few dollars off the price,' Warren ad-libbed, and the audience roared again; they were beside themselves.

I started laughing and completely forgot my lines. Warren couldn't remember his either and the pair of us realised we'd lost it altogether; neither of us could think of how to get out of the jam.

'I think that might be my brother,' I said as I exited through the door. I ran round to the stage manager at the prompt corner. 'For fuck's sake give me a line – we're both completely lost!'

I walked back on and managed to get something out and somehow or other we got on track again. Funny, but really rather terrifying, I'd got lost onstage with an icon.

48

Family Man

We had to make a move; Eloise was about three and school was starting to be discussed. She was enrolled in her first nice little, grossly overpriced, hip neighbourhood nursery and we were already being inculcated into the one thing we both instinctively knew we had to avoid, the 'parent' trip, London-style. We just weren't up for it, either of us, but the more laid-back style of Normandy was a possibility. The house in France had no mortgage and it was just sitting there. Clare and Eloise had got to know it a little already, and anyone who came to spend time there always fell in love with it, so we thought: *OK, let's do it, let's just pack up and go.*

I really do believe that that time in France was the making of Clare and the girls – both on their own and with me too as a complete family unit. It let us become a family because all the distractions, deflections and barriers that a modern urban lifestyle throws in your way are reduced to a bare minimum, and so life becomes much more simple and uncomplicated.

Obviously it was made more difficult by my working situation with television and theatre commitments. I was commuting between Normandy – where the family actually lived, with all the school and babyminders, music lessons and horse riding, sleepovers and school fetes that even rural life involved – and London to earn a living. But in spite of the time I had to spend away, our time in France made me feel a part of a family. We grew up together and finally I felt bonded into that unit too. I have experienced it. I have been a part of its ups and downs and have learned what it is really like.

Patrick, my mate from a village outside Livarot, drove over to us in a hired van. He and I loaded it with all our worldlies and, using an ingenious system I engineered, we tied all those endless plastic and steel children's little slides and bikes inside six of those big bags that they bring the sand in, the half-tonners, and we roped them all down on to the roof rack of my beloved old Mercedes station wagon. Somehow we managed to accommodate the lot.

And so with Eloise, Clare and myself squeezed into the merc and with Patrick in the van, over we went on the ferry to Caen.

When we arrived, we unloaded it all and just got on with it. We made a life in Normandy.

It was certainly new. The relationships that Rachel and I had shared with the locals couldn't be replicated and now they were history. My old friends in France had become mystified by the fact that Rachel no longer came with me to the house. After three years of making excuses, I finally let them know that we'd split up and that there was someone new in my life. 'It was complicated,' I explained to them, picking my way through the unfamiliar French vocabulary of relationship breakdowns. 'You see, we shared the costs of our life between us, depending on who was working at the time. Over a period of several years, the balance had switched and I was in her debt, and six months after we had broken up, I'd been to see her to talk things through and she'd said to me, "You know Larry, when you got that job on *Peak Practice* and all that money, I knew then that I should have insisted we spend six months apart to see whether the relationship was bigger than the money, but I wasn't brave enough."'

They took it as I'd known they would: very seriously. They were sad that it had broken down and I think they found it hard to accept that there was a new woman in my life and that

Rachel would no longer be a part of theirs. But they did their best to accept Clare. For them, though, life had changed and it has never really been the same. Albert stopped dairying and so Noel stopped milking; and they all stopped making hay.

Clare is far too much an individual to even contemplate the possibility of taking someone else's place. People were hospitable and invited us to dinner, but it just didn't work. The relationship they'd shared with Rachel was something special and it was just too sad to even attempt replacing it, so we sort of kept ourselves to ourselves.

School was the first thing to sort out once we had settled into the house. Eloise was already three and they like to start them young over there. I took her into the little village school and spoke to the headmistress, Madame Maupas.

She didn't speak a word of English, so on I ploughed and explained that both Clare and I were actors and wherever the child was educated we would be separated at certain times, so, as I'd been involved in the place for years, we'd decided that a French education was perhaps the way to proceed. She smiled, stroked Eloise's head, and the next morning Eloise started school. Just like that, in at the deep end, the only English kid in the school.

I took her. Clare was beside herself; she knew if Eloise changed her mind she wouldn't be able to deal with it. We were all so nervous. But Eloise just took to it like a duck to water and within two years was top of her class in French. We'd become a little immigrant family in rural Normandy.

49

Gavin and Stacey

I remember back in the early nineties making *Get Back*, the comedy series Marks and Gran wrote and produced for the BBC. Jane Booker, who was playing the wife of my character, was telling me about her husband having got a small part in 'some funny little film – no money, but it's a good script and he's enjoying it.'

The 'funny little film' turned out to be *Four Weddings and a Funeral* and Jane's real-life husband was the brilliant actor James Fleet – who was brilliant before the film but only noticed to be so as a result of it. It's certainly the way it goes: now and then you get a lucky break.

There will be people around now who will remember me saying that I was working on 'this little comedy series; not much money but it's a good script and I'm enjoying it.' Who would have thought that within a couple of years, that 'little comedy series' would etch its name on the TV hall of fame in letters 200 feet high, having made itself a part of the lives of literally millions of people from every walk of life, in every corner of Britain. It was a joy to be a part of it. It was a glorious accolade, a fabulous 'gong' to pin to your chest, particularly as you join the senior set and start to settle down to play dads, uncles, bosses, and finally old men.

The summer of 2006 had been a good one for me. Sam Shepard's play *Fool for Love* with Juliette Lewis and Martin Henderson was at the Apollo Theatre on Shaftesbury Avenue and it was my third successful time in that theatre. We were due to close and I was just beginning to get the 'I'm never going to work again' blues, something actors always suffer from when a contract draws near to its end. Juliette and Martin were heading off to other projects and Joe Duttine, the fourth member of the cast, had got a leading role in a new TV series. So when Teresa Hickey, my agent, rang to tell me about an audition for a new comedy series, it at least flagged up a tiny island of hope out in the sea of despondency.

'They want you to go in and read on camera,' she said. 'We'll get a copy of the script delivered to the stage door.'

In fact the following evening an envelope containing two scripts was waiting for me. I ran up to the dressing room and ripped open the envelope immediately. On the front of the A4 document, it read:

Gavin and Stacey
Episodes One and Two
by James Cordon and Ruth Jones

Neither name meant anything to me, but it was being cast by Toby Whale so I knew it had – at the very least – to be something special.

Toby had put in a note that read: 'Take a look at the part of Mick, Gavin's dad', and he listed the scenes they wanted me to read with them. Immediately panic started to set in. Reading in front of a camera in a room full of strangers. How many jobs had I lost when doing just that? My career was littered with the spaces they'd left. Auditions are just not my thing, and as for filmed auditions, I'd rather have my eyes pierced.

However, it was all fixed up for a meeting at Spotlight's offices for eleven thirty the following morning, and boy did I need a TV series. It was years since I'd had one. It was a comedy series at that. I was so desperate to get the part of Mick; so sick with fear at the thought of the trial I had to go through. I knew that any actor in the world would kill for a sniff of an audition for something like this.

I didn't sleep a wink that night.

I sat in the waiting room and ran through the scenes for the ninetieth time. I was Mick, at least a large part of me is Mick: my nicer side, my mum's side, my feminine side.

I'd have to somehow convey that to whoever I would be meeting, though, and all I had to reassure me was that at least Toby Whale thought that I was right for the part. But then of course Toby would think other people were right for the part too. My poor mind raced until I found myself in the room saying hello to Chris Gernon, the director, Ted Dowd, the producer, and Ruth Jones, one of the writers.

Chris Gernon had spent years working her way up the chain of command in television and proved her skill in comedy direction countless times. She is a real team player in a business where too often directors forget how important that can be. The power the director is entrusted with can prove intoxicating. It's their interpretation of what is on the page that finally shows in millions of living rooms, and Ruth and James knew that whoever was going to handle the birth of their baby had to be someone they could both become at one with. It was a huge demand to make of someone but the powerful, loving, trusting and human qualities that Chrissie overflows with made her the obvious choice. A keystone was laid.

There was lots of chat about *Fool for Love* and lots more chat about the scripts and how Alison Steadman was going to be playing Pam. Alison was another keystone of *Gavin and Stacey*; she, Ruth and James had bonded during their time together on *My Fat Friends* and so once the project started to materialise Pam began to come alive along with Nessa and Smithy. They told me how they all thought I'd be perfect for

Mick. I couldn't help but wish that if they really thought I'd be perfect, couldn't they just give me the job?

'Would you mind reading a bit?' Ruth asked. 'And if it's all right with you, Ted Dowd, our producer is going to put it on camera so James can have a look at it in New York. He's about to finish *History Boys* and won't be back for a couple of weeks.'

'No, of course not.' I smiled sweetly through my pain. 'Let's do it.'

And so do it we did. I seemed to be getting it right, though comedy is so hard to judge. I personally would rather make them cry than laugh, but by the time I said my goodbyes and Toby had walked me, shaken and empty, to the top of the stairs, reassuring me I'd done really well, I was sure I'd blown it.

And I was right. I had. But not completely. I was straight on the phone to Teresa.

'It'll be the director who's not convinced,' I told her. 'I'm sure the other two were sold on me, but there was something that didn't quite click with Chris Gernon.'

'You're right on one hand,' she said that evening, 'the director was the problem, but you haven't completely blown it, they want you to go back again and read with Alison.'

Oh fuck! I've got to go through the whole thing again! I thought as I looked at myself in the mirror, a mad little affectation of mine: talking myself through things with myself, so to speak.

'Show me how you played Mick. Read me that first scene and I'll be Pam.' Clare, my other half, had decided to get involved. She'd read the scripts and realised straight away that this was gold dust.

'No wonder they didn't like you,' she said when we'd read the scene. 'You don't get it, do you?'

'Of course I get it. What do you mean I don't get it?'

'So tell me what's funny then . . . hmm?'

'It's you know, it's what young people laugh at. You know . . .'

'Yes and you don't get it. Just like you don't get *Friends*.'

'All right then, so how should I play it?'

'Don't try to be funny. Make him find everything Pam does and says funny and make it look as if they have a lot of great sex.'

'But this is a reading. How the fuck am I supposed to do that?' I laughed out loud.

And Clare smiled and said, 'Just like that.'

So we worked on the scenes and one by one she got me to let the Mick side of me come through.

Poor old Alison. How must she have been feeling? How embarrassing for her. We'd worked together years before on a film for television called *The Wimbledon Poisoner*, and we were also connected through a mutual friend, Stephen Bill. In fact, by sheer coincidence I was going to be seeing Ali very soon anyway. She was coming to France to visit Stephen and I'd invited them all to come for dinner. And now I had to audition for a part with her in a show she was already cast in. There was plenty of potential embarrassment all round.

But the next day we read together back at Spotlight and Ted filmed, Ruth laughed, Chris directed and I got the job.

I didn't know that of course when I walked down those stairs again. They still had some other poor soul to run through the wringer and, as the choice had to be unanimous, with James still over in the Big Apple, D-Day wasn't going to come at all quickly.

By now I was back in France. My agent had told me there would be no decision until the following day. Alison and her other half, Michael Elwyn, were coming with Stephen and his family for dinner that night. I was skint and couldn't quite figure out how to budget the meal: splash or simple? Employed or unemployed? I decided to throw caution to the wind and go for splash. I was cooking ribs of beef, grilled over oak cinders, Norman-style.

It was a good decision. An hour before they arrived, Teresa called and told me I'd got the job.

What a relief for everybody, Alison especially. She told me how embarrassed she'd been and had literally been forced into doing the auditions. It turned out she'd worked with the other actor as well. What an evening we had. I even managed to get Clare to play the piano – which was no mean feat – and we all sang and laughed and drank the night away.

But I still had to get that character spot on camera. I had to put my money where my mouth was! A couple of weeks later I found myself sitting next to Alison with a crowd of strangers around a table set with scripts, pencils and bottles of water, preparing for the dreaded read-through routine again.

'I'm Larry Lamb and I'm reading Mick,' I said when it was my turn to introduce myself. I didn't want to tempt providence, I still wasn't sure I could do it, hence the subtle use of the word 'reading' where the other cast members said 'playing'. After a few disappointments in the past, I was still very wary about making it through. I still lacked the confidence that I could pull off comedy on film. The pressure was really on. All the heads of the various departments that would make the programme happen were there: representatives from the upper echelons of the BBC who were backing the enterprise, and the executive producers from Baby Cow who were producing the show; the room was literally packed to the rafters. There was so much riding on this. I felt that fear ball forming again deep down below, starting to work its way right through me up into my lungs and heart, gripping at my throat, taking me over from the inside out, daring me to overcome it.

And so we started. And gradually, gradually, giggle by giggle, titter by titter, the phenomenon that millions of people now hold so close to their hearts started to come off the page and into the ether and my fears started to ebb away. Mick came alive and I became Mick and Mick became me.

There we were, having read it all through, and it had already become part of our lives. We kissed and we hugged and this new-formed family of writers and producers, technicians and actors and one fabulous director all became a part of TV history.

The BBC were so completely sold on the potential of what they saw on paper when *Gavin and Stacey* was pitched to them that a series was green-lit almost immediately. In days gone by that sort of thing was the norm: if a chief executive was convinced that the project was a 'winner' then money would be provided to turn the scripts into episodes. Rarely does that happen any more. There are all sorts of precautions taken, endless readings in front of streams of executives, rewrites and recasts and then maybe a pilot episode too. Caution all the way. But none of that was to be in the case of *Gavin and Stacey*. It was ordered immediately!

Ruth and James have a kind of big sister, bolshie brother relationship and there is a real, almost blood bond between them that comes out of mutual respect. Like all great writing teams the power flows between them and the creative energy that they engender switches back and forth. They really write it together and then spend countless hours arguing about how they can hone and perfect it. They miss nothing, they nurture every detail and every nuance. They are ruthless and passionate perfectionists both.

The cast was taking shape. Rob Brydon *is* Bryn, the archetypal geeky uncle. We might not have all had one but we do now! He is rocket-fuelled and has such creative energy, he is a true genius. Ruth and Rob had been buddies since acting school days and his character – just like Alison's – was something that he'd helped create, just by being 'organic' I think Bryn would call it.

Melanie's warmth and subtle strength made her an obvious choice for a gentle, loving widowed mother and mother-in-law-and who on earth could have inhabited Doris, the lascivious and bubbly red-hot mamma next door like Margaret?! Steffan, a true Welsh sex-bomb, was inspired casting as Dave.

Mathew and Joanna were yet to be cast, the balance between them and the total belief in their love was a huge hurdle to overcome. Fortunately the creative team had enlisted one of the most inspired casting directors in Britain, Toby Whale. His encyclopaedic knowledge of actors enabled them to match. And match and re-match again until these two now iconic individuals were put together. We all fell in love with them as their characters fell in love, their instinctive skills as actors drawing us deep into their world.

Even before it was filmed we all knew, that this was a jewel, a star in the firmament, and that we'd all been given a wonderful gift, to tell the story of a young couple who fell in love.

And everyone loves that.

50

Coming Home

Eva-Mathilde had been born in the summer of 2003 and, over the course of the next four years, I lived between London and Normandy. With Clare and the girls enjoying a French rural idyll and me commuting between there and London, the situation was finally began to take its toll. I was a family man, but at what cost? I seemed to spend so much of my time in the car or on a ferry, it was a life on the run. I would dash back home at the slightest opportunity to relish the warmth and joy of being with my girls. It was just about sustainable with television jobs lasting a few weeks, and if I was working in theatre I somehow managed to get home for a thirty-six-hour weekend, but I would end up on my knees by Monday evening. The times I looked forward to were the periods between jobs when I could just be Dad and get on with life in the country, which invariably meant fixing or building something at the house. It was a wonderful way to live, the girls were both totally bilingual and they were living in a kids' paradise with acres of space, barns, trees and a lake to play in. But it couldn't go on indefinitely. Something had to give.

Gavin and Stacey proved to be the turning point. I was running between Cardiff and home for six weeks and it pretty near killed me. I would leave the location usually at about six or seven on a Friday night and race to Portsmouth to get the night boat and arrive home at La Cour on Saturday morning, completely exhausted. On Sunday afternoon I'd be off again, racing back for the teatime boat. With the three-hour drive from Cardiff to get through, I would get back at about one o'clock in the morning ready for a five thirty a.m. wake-up call to start the week's filming. As if that wasn't hard enough, I then got *EastEnders*.

I managed to handle both shows for the most part because the BBC had by a miracle managed to co-ordinate the shooting schedules, but when it came to the simultaneous filming of two Christmas episodes – one in London and one in Cardiff – that proved to be the final straw.

Filming Christmas in October is a rather unsettling experience anyway – it puts you right out of sync, the summer isn't fully out of your mind and suddenly there are Christmas decorations and trees and gift-wrapped parcels and cards everywhere. To be doing it in two shows was mind-altering.

I remember spending an entire day sitting at the head of the table in Walford being involved in a cataclysmic family meltdown, my plate loaded with Christmas fayre, cooling and congealing in front of me, the scent of cold cooked Brussel sprouts pervading the air. As if that wasn't torture enough, as soon as filming ended, I was running from the studio, stripping Archie's costume off as I went and getting myself into the back of a waiting car to try and sleep on my way to Cardiff. I'd slip into bed just before midnight and then get up again well before dawn to change into Mick. I was back at the head of the table, only this time in Billericay, having a joyous time with my glorious family and friends – as far removed as life could possibly be from a Mitchell family freak-out, apart from that stink of Brussel sprouts that is . . .

Fortunately I was being used as little as possible on both shows. Where possible Mick would be 'in the other room' when people were calling out to him from the lounge. My character would be offstage while I was curled up in the back of another car hurtling down the motorway through the night to get back to *EastEnders* with perhaps enough time to snatch a couple of hours' sleep in the dressing room before it started all over again.

As I filmed those two important episodes simultaneously, I realised that was it. It had to change. We had to move back to London. I still wasn't sure how long Archie would last on the Square, I was desperately hoping he might get a stay of execution and that I would be able to sit at the corner of the bar reading my paper, drinking my tea and plotting dirty deeds forever. Decisions like that come from up high at the Beeb and their policy is that it's the character that matters, the actor is a pawn and has no real say in it. The plot controls all.

But Clare and I had to make the decision and the decision we made was to come back to England. It was sad to say goodbye to our home in France but David and Susie Pearl, dear friends, had loaned us a lovely place to stay in London and we'd got the girls into the local school so that was that. La Cour would go back to being a holiday home and our French period was over.

51

The Machine

'I know you've been in some popular television shows, Larry, but this is going to change your life!'

So spoke the oracle, Clare. She'd had first-hand experience of the effect that *EastEnders* can have on the life of an actor. And boy was she right.

As a teenage actress herself, she was Nick Berry's real-life girlfriend back when he got the role of Simon Wicks. She'd seen how deeply the series penetrates the day-to-day workings of British society. *EastEnders* is not just a television series, it's an institution, and for someone like me who has moved from job to job over the years, it basically put me on the map. Sure I was a known 'face off the telly' but, just as Clare had predicted, this was way beyond anything I'd experienced. Millions of people now instantly recognised me.

'Archie Mitchell is going to be an enormous character in the series,' the executive producer, Diederick Santer, told me as I was given the basic outline of the man he and his writing team were still in the process of designing. 'He's a deeply complex character and I feel you'd be perfect for the job.'

So what do you say apart from 'sign me up!' It was too good a part and too tempting a character to possibly resist and, coupled with the fact I would be playing Peggy Mitchell's new romantic interest, I was sold. I was going to be Phil Mitchell's long-lost uncle and father to two wayward daughters, Ronnie and Roxie – and that was just for openers.

'Just come and join us for six months so we can see how
Archie works in the show and you can see how you feel about
us,' Diederick continued.

And so I became a part of an amazing television production machine. If not unique in the volume of viewing hours it
produces, it is certainly unique in the volume of quality prod-
uct it turns out – *sans pareil*.

The buildings that house this 'machine' – I have to call it
that because it's the only way I can grasp the enormity of what
it is and what it does – are all rather drab. But what goes on
day by day for fifty weeks of every year within those walls is
truly mind-blowing.

There are about 500 or so people involved in the creation
of *EastEnders*. Working on a hundred hours of television that
has to be plotted and planned months in advance. Story-lines
are worked out perhaps a year or more before they ever erupt
on to the screen. Hours are spent just thinking about the
way the various plots in different characters' lives interrelate
and flow: births, deaths, marriages are all discussed, argued
over, fought for and sometimes dropped. There are meetings,
endless meetings, to talk about characters that will have to be
invented and how their backgrounds – who they are and how
they fit into the story – will work in the big, bubbling cauldron
that is Walford.

It's all done against the clock that ticks on relentlessly, year
in year out. Once the storyline has been agreed upon by the
executive producer and his writing team, then that story has
to be slotted into the overall plan of the series. The scripts are
involved with several stories simultaneously, so a balance has
to be achieved in the scope of each episode – some stories
will feature for a week or so and then be superseded by others
that have been creeping up on the sidelines. It all has to be
carefully concocted and each element properly prepared and
never under- or overused.

The script editor in my time, Dominic Treadwell-Collins, and Simon Ashdown, the head writer, got me into the studios with director Clive Arnold and Diederick to nail down some of Archie's character. They gave me the once-over and fired question after question at me. They were looking for elements of my life that might be included in the extra-specially complicated character I was to play. 'How well off is Archie? How has he made his money? What sort of house does he live in? How much and why does he want to get back into Ronnie's life?' On and on: questions, questions, questions.

About a month after the meeting, I got the scripts that would introduce Archie into the series. They sent me three of the four that would cover his first appearance and bring him and the girls and Peggy together under one roof for the first time. A day or so later, the fourth script arrived. I phoned Simon Ashdown, the man who had actually taken everything that came from the first meeting and put together this new man. 'Simon, I've just finished reading the four episodes and it's a lot darker than I thought it would be. I'm worried that Archie might actually be a little bit of a psycho. Do you think we could perhaps lighten him up a bit, make him a bit more—'

'A bit more likeable?' he asked me. I sensed just the tiniest nuance of defensiveness in Simon's voice. 'Well, obviously we can always do that, Larry, but in my experience the nice guys aren't nearly so interesting and—'

'Simon,' I jumped in. 'Let's just forget this conversation, can we? Let's forget my stupid suggestions and just do it the way you've written it. You're absolutely right. If you left it to me, I'd turn him into another Mick Shipman.'

And that, fortunately, was that. Archie was there on paper; all I had to do was join up the dots. He was an amalgam of bits of me, bits of my dad, bits of my uncle Bill and, I feel sure, bits of Simon. He'd created a deep, dark and terribly damaged man.

Of course getting the character right and putting him into the story was the first stage; next we had to figure out what he looked like, how he dressed, how he did his hair and what he lived in. We then entered the other side of the machine, the side that shows the public what sort of person this is that they are getting to know: little clues; details that present the image of the character. The art side.

Di Humphreys is the costume supervisor, and she has the job of co-ordinating the literally thousands of items of clothing, shoes, jewellery, uniforms and fancy-dress costumes; in fact anything and everything that any one of the hundreds of characters might be wearing. Every single item of every single outfit is a cog in the machine. It all has to be accounted for, stored, cleaned, ironed, maintained and be ready at the drop of a hat to be pulled from the racks and fitted there and then to the appropriate character. She has a team of design assistants, seamstresses and dressers who take care of everything on a day-to-day basis. Each block of four programmes, one week's viewing, will have a costume designer who will actually be responsible for the overall look of that week's two hours of drama.

Steve Paciello was the designer who gave Archie his 'look'. I met Steve on my first visit to the studio and he and Di gave me the once-over to see what sort of colours suit me and what style and cut of clothes would be right for the man. They really 'got' him: smart but certainly not too formal, casual but never sloppy, all carefully considered and talked through in Di's little office. After a week or so of Steve prowling round the West End stores I tried on Archie's new wardrobe. Not only did it all fit perfectly but it also helped me find Archie. I could feel him coming together. It was me in some ways, but in others not me at all. And trying on those first outfits I stood in front of the mirror and sensed Archie coming to life.

Hair and make-up aren't major factors in an actor's life. Actresses spend hours 'in the chair', but once I'd chatted with Karen Perkins, the make-up supervisor and we'd agreed on Archie's hairstyle, I was pretty much set up. A bit of a tan and the hair neat and trimmed regularly and I was all set to go.

One of the young assistant directors walked me through the studios back upstairs to meet Barbara Windsor, and there she was, waiting to greet me.

'Ooooh, aren't you tall? How are we going to manage?' She seemed so tiny, so neat and petite. I felt like I'd known her all my life.

'Don't you worry, we'll make it work; there's plenty of girls who like tall blokes and it doesn't stop them, does it? We'll be great together,' I said as I bent down and gave her a kiss on both cheeks.

'I'm so happy you're coming into the show,' she said, holding my hand between hers, looking up at me with those little-girl eyes. 'I'm sure you'll enjoy it; everybody's thrilled you're here.'

What a welcome this was, what a way to land in a big new job.

Barbara was fabulous – right from the first moment we clicked. Most people assume we already knew each other, but in fact we'd never met. We're actually both from the same neck of the woods, though, and we shared a lot of mutual friends and acquaintances, so it was a perfect match.

We had in fact come very close to meeting a couple of years before at John Bardon's sixty-fifth birthday. Wendy Richards had just left the party and Barbara was expected at any moment. 'Is that political?' I asked John. 'Course it is, son!' he said with that wonderful, all-telling wink of his.

That little insight, long before I'd become involved with the show, was an indication of how things were 'on the Square' back in the old days. By the time I arrived, Barbara was the undisputed head girl, and when Barbara is the leading lady, everything has to operate with a certain style. No petty bitching and grand behaviour is allowed. 'We're all in this together; forget your personal likes and dislikes because they aren't allowed here. We smile and get on with it.' That was always her attitude.

At times in the history of the show there had been a terrible atmosphere: people would act scenes onstage involving real emotion and then completely ignore one another around the studio. Barbara set the tone at a higher level and nothing like that would be tolerated now – the atmosphere on- and offstage was just perfect. Everybody got on.

My first scenes to be shot were not actually done at the studio. The BBC had really pushed the boat out and hired a beautiful mansion a few miles into the green belt from Borehamwood. This was supposed to be Archie's pad down in the West Country near Weymouth.

I arrived at least an hour too early, as is my habit, and made up and costumed Archie. I waited impatiently in a caravan dressing room for my first big entrance.

Chris Dall, the long, lean first assistant director, welcomed me to the set, and Clive Arnold, the director charged with bringing Archie to the public, introduced me to Barry Austen, the senior lighting director, and Duncan Unsworth, the head cameraman, and that was it, introductions over, we were off.

Clive had been involved in setting Archie's character up, and so we'd already got to know each other. In a situation like this – with so much hanging in the balance – it was a real bonus to be working with a director I'd already got to know. It was still nerve-wracking all the same, though – for all concerned. Everyone on that set was aware of the importance of these opening scenes. I had to 'give them' Archie right from the word go. There was no room for half-measures; they had to be sold.

We did a few little bits and pieces first, just to let me get a feel for this totally alien situation. Samantha Janus and Rita Simons, who played Ronnie and Roxy, were there, and Barbara and Rob Kazinsky, who played Sean, and scene by scene we worked our way through the day. Gradually, in this big, beautiful house, I began to be the character, with his daughters, his brother's widow and his prospective son-in-law talking outside. It all began to feel so real. The design department had managed not only to make sure that house looked like it fitted Archie, but in doing so had enabled my Archie to fit the house. At the end of my first day, Barbara and the entire team gave me a welcoming round of applause. I'd made it. Archie was launched and I'd been accepted. I was a part of the 'machine'.

Away from Borehamwood, the shooting schedule on *EastEnders* is so finely tuned that there is virtually no time allotted for the luxury of rehearsal. The actors assemble out in the lobby of the main Studio, waiting to be called on to the set by one of the assistant directors. The whole operation is timed down to the second, and the first assistant director will have all the actors for the next scene to be shot waiting at least two or three minutes before the scene being worked on is finished. As that scene is cleared by the technical department as 'Scene Complete', the actors leave the set and the ones for the coming scene file in. They gather around the director and read the scene. In general they know their lines, though most still carry the script just to prompt themselves. They read it a second, third time and that's it, off you go.

The cameras, four or perhaps five, are arranged around the set; the sound men position their microphones so as not to be seen by the cameras; the director sits in front of the monitor and that's it. There's none of the luxury of Hollywood's take after endless take: four or five and it will be done and then it is, 'May we have the actors for scene . . . ?' and on they go.

Hour after hour, day after day. The machine runs on and on.

Rona McKendrick, the chief production manager, assigns the episodes to the production managers, who run each block of four episodes; the margin for error is just minutes. A tight ship was always the way the BBC operated, and Ms McK and her team keep it that way. Even when, in my second year, the whole operation was brought to its knees by the snow, they worked around the clock to somehow or other do the impossible and accommodate the weather and the chaos it had caused. It was little short of a miracle.

But of course I still had the real baptism of fire to go through: my first scene with Barbara in the Queen Vic. Suddenly, there I was in the bar of the most famous pub in Britain, Peggy behind the pumps and me at the bar. It had been years since I'd worked in a multi-camera studio – these days most TV is filmed on one camera so that every scene has to be shot from every actor's point of view. We did our first scene and Barbara wandered away. I stood there waiting for my turn in front of the camera, but that was it, the scene had been recorded. I'd already done my bit and every bit of my performance was on tape. Barbara was standing off to one side giggling. 'You soppy sod,' she laughed, 'it's all done!'

When an actor joins the cast of *EastEnders* as a newly recruited 'regular', he or she is linked up with a member of the acting company who will act as their guide – someone who can mentor them in the first weeks and put them wise to the way things actually run. Steve McFadden was to be my mentor. Carolyn Weinstein, the company manager – who basically mothers the cast, answers all questions or gets them answered, and generally featherbeds the day-to-day studio life of the fifty or so ongoing characters – sets this up. She considered Steve, as the senior male actor, to be the person best suited to looking after me.

Steve was actually the first actor I met when I'd come in to talk about the character. I was waiting outside Diederick's office when someone I assumed to be a dispatch rider walked into the open-plan area in a crash helmet carrying a brown paper envelope. As he came towards me, he lifted the visor, and I realised it was Steve.

'Really pleased you've joined us,' he said. 'You probably won't remember it, but we have actually worked together before.'

'Well,' I started, 'you know whenever I've watched you on the show, I've always thought there was something ringing a bell. What was it on?'

'*Buster*,' he said. 'It was my first job out of RADA. I was one of the gang that held up the train. I drove one of the lorries.'

'Of course! I remember you in your uniform. You really did look like a squaddie, unlike everybody else, who looked like gangsters in disguise!'

And so mentored and mollycoddled, I started what was in theory a six-month stint as the new man in Peggy's life. Gradually, even though I wasn't necessarily doing scenes with them, I began to meet all the other cast.

The entrance to Studio A – which houses the Vic and all the rooms above – is like the reception area of a rather naff, second-rate hotel. There is absolutely no glamour whatsoever but, behind the desk – 'The *EastEnders* Help Desk' – on a half-a-day-each schedule, sit the two guardian angels of the cast, two of the kindest, warmest, most patient women I have ever run into: Jackie and Angela, Angela and Jackie. Whatever way you say it, these are two people who take care of all the little things that a personal assistant would handle – but for fifty actors. Nothing is too much trouble for them and they are absolutely integral to the running of the show. I cannot imagine what it would be like without them.

It's in this tiny reception area that the cast gather to wait to be called on to the set. It's really the hub, the meeting place, and sooner or later, as you sit and wait and everyone passes through, you get to know people. Sid Owen (Ricky) and Perry Fenwick (Billy) were two of the gang I got to know early on. I didn't have so much to do with them in my initial storyline but they are both really old Walford hands. They've seen hundreds of people come and go and both of them were quick to tender a warm welcome. I have tenuous connections to both of them: Perry is a long-time friend of Ray Winstone's, so we had him in common, and Sid is an old mate of Nick Berry, my other half's ex of old. So we sort of knew about each other.

Sadly John Bardon had fallen victim to a stroke by the time I arrived on the scene, so I was denied working with him again, but he did come back in to film a few scenes so I got to see him anyway. He was constantly surrounded by all the members of the cast who'd grown to love him as I had. They clustered around him, relishing every minute of his company.

I'd been pulling up some floor covering in the back kitchen of the Normandy house when I'd got the call from my agent asking me to be a guest on John's *This Is Your Life*. I stood in the studio with Michael Aspel and John about a month later as the episode was being recorded. 'You know, John, as I was pulling up that false tile floor that you'd laid so precisely all those years ago, I was thinking to myself: not many people have had a floor covered by Jim Brandon – and two seconds later I had my agent on the line asking if I'd be a guest here tonight. Christ, I thought, the old bastard's haunting me!' How we'd laughed about that one and, stroke or no stroke, that extraordinary spirit of his still shines through. He's a brilliant performer.

And, as in the show, his devoted 'wife' June Brown, dear old Dot Cotton, still visits John and sits with him and reads to him – colleagues and friends, the 'art' having been taken over but never extinguished by life.

Patsy Palmer and Cliff Parisi were two others who made me welcome straight away. Both of them combined busy home lives with their 'day jobs'. As did Pam St Clements, so different from her character – she's a witty, rather mysterious middle-class woman offstage, a thousand light years away from her Walford persona. She's been there forever and seen it all and she obviously enjoys the double life that being one of the mainstays of the show allows her.

Adam Woodyatt enjoys it so much that he lives in the heart of the country and commutes to and from Walfordland in his top-of-the-line Maserati. That's really enjoying it. But in the same way that Ian Beale adores his family, Adam dotes on his. He's a loving father and husband on and off the screen.

Of course a lot of my time involved shooting scenes with my two wild daughters, who were even crazier offstage – I have to say – than on! Their relationship as actors is one that many sisters would envy. They are both young mothers with children and husbands to accommodate and they spend a lot of time at the studios. Being with the pair of them is pure joy. They share the most outrageous and totally unprintable vocabulary and rarely did a day go by during my two years with them that we weren't in stitches. 'Dirty Daddy', they called me, and to me they will always be my 'Two Slappers'. They really were my daughters.

Scott Maslen and Nitin Ganatra were two other actors I'd worked with before. Scott had still been a regular in *The Bill* when I was there and his zany, Chaplinesque style of physical comedy still managed to make me cry with laughter.

Nitin and I had done a series of workshops together and then suddenly there he was doing brilliant comedy acting in *Bride and Prejudice* and here we were on 'The Square' together: him delivering mail to me at the Vic.

Linda Henry and Cheryl Fergison are another two whose relationship on screen extends into the real world – they absolutely adore each other – and their vicious ribbing of one another (and anyone else who might be passing) is hilarious.

'Would you have stayed in *EastEnders* if they'd asked you to?'

How many times have I been asked that question?

My answer is always the same. 'I would have stayed there until they carried me out in a box!'

But when you get involved with a show like that, you have to try and stay real. You're only there because of the story; it's not the other way round. Sure it would have been great to have a well-paid job, working with people I liked, but the story needed an end. It had to reach a dramatic crescendo, otherwise what would Archie have done? Sat around the Vic plotting against endless enemies? No, the reason that Archie became such a memorable character is because the audience witnessed his rise and then were party to his fall. That is good drama. The writers took the audience on an extended roller-coaster ride and, in the end, the villain got his comeuppance.

I miss them all: all the ones I've mentioned and all the ones I've not. All the directors, the assistant directors, the fabulous, unbelievably supportive supporting artistes, the lighting crews, the camera crews, the art departments, the props men, the tireless, ever-smiling make-up artists and members of the costume department, the producers, the

writers, the script editors and security crew; in fact everyone who makes up the incredible, creative, all-embracing,
unforgettable 'machine' that is *EastEnders*. My love and
thanks to you all.

The Finale

Looking Back

On the eve of her seventh birthday, my youngest daughter, Eva-Mathilde, couldn't sleep. She couldn't keep her eyes closed and was just too excited by the prospect of tomorrow's big day.

'I need a proper sleeping mask, Daddy, or I'll never sleep,' she said, and then she paused and snuggled herself further into my arms. As she did so, she said, 'My friend was very sad today. Her mummy and daddy have split up because they had a big argument. She was crying.'

We both wriggled a bit, adjusting our nest in her bed, and I whispered, 'That's sad, isn't it, darling? But perhaps her mummy and daddy will make up and be friends again.'

She didn't really respond to that suggestion. She moved on in the way children do. 'She is my BEST friend.'

'Did you give her a cuddle to make her feel better?' I asked.

'Yes, Daddy, I did.'

Perhaps I've got it right – at least a little bit right. My kids are the ones who are from a home where their parents don't fight – apart from the odd barney, but nothing the little ones would ever know about. My kids are living the lives that all kids should live: happy to go off each morning, not carrying domestic worries with them, free from all concerns, free to have a childhood.

Back when I'd jumped ship for the final time and started yet another new life – this time with Clare, almost twenty years my junior – I said to the very wise man who was psychoanalysing me, 'I want to get it right. I want to have a proper family life. I want to prove to myself that I can do it.' He gave me one of his frighteningly profound stares, which asked everything and said nothing. 'I've got to get it right,' I heard myself say yet again.

Again, I'd run away from a relationship, but this time it was to make a family, specifically to have children and to try and create the thing that all my life I'd craved but never achieved. This wasn't just a crazy falling in love, it wasn't about wanting the romance of it all to envelop me and fly me off to La-La Land. No, this time it was a mating call. I wanted to have children, to start a family, and to try and do what I'd attempted but never accomplished. My son was eighteen at the time and would soon be a man. I couldn't let it just stop with him.

Back then I'd told Mr P in one of my sessions, 'I've come all this way and now there is a fork in the road ahead of me and one way means carrying on with Rachel and it is cosy and loving and really easy, but the other branch is the only one that goes the way I hope it goes, or the way I think I want to go.'

He pierced me with his all-seeing eyes, his fearsome mental energy encouraging me to order my thoughts, willing me to think more clearly.

I knew more than anyone just how difficult it would be for me to stick to my guns. The relationship that Clare and I were in was – on the surface at least – destined for disaster. We were both 'damaged goods', but could that perfect family that we both longed for and needed perhaps be achievable? Through the first year, the break-ups and the make-ups were dizzying, and on several occasions it had become so crazy that we couldn't really figure out whether we were together or back being single again.

We were both impossible to live with and I continued to

worry about whether we'd made the right decision in trying to make this work. I talked it over with Mr P and he kept making me think, making me talk, making me figure it out. He never advised but he made me understand that I would always have to answer to myself. I'd learned enough about life to know that I would constantly seek to put it all right, to try to die a contented old man. I didn't want to be torn and sad, knowing I'd screwed it all up.

I would never be satisfied with life until I'd achieved the dream, the one I'd learned about as a little boy in those occasional magical moments when my mum and dad appeared to loved each other. Those brief, fleeting moments when there was a sense of wellbeing and peace.

Now, all these years on, my little girls live happily. They always include a big bright spiky sun up in the sky above the scenes they draw and, although they laugh and moan, argue and squabble through their lives, they never have to worry about their mum and dad. This is what I got when I tried. It is the life I knew I was due. It certainly hasn't been easy and, after everything that has gone before, it fell as though I was trying to work it all out back to front, inside out: it was like trying to learn to do up a bow tie without a mirror.

It took me nearly fifty years to figure it out and to get to that point. So now, in my sixties, I'm the father of little girls and the partner of someone only a year or so older than my long-lost first daughter. That's the price I'll have to pay for having taken so long to get it right.

It's as if I've managed to organise the perfect party, the one where everybody is going to have the best fun – guests and host alike – but now what I know is that no matter how good it is, I'm going to have to leave before it ends. That's what I hadn't figured out. That's what I never realised: that by leaving it so late to start making that family, I wouldn't be able to see it through.

53

Halifax to Hollywood

So finally, after actually living all the stories of my life, I finished up featuring strongly in the two most popular programmes then showing on British television, and I was doing it simultaneously. For two years running, I played the villain of the piece in *EastEnders* and the nicest dad in the world in *Gavin and Stacey*. And, with the coverage of those two shows, suddenly, after thirty-odd years as an actor, everybody in Britain seemingly knows who I am. Cliff Jones, a Welsh footballer I'd idolised as a boy said to me, 'Hello it's Larry Lamb isn't it? I thought you were great in Cagney and Lacey.'

I laughed, 'I think I was actually better in Gavin and Stacey.'

My son, fed up with nagging me to write those stories, starts nagging his agent to get me a book deal. And he gets me one. A good one! When I came to write this book, I realised that I'd have to go back to some of the places that featured so heavily in my life. I wanted walk their streets and meet those people again.

When I started out in this business as a professional, it wasn't with any other end in view but to become a movie star. I'd done so well in what I was doing, I figured that it would obviously go the same way in acting. Little did I know just how 'pie in the sky' that theory was, and how elusive the possibility of making it to the top in show business actually is! Statistically, only about a quarter of all professional actors ever make their living by acting. Most of them have to do other jobs to finance their passion. If somebody had pointed out to me that simply being able to say after thirty-six years as an actor that one has made a living at it rates one as a success in the profession, I have to say I'm not sure I would have quite so readily taken the plunge. But I was young and free of responsibility, and able to do whatever took my fancy. And, who was to say, maybe – and I wasn't really interested in statistics – I could make it big.

And so now I have actually been a professional actor for thirty-six years, I have to face the fact that I haven't done what I set out to do, but instead I've had one hell of a career. And, more importantly, I've learned how to act. When I started I just assumed that as I was an actor, obviously I could act. It went without saying. What I now realise is that it took me almost thirty years to learn how to do it, to get to the point where I knew I wasn't kidding myself, to get to the point where, out on a stage in front of an audience of experienced theatregoers, I was in charge – in charge of myself and there-fore in charge of the job I was doing. Completely in control, able to deal with whatever might crop up. It had taken me that long.

All the hours of television and the various cracks at film acting, they all added up to a list of credits that proved I'd made some sort of a mark, but the real proof for me was the way I felt out there, with 800 pairs of eyes absolutely focused on what I was doing. No nerves, no sense of anything other than being that character.

To have come all that way from a little theatre in Bremerhaven on an American military base in occupied Germany, I'd been terrified, my knees knocking uncon-trollably. And now, there I was on the stage in the West End of London in a play by one of the greatest playwrights the world has ever produced, and thoroughly enjoying it. That has been the journey that I didn't even realise I was on. What I thought I wanted to do was win the lottery of stardom, but all I'd done was buy a ticket. I had no conception of what was really involved, not the remotest inkling of how lucky one has to be even getting your first job as an actor, or of how the odds are stacked against you. I'd been lucky in what I'd been doing before because I was a bigger, noisier, more noticeable fish, but when you get amongst the actors, you realise just what small fry you've suddenly become. And what do you know? They've all got tickets too.

I'd bounced into the business as a reasonably talented amateur and, sadly, as with so many other elements of my life, I had taken the ease of my entry for granted; it was as if that was obviously the way it was meant to be. I had a lot to learn. There was of course nobody to coach me, per se; it had to come with exposure and the gradual realisation that there was in fact something to be learned. It wasn't just about talent – that raw material was a given – what I had to get into my head was that there is a craft involved too. There are tools to be mastered and skills to be honed. The all-important element of luck, the other intangible component, did stand me in good stead. Over the years I've kept on being in the right place, time after time; but that can only go on for so long, and the longer you stay in the race, the tougher the competition gets.

In Britain most actors are formally trained, and the level of instruction is partly what makes our players amongst the most highly respected in the world. With the great proving houses of the National Theatre and RSC drawing actors ever onwards and simultaneously providing a canvas on which to highlight the talents of directors, writers, designers, and all the other varied and wonderful disciplines of the theatre, these centres of excellence keep the standard of plays and players constantly at the cutting edge. And so, by following the advice of dear old Janet Roberts and the wisdom and foresight of Jeremy Brett, I came back to England and, having not had the training, was able to learn by osmosis. I was lucky enough to have some of it, perhaps enough of it, rub off on me.

I knew when I set out on this writing job that I would have to revisit two of the places that figured so massively in my life as an actor. The first was obviously Nova Scotia, where I got the opportunity to dare myself to take a shot at the dream. It was there that I'd achieved a level in my former life that I could have been satisfied with. I was twenty-seven years old and I'd made it. I had a good job and I was doing well; but it was not enough, a wider world drew me on. I knew that I needed the inspiration and input of educated people, my horizons needed broadening, and the theatre – and more importantly the people who made their lives in it – offered that. And somehow or other I'd picked up on the fact that if you wanted to be a movie star, the theatre was where you had to start. So I threw caution and a career to the winds and started a new one from scratch.

The second significant location was Hollywood, or the entertainment industry's share of LA – be it Beverly Hills, Bel Air or Malibu or, in my case, Venice Beach, the glorious old seaside town where I'd decided I would settle whilst I made my final assault on the summit. Where I'd established my base camp. Then, in the early summer of 2010, I got an invitation to a wedding – a Hollywood wedding at that. My colleague and friend Steven Moyer, star of *True Blood*, was going to marry his beautiful leading lady Anna Paquin. It was all hush-hush, with not a word to be breathed to anyone, but I knew it was a sign. I was going back to Hollywood. The wedding was to be on 21 August, right around the time I knew I had to be in Nova Scotia if I wanted the best possible chance of good weather. On top of it all, my agent had been nagging me to get out to LA anyway to talk to his partners and get myself properly represented in Tinseltown where *Gavin and Stacey* had become a must-see. The whole puzzle slotted together. I was off on a two-week trip back down the memory lane of my life from Halifax to Hollywood!

54

Homeland

I was back in Nova Scotia and it was 2010. The last time I'd set foot in the place was during 1978, thirty-two years before. During those years, my life had completely changed. In that time, I'd discovered fatherhood for myself, and it was a very different picture to the one my father painted. Although I didn't know it back then in 1978, within a year I would become the father of a boy, a boy mothered and nurtured by a woman far stronger than me. Via that child, and through the strength his mother passed on to him, my boy taught me to be a dad and now, as I'm on the early approaches to old age, I have the strong male figure in my life that I never had, the strong male figure that all men need, the one they know they can trust no matter what – and it's my son!

Meeting George's mum was the first real mating call I'd had. I instinctively knew that I wanted to have children with this woman. She was the one. All those nights spent scoping out the prey in the Eager Beaver bar; all those 'Would you like to dance?' and 'D'you wanna come back to my place?' questions could come to an end. In an almost identical scenario, I found Linda, George's mum. I found it ironic that during my first few years as an actor, that old way of life – the predatory male, always alone, always on the lookout in the places where the females were definitely on show – had gone by the board. My life wasn't like that any more. I worked in an industry where I was constantly surrounded by women and I didn't have to go out to seek groups of them. They were there working right alongside me. On this one unusual night, my life changed completely. I began the journey to find a father. But the way to that beginning had started somewhere else. On the other side of the Atlantic.

On paper at least I'd been sent to Canada to do a very specific job of work. No mistaking that. It was 1973, I was coming up to my twenty-sixth birthday and the company had entrusted me with a huge responsibility. Obviously I was flattered, and from the projects I'd already finished for them, I knew that I was actually capable of doing the job. But I was distracted; my mind wasn't focused on that job. I had other fish to fry.

It took me no time at all to realise that having my temporary living quarters in Keddy's Motel, Truro, suited the company, not me. The only place to be in Nova Scotia once the sun went down was Halifax, the provincial capital. There was life there; it was where the action lay. And I wanted action, big time.

I'd lived through a long period of trying to resign myself to the fact that I was married. A period when, from the beginning, I'd known it wouldn't work. But initially I'd been too weak to avoid it, to be truthful about how I felt. In the end I'd had to face the truth, that I couldn't be tied down to one person; once I admitted it, I'd broken free. It had taken so long and it had been so painful because everything about Jacquie was so obviously right, but I knew I just wasn't ready. And therein lay the hard point. The fear of spurning the 'right one' – what if she were to prove later to have been the only 'right one'? What then? How would I deal with that for the rest of my life?

In the end I'd decided to face that possibility. To strike out on my own. And then the opportunity arose, and with absolutely no knowledge of anything but the name of the place and where it sat on the map, I came to Nova Scotia, the place where I became a new person, the place where I became an actor.

I hadn't been back, but I had managed to fall in and out of contact over the years. In 1984, I got a call from my agent to say she had someone on the line who was an old friend of mine from Nova Scotia. 'Robby Parker,' she said, 'he's at Heathrow Airport en route to Canada. He's missed his flight and there's not another one until tomorrow.'

'Robby,' I shouted down the phone, 'get in a taxi and come here right now!'

It turned out that Robby had been on his honeymoon: 'We were up in the Golden Triangle just inside Burma when I got a cable at the American Express office telling me that the licence had come through to start construction on what's going to be the first ever tavern in Enfield. Work has to start immediately or the licence will be revoked, so I left Jane on an elephant somewhere in Burma and ran for the airport.'

We talked all night up in my flat on the North End Road and, first thing in the morning, as the boys were setting up the stalls in the market on the street, we walked down the stairs and said goodbye again.

'Robby?' I'd asked him, I just couldn't resist. 'What did you all think when I went off to be an actor?'

Robby grinned and shook his head. 'Well, we just thought you'd be back, but you never did come back.'

Then, sometime in the early 1990s, I picked up the phone and this very familiar voice said, 'Larry Lamb?' I broke into a smile, knowing that this was going to be good.

'Joe Scott,' said the voice.

'Lord thundering Jesus,' I said. 'Joe fucking Scott? What in the name of . . . ? How are you, man? How on earth did you get my number?'

'Girl came into my office looking for a job so I said to

her, "What are you good at?" She said, "I'm good at finding people," so I wrote your name down on a piece of paper and said to 'er: "Find this guy, Larry Lamb," and that's why I'm on the phone.'

And in the way blokes do, about fifteen or so years later I got a call from Joe again to say he was passing through London with Caroline, his wife, on the way back to Halifax. I drove out to Heathrow and as I looked across the big airy atrium of their hotel, I couldn't understand why this old geezer was standing up way across from me and waving. I realised it was Joe and he wasn't twenty-eight any more.

A week or so later, Joe called me with Jimmy's number.

I phoned him at the Curly Portables tavern that Robby had left his honeymoon to rush back and build.

'Can I speak to Jimmy Senor? It's Larry Lamb calling from London, England.'

There was a pause and then Jimmy came on the line, 'We're not hiring!' I knew nothing had changed and it was as if I'd never left.

'Hello?'

'Robby? It's Larry.'

There was a really long silence 'Lamb?'

'Yes,' I said, my face grinning as I waited to hear what he would say.

'My God . . . I think of you so often.'

And now all those years later I was flying in over the province, the endless, madly convoluted coastline, the countless jewel-like lakes cast in their vast velvet setting of scrub pine and mixed forest. It was August 2010, thirty-seven years on from my first setting foot in the place.

I wanted to try and discover just what it was about Novia Scotia that had left such a lasting impression on my soul.

At six o'clock the next morning, I found myself sitting on the porch of a log cabin overlooking a broad stretch of sea that is the St Lawrence Bay. It's probably 200 miles or so across to Quebec, and somewhere out there are the tiny French islands of St Pierre and Miquelon, and further still the wild shores of Labrador. The sky was clear, there wasn't even the tiniest puff of cloud, and there was a slight chilled breeze blowing from inland. Our sea-wet towels and 'bathers' fluttered gently on the big pine banisters that skirted the cabin porch. The sun was warm across my face and I sat and tried to tell myself how lucky I was to be there again, I knew that breaking free and running away had been the right thing to do back then. My life – and all that has come from it – happened because of that move.

It empowered me; it set me free mentally and physically to become the person I didn't even know was in me.

The place had changed, as all places do – there were more buildings, more cars and more people, but it was the same really, and all we are is older. Coming here all those years ago changed me. I wrote this poem about it.

My Home from Homeland
It's been too long to not come back
Those parts of lives we've missed
Episodes and chapters related
As we've developed and grown in isolation
What you have now and what you've become
What we have in common and can now compare
Who you are and what you were
What I was and who I am
Learning the lesson of what that separation means
In terms of what you've missed together
You and your house and me and mine
Our wives and lives, our photographs and friends
Thirty-two years too easy to say – but impossible to regain
But the root of friendship is planted deep

You're just the same – you haven't changed
You're you in a different – better – form, that's all
But now I know what I am – and who I am
That bond just picks up, knits itself back into the pattern
And just how rare that is and just what a treasure –
What a joy to feel again – but now in maturity
With all that growing-up time in between
Somehow cementing the friendship – pulling it together
No negatives, not sad, just life
Sure we should have been together, sure I should have
kept
     in touch
But as I hug you and kiss you goodbye and the tears well
     up
I know that it is back together and that from now until the
     end
That's how it will stay – firm and fixed

55

Making it to Hollywood?

It was 1988 and I'd just flown into LA from Acapulco, where I'd been 'going loco', filming *Buster* along with Phil Collins and the gang. Ervin Zavada, the CBS exec from my *Christopher Columbus* days had invited me to come and stay with him and his family. Erv was the archetypal American executive and I was the hungry actor. Something between us had clicked. I think in part it had something to do with the American thing: whenever I'm there I just pick up from where I was, and I never really felt like I'd left. Erv had started his career in the mailroom of CBS and had worked his way up the chain of command. Czech-American, he was of medium height, round faced and bearded, a warm, happy-go-lucky family man. And we found each other on that job, and in the end he'd lived with me at my flat in London for about five or six months whilst *Christopher Columbus* was put together in the labs and studios around Soho. I can remember him saying, 'Larry, would you police up your living area?' and it always stuck in my mind.

This little visit was going to be a trial run just to get a feel of the place from the inside. I had a featured part in a mainstream movie that was going to be released in America, in Hollywood. Now I had no excuse not to go there and try and make a go of it. So Erv met me at the airport with Derrick, his son, and took me to his home in Westwood.

I spent about a week driving around the city of Los Angeles and immediately realised that this part of America – one of the areas I didn't know first-hand – would be somewhere that I could live.

Erv and his wife, Nancy, were really wonderful hosts and they made a guest feel completely at home. I was really just there to get a taste of the city, but the film was definitely going to go the whole way and would have a launch in LA, so Erv made every effort to ensure that when I eventually returned with the film I would know how the place worked.

Buster enjoyed a reasonable success in London. Phil's fan base ensured healthy audience numbers and the soundtrack recording was on sale all around the world during the build-up. There was a slight hiccup when Buckingham Palace vetoed Prince Charles attending the premiere, but in the end we did all get the red carpet treatment in Leicester Square. In fact, as I stepped out of the limo, a huge cheer went up . . . for Ringo Starr in the next car. The film went down well with the audience and didn't fare too badly with the press.

I was a bit disappointed that Phil wasn't able to give me a leg up when it came to LA but I had to assume that budgeting restrictions even touch multi-millionaire rock and roll kings and so I had to take it on the chin that there would be no opening for me in Hollywood. In the end I decided to go at my own expense.

So when I walked out poolside at the Sunset Marquis, the ultimate rock-and-roll home-from-home in Hollywood, Phil and the gang were a little gobsmacked and delighted that I'd made the effort.

I have to say it was a bit overwhelming to be exchanging nods and bits of banter with Alice Cooper over hamburgers and, later on, when Phil introduced me to 'The Boss'.

'Hi Larry, howyadoin?' Mr Springsteen greeted me.

'All right, Bruce, thanks, all right.' I was a bit blown away.

★

Edward Duke was on tour with his one-man show, *Jeeves Takes Charge*, and he asked me, 'Laredo darling, have you got a Tinseltown agent?'

'Well, not really, I'm here under my own steam so it's a bit difficult.'

'I'm going to phone a friend of mine and let him know you're there,' he kindly offered.

Things started to happen very fast, and within about half an hour I heard an English voice on the phone. It was an agent friend of Edward's friend. 'I just had a call from Sheldon Larry, who's a friend of Edward Duke, saying that you might be seeking representation in LA?'

'Er, well, yes,' I spluttered. *Blimey*, I thought, *they don't hang around.*

'Well Larry, by the strangest of coincidences I was in the cinema two nights ago, watching *Buster*, and I was wondering to myself if that actor playing Bruce Reynolds was represented in the US? And so here I am talking to you on the phone.'

By the end of the following day I'd been contracted to Writers and Artists, at that time a very successful mid-range agency, and by the end of the day after, I'd driven all over LA, meeting a whole string of seemingly very accessible people who might be looking for someone like me in the upcoming pilot season. Actors traditionally fly into LA in the January of each year to spend two or three months attempting to land a role in a pilot TV series which might just – with a great deal of luck, to say nothing of industrial quantities of blood, sweat and tears – lead to fame and fortune.

'Larry, you should really stay in LA over Christmas, because things start hotting up very early in the year. If you have to go back to London, make it as short a trip as you can and just get back here ready to go.'

Everything was set, Erv was delighted, and before I left to spend Christmas back at home, I'd sublet a small apartment in a beautiful old seaside house just along from Venice Beach. Christmas and New Year flew by, and by mid-January I was getting my first taste of being a Hollywood actor: I was UNEMPLOYED.

All those easy meetings back then in quiet December suddenly got very edgy and extremely important – and there were lots of them. LA is enormous; it was like waking up in Kilburn and having your first casting of the day at Eltham at 9.30 a.m., your second at 11.30 in the West End, the third out in Hounslow and the last one of the day at 5.45 p.m. in Walthamstow. I seemed to spend hours in traffic jams, and at times I felt like I was in a supermarket parking lot that was on the move.

When I finally arrived at the auditions, turning up at the security guard shack at the entrance to somewhere like Warner Bros Studios was pretty daunting. I was sitting in a waiting room with a bunch of actors who are all rather like you, all of you desperately trying to focus on the task at hand: to convince the panel of people sitting around the table on the other side of *that* door that you are the man they've been waiting to see. The casting person would come out, always delighted to see you, and in you'd go to confront two, six or eight people – nobody ever tells you what or who to expect. You shake all their hands and off you go, no niceties, no chit-chat, you just read like your life depends on it – and of course it does. The stakes are so high, your life can change there and then, just like that. This could turn out to be the most important moment of your life.

I would walk out, try to forget it and walk down to the car, ready to get going to the next one. Day after day it was the same in pilot season and I kept doing it. I hit the road and drove from casting to casting.

But something wasn't right; something big was amiss. When I'd been on my way home from Acapulco and was stopping over to scope the place out, I just hadn't figured George into the equation. Try though I might, I couldn't leave him behind. Going away on jobs was one thing, but if I went through with this now, it would mean coming to live in another world. It was impossible to follow this through. I had to go back. After all, what on earth could there be in the world that was more important than watching my little boy become a man?

The agency were very gracious about it; I gave them a plausible excuse. I had to try to save face on all sides: we'd both made big efforts and laid out some cash, but that boy was bigger than all of it. He needed his daddy and, as the future would reveal, his daddy needed him.

And so now, all those years later, I sit at my desk at the Venice Beach house, just down the road from Ocean Park where I landed then and from where I left, writing stories about my life. The place I'm staying in, and the clothes I'm wearing – even the glasses I'm seeing these words through – have all been carefully chosen by a master.

Everything that I am now is because of that son who now fathers me: the little boy I couldn't leave behind.

Picture Acknowledgements

Author's collection: 1 - 5, 6 (middle and bottom), 7, 9, 11 (middle), 12, 13 (top right, middle and bottom), 14 (top right), 16 (middle right and bottom). © Alamy: 6 (top left)/ photo Mirropix. Courtesy Baby Cow Productions: 15 (middle and bottom). © BBC Photo Library: 15 (top left and right). © Neil Cooper: 16 (top left). © Corbis: 11 (top)/ photo Robbie Jack, 11 (bottom)/ photo Rune Hellestad. © The Kobal Collection: 8/ photos NHF Productions. © Press Association Images: 14 (bottom)/ photo Ian West. © Rex Features: 10 (top) and 14 (top left)/ photos ITV, 10 (middle and bottom)/ photos Fremantle Media Ltd, 13 (top left)/ photo Nikos Vinieratos.

Every reasonable effort has been made to contact any copyright holders of material reproduced in this book. But if there are any errors or omissions, Hodder & Stoughton will be pleased to insert the appropriate acknowledgement in any subsequent printing of this publication.